EUGENE O'NEILL AND ORIENTAL THOUGHT

A Divided Vision

By James A. Robinson

SOUTHERN ILLINOIS UNIVERSITY PRESS
CARBONDALE AND EDWARDSVILLE

Permission to quote from the sources listed below is gratefully acknowledged.

Collection of American Literature, Beinecke Rare Book and Manuscript Library, Yale University: O'Neill letters, manuscripts, typescripts, and notes.

Coomaraswamy, Ananda K., *Buddha and the Gospel of Buddhism* (Harper & Row, Publishers, Inc., 1916). By permission of Dr. Rama P. Coomaraswamy, executor of the estate of Dr. A. K. and Mrs. D. L. Coomaraswamy.

Harcourt Brace Jovanovich, Inc.: Quotations from T. S. Eliot, "The Waste Land," in Sculley Bradley et al., eds., *The American Tradition in Literature* (New York: W. W. Norton & Co., 1974).

Harper & Row, Publishers, Inc.: Poetry given on the dedication page, from Huston Smith, *The Religions of Man*, 1958.

Random House, Inc.: Eugene O'Neill, *Nine Plays*, 1954; *The Plays of Eugene O'Neill*, 3 vols., 1954.

Eugene O'Neill letters, manuscripts, typescripts, and notes copyright © 1982 by Yale University.

PS3529
N5
Z794
1982

Library of Congress Cataloging in Publication Data

Robinson, James A.
    Eugene O'Neill and Oriental thought, a divided vision.

    Bibliography: p.
    Includes index.
    1. O'Neill, Eugene, 1888–1953—Criticism and inter-
pretation.   2. O'Neill, Eugene, 1888–1953—Philosophy.
3. Philosophy, Oriental.   4. Asia—Religion.   I. Title.
PS3529.N5Z794   812'.52   81-14428
ISBN 0-8093-1035-X   AACR2

When I behold the sacred *liao wo** my thoughts return
To those who begot me, raised me, and now are tired.
I would repay the bounty they have given me,
But it is as the sky: it can never be approached.

* A species of grass symbolizing parenthood.

To my mother and father

Contents

Acknowledgments

Numerous individuals and institutions have assisted me in the research and writing of this book. First, I am grateful for the generous support of various fellow O'Neill scholars. Kathy Lynn Bernard provided me with a free copy of her excellent dissertation on O'Neill's library, and gave me information on O'Neill's research. Louis Sheaffer and Barbara Gelb responded promptly and helpfully to my inquiries, as did Frederic Wilkens of Suffolk University. Travis Bogard shared his opinion of the manuscript with me, and suggested ways in which details of my argument might be strengthened. His colleague at the University of California at Berkeley, Frederic I. Carpenter, requires special thanks here. His published ideas about O'Neill and Orientalism inspired my thesis; his advice and encouragement sustained me in the early stages of my work; and his perceptive criticisms of my first draft assisted me in my revisions. Indeed, this study might not have been conceived, written and published without the help he has given to a fellow scholar whom he has never met.

Another O'Neill scholar closer to home has also been invaluable to me. Jackson Bryer, my friend and colleague at the University of Maryland at College Park, helped guide me to my thesis, advised me countless times during the process of composition, and assisted me in the search for a publisher. My thanks to him, and to other Maryland professors: George Panichas and Carl Bode, whose constructive criticism aided me in my revisions of chapters one and three respectively; Robert Coogan, whose knowledge of Roman Catholicism (and association with Catholic clergy) contributed to my third chapter; Joseph Mancini, whose enthusiastic interest helped me develop and synthesize my ideas; and Theresa Coletti, whose moral and practical support I deeply appreciate. My gratitude also goes to the excellent secretarial staff in the English office, nearly all of whom participated in typing final copy. Finally, I am indebted to the General Research Board of the University of Maryland, which provided me with release time to pursue this study, funds that facilitated my research outside College Park, and a subvention that helped defray the cost of publication.

I wish also to express my appreciation to those who oversee the O'Neill collections at three university libraries. The Rare Book Room staff at Princeton's Firestone Library made available to me manuscripts and correspondence relating to "*Anna Christie*" and *The Fountain*. Donald Gallup's staff at Yale's Beinecke Library furnished numerous letters, manuscripts, typescripts and notes on the other plays considered here. The Rare Book Room curators at C. W. Post Center of Long Island University, especially Jean Goldberg, allowed me to examine O'Neill's personal library, given to them by John Pell; that collection thus constitutes the source of my frequent unattributed references to books O'Neill purchased, read and annotated.

Finally, I am grateful to three individuals who contributed in less direct, but no less important, ways to this work. Robert W. Daniel of Kenyon College supervised my honors thesis there, educating me in the nuances of style and structure. Louis J. Budd of Duke University directed my dissertation, teaching me the basics of scholarship. My wife Susan has supported me in a profounder manner, offering an unstinting patience, concern, understanding, and love that allowed me to meet various deadlines that had to be met. I quite literally could not have done it without her.

Bilbao, Spain   JAMES A. ROBINSON
18 June 1981

Epigraph

Perhaps I can explain my feeling for impelling, inscrutable forces behind life which it is my ambition to at least faintly shadow at their work in my plays.
—O'Neill letter to Barrett Clark, 1919

The thing that is called Tao is eluding and vague;
Vague and eluding, there is in it the form.
Eluding and vague, in it are things;
Deep and obscure, in it is the essence.
—*Tao Te Ching*, book 21

I'm a most confirmed mystic, too, for I'm always, always trying to interpret Life in terms of lives, never just lives in terms of character. I'm always acutely conscious of the force behind—(Fate, God, our biological past creating our present, whatever one calls it—Mystery, certainly)—and of the one eternal tragedy of Man in his glorious, self-destructive struggle to make the Force express him. . . .
—O'Neill letter to A. H. Quinn, ca 1925

But the man who knows the relation between the forces of Nature and actions, sees how some forces of Nature work upon other forces of Nature, and becomes not their slave.
—Bhagavad-Gita

I became drunk with the beauty and singing rhythm of it, and for a moment I lost myself—actually lost my life. I was set free! I dissolved in the sea, became white sails and flying spray, became moonlight and the ship and the high dim-starred sky!
—Edmund in *Long Day's Journey Into Night*

Those who realize that all this world of our experience is a Becoming, and never attains to Being, will not cling to that which cannot be grasped, and is entirely Void.
—The Compassionate Buddha

Off and on, of late years, I have studied the history and development of all religions with immense interest as being for me, at least, the most illuminating 'case histories' of the inner life of man.
—O'Neill letter to M. C. Sparrow, 1929

1

A Divided Vision

And what do you think was his next hiding place? Religion, no less—but as far away as he could run from home—in the defeatist mysticism of the East. First it was China and Lao Tze that fascinated him, but afterwards he ran on to Buddha, and his letters for a long time extolled passionless contemplation so passionately that I had a mental view of him regarding his navel frenziedly by the hour and making nothing of it! . . . But the next I knew, he was through with the East. It was not for the Western soul, he decided.

The speech appears in *Days Without End*,[1] written in 1932 by Eugene O'Neill; the person described is John Loving, whose spiritual and intellectual history strongly resembles O'Neill's; the speaker is Father Baird, a Catholic priest who helps Loving finally find salvation through Christ. But the conclusion's explicit affirmation of Christian faith, totally unique in the playwright's drama, is regarded by nearly all O'Neill scholars as a temporary aberration in his modern, tragic vision. Those same scholars largely agree that the flirtation with Oriental thought described above was only slightly less evanescent. After all, they have the word of the artist himself to this effect. Writing to Frederic Carpenter the same year he completed *Days Without End*, O'Neill admitted that "many years ago" (like John Loving) he "did considerable reading in Oriental philosophy and religion." But, he continues, "I never went in for an intensive study of it." Moreover, he eventually concluded that Eastern mystical systems were not appropriate to the needs and

1. *The Plays of Eugene O'Neill* (New York: Random, 1954), 1: 503.

concerns of Western man. Hence, the letter claims, "I do not think they have influenced my plays at all. At least, not consciously."[2]

Not all students of O'Neill's drama have been as willing as the playwright to discount an Oriental influence on his work, however. First, the "defeatist mysticism" mentioned by Father Baird has long been recognized as a prominent feature of O'Neill's art. Arthur Hobson Quinn asserted as early as 1926 that the "poet and mystic" in O'Neill constituted the profoundest part of his temperament.[3] Quinn, it should be noted, saw O'Neill's Celtic background as the source of these qualities; but in the later tragedies especially, the mysticism is so defeatist that it corresponds more closely to the Eastern than to the Irish vision of existence. More recent critics dismiss the playwright's disclaimer of interest in Eastern thought, but limit its impact to a few plays from the 1920s, mainly *The Fountain*, "*Marco Millions*," *Lazarus Laughed* and *Strange Interlude*; Doris Alexander and I. M. Raghavacharyulu are the most prominent members of this school.[4] Only one O'Neill scholar—Frederic Carpenter, in the 1964 and 1979 editions of *Eugene O'Neill*, published by Twayne—has asserted that O'Neill's vision betrays deep and consistent affinities with Eastern mystical thought, particularly in his emphasis on the transformation of emotion.[5] A 1966 essay by

---

2. Quoted in Carpenter, "Eugene O'Neill, the Orient and American Transcendentalism," in *Transcendentalism and Its Legacy*, ed. Myron Simon and T. H. Parsons (Ann Arbor: Univ. of Michigan Pr., 1966), p. 210.

3. *A History of the American Drama: From the Civil War to the Present Day* (New York: Appleton, 1936), 2: 201–2.

4. See Alexander, "Lazarus Laughed and Buddha," *Modern Language Quarterly*, 17 (Dec. 1956): 357–65; "*Light on the Path* and *The Fountain*," *Modern Drama*, 3 (Dec. 1960): 260–67; *The Tempering of Eugene O'Neill* (New York: Harcourt, 1962), pp. 215–19; and Raghavacharyulu, *Eugene O'Neill: A Study* (Bombay: Popular Prakashan Pr., 1965), chaps. three and four *passim*.

5. *Eugene O'Neill* (Boston: Twayne, 1964), pp. 175–78. In both the 1964 and 1979 editions, Professor Carpenter mentions O'Neill's Orientalism frequently, and these references form a kind of *leitmotif* to his thesis concerning O'Neill as a romantic writer. However, he offers a sustained discussion of O'Neill's affinities to Eastern mysticism only twice. Chapter two, "The Pattern of O'Neill's Tragedies," interprets the late plays as "transcendental" tragedy, in which "the veil of Maya"—which O'Neill views as "the substance of life itself"—"seems to be torn aside," permitting one to achieve "an approximation of Nirvana" (p. 79). The book's concluding section, on O'Neill's theory of tragedy, claims that the playwright "reaffirmed the age-old belief, typical of the Eastern world, in the primacy of emotion"; and that O'Neill "described man's goal as a mystical experience resembling that of Nirvana—'the

Carpenter further describes O'Neill's Orientalism as "the most important and distinctive aspect of his art," though also "the most difficult to define."[6] Thus, a minor but significant branch of O'Neill criticism has for some time held that Eastern religions illuminate some important aspects of his art; but so far, no extensive study of the subject has been attempted.

This book is just such a study. From the early sea plays through the final tragedies, I contend, O'Neill's affinity to Eastern mysticism informs his dynamic vision of reality, influences the values and attitudes of his protagonists, and shapes the symbolism and structure of entire plays. In addition to his own Oriental research, other factors help account for this pervasiveness. Numerous concepts of the Western thinkers he most admired—Emerson, Schopenhauer, Nietzsche and Jung—either paralleled or drew upon Oriental mystical theories. Moreover, O'Neill had intimate and lengthy relationships with two individuals who were themselves intrigued by Eastern religion and culture. Early in his career, his companion Terry Carlin introduced the young writer to Indian philosophy; years later, his third wife, Carlotta Monterey, helped reacquaint him with Chinese thought. Seeds cannot take root, however, if they fail to fall on fertile soil; O'Neill was nourishing ground indeed. Religious by nature, he distrusted rationalism, and searched incessantly for a mystical faith to replace the Catholicism he had abandoned in adolescence. That search inevitably led him to Hinduism, Buddhism and Taoism. Their mysticism corresponded to his own, and their relatively non-dogmatic approach to spiritual questions comforted a man who longed to diminish his constant sense of personal guilt. Nor was this personal movement toward Oriental thought unusual. Like many other artists of his time (Pound, Eliot, Hesse, Artaud), O'Neill perceived spiritual stalemate as the legacy of traditional Western culture, and sought solace in the serenity of the East.

But my aim is not simply to demonstrate the influence of particular Oriental sources on O'Neill. Rather, I propose to illuminate the tension in O'Neill's vision between two contrasting philosophical traditions. At its deepest level, his drama recurrently mingled West-

---

discovery of meaning' through the transcendence of all hopes and selfish illusions" (pp. 175, 179).
6. "Eugene O'Neill, the Orient and American Transcendentalism," p. 208.

ern and Eastern approaches to personality and reality. His professed belief in struggle (against self, society and fate), his drama's preoccupation with psychological conflicts, his quest for a new faith—all reflect the values of modern European and American culture. As the heir of a dualistic Western tradition that divides self from God and nature, however, O'Neill discovered himself bound within an isolated ego, prone to guilt. That isolation tormented him, and his mystical, "Oriental" side endeavored to heal the breach between subject and object by emphasizing the unity of soul and cosmos in a sphere beyond moral categories. That realm might be reached through passive self-contemplation, which led to the liberating intuition that the ego was an illusion—as were numerous other categories and dualities fostered by man's reason. The Eastern dimension of O'Neill's nature attempted to reconcile such dualities—between male and female, life and death, being and nonbeing—by viewing them as contraries participating in the same dynamic process. These dualities were of necessity the raw material of his art, since they generate the multitude of conflicts that form the core of Western drama; and O'Neill was traditionally Western in his reliance on conflict to create involvement and suspense. These conflicts are indeed the central "facts" of his theatre. But while he conceded that "facts are facts," he believed "the truth is beyond and outside of them."[7] O'Neill's drama represents a continuing effort to present facts while simultaneously moving beyond them in a quest for mystical truth. By so doing, he hoped, through the therapy of artistic creation, to synthesize the Western and Eastern sides of his own divided nature.

Generalizations about "Western" and "Eastern" thought can be both arbitrary and misleading. Nearly every concept found in Oriental mystical religions is duplicated somewhere in Occidental philosophy, particularly that of the last two hundred years. Nonethe-

7. O'Neill to Kenneth Macgowan, 29 Mar. 1921; quoted in Louis Sheaffer, *O'Neill: Son and Artist* (New York: Little, 1973), pp. 52–53.

less, differences of degree and emphasis do obtain between the two intellectual traditions; and these differences become apparent when we examine the major assumptions shared by Hinduism, Buddhism and Taoism that made these systems attractive to O'Neill. Their primary belief is that an impersonal spiritual force or state, an ultimate reality beyond all human thought or language, is available to man. It is termed Brahman by Vedantic Hindus, Nirvana by Buddhists, Tao by the Chinese. All three "ways" have as their goal the mystical union with this force or state. Man's rational faculties, however, cannot achieve this union. The reason is enslaved to the phenomenal world, laboring constantly to define and categorize it—a mistaken endeavor based on man's ignorance of the seamless unity of the universe. The major false distinction created by rationalism is that of the separate ego. This concept—vital to Western thought— is repudiated by all three systems, which agree that the individual personality possesses at best a provisional reality. They also perceive the phenomenal universe (including human "identity") in an eternal flux that frustrates our normal human desires. Hence, all three urge an attitude of non-desire that will liberate one into a blissful state where action is no longer required. This renunciatory ethic is shared by Christianity to some degree; but unlike Christianity, Oriental mystical faiths relegate the will to a limited role in the process of arriving at the desired bliss. One is enjoined to assume a passive, meditative stance that allows an intuitive apprehension of the oneness of the universe. That knowledge—not selfless love, or pursuit of the Good—permits liberation from the pain and confusion of normal human existence, as well as freedom from its artificial ethical categories.

The universe in flux perceived by Hinduism, Buddhism and Taoism should not be confused, however, with the Judeo-Christian view that the cosmos evolves in a linear fashion. The Eastern conception of time is predominantly circular, not progressive. The Indian mystical faiths picture the soul on a wheel of *samsara*, subject to perpetual transmigration until liberation is achieved; Brahman itself evolves and dissolves according to an eternal rhythm that creates and disintegrates the phenomenal universe. This motion of Brahman also points up the importance in Oriental mystical thought of non-being (a concept generally frightening to the West).

Buddhism presents the extinction of the self as the way to Nirvana; Hinduism identifies ultimate reality with the void; Taoism proposes that vacancy and plenitude are *yin* and *yang*, rhythmically alternating with one another. Indeed, Taoism argues, the same cyclical pattern characterizes all supposed oppositions. Heaven and earth, male and female, motion and stillness are all complementaries, containing the seeds of each other within themselves and engaging in an endless ebb and flow. This unifying, dynamic polarity also pertains to the cycle of life and death that governs human existence.

In Oriental mysticism, then, a monistic rhythm characterizes the processes of time, the material world, and human destiny. This idea particularly intrigued O'Neill. He longed to view his own inner conflicts as part of a larger, meaningful whole, and consequently endeavored in his drama to rhythmically unify numerous oppositions. His own tormented personality, along with his mystical distrust of reason, led O'Neill to the purchase and reading of the volumes on Hinduism, Buddhism and Taoism that chapter two will discuss. The same causes directed him to romantic philosophers like Schopenhauer, Nietzsche and Jung, all of whom studied and incorporated into their thought certain monistic Eastern assumptions. The third chapter will examine these figures (and another prominent O'Neill source, August Strindberg) in the context of modern romanticism, a major Western tradition that stimulated and reinforced O'Neill's interest in Oriental thought. The two other traditions discussed there, Roman Catholicism and American culture, were equally important in this respect. Despite its guilt-producing morality, Catholicism encouraged young Eugene to develop a mystical vision that eventually led him to turn East. Despite its prevailing pragmatism and materialism, American culture spawned a quasi-Oriental movement—Transcendentalism—that influenced O'Neill via the philosophy of Emerson. And at the time his mystical, experimental plays were produced in the 1920s, American society was experiencing a surge of interest in the Orient that helped generate remarkably receptive audiences for mystifying drama like *The Great God Brown* and *Strange Interlude*.

The traditions described above mingled elements of Eastern and Western thought, usually stressing the latter. The examination of selected O'Neill plays in the final three chapters reveals a similar mixture and emphasis. Because of the constant pull of Western philosophical and theatrical traditions in his sources and personality, O'Neill's journey East was complex and intermittent. Indeed, the first phase of his career, from 1913 to 1925, is heavily Western in its realistic psychological portraiture and its traditionally tragic outlook. For instance, his series of one-act sea plays, which view the sea as an "ironic life force" and tragic antagonist, reside firmly within the European theatrical mode of naturalism. But the serene stillness of *The Moon of the Caribbees* offers the first glimpse of the mystical, Oriental side of O'Neill; and the later, full-length *"Anna Christie"* hints at a possible Vedantic influence in its picture of an amoral divinity that weaves webs of illusion around the confused characters. That Brahmanic force also informs the protagonist's mystical vision at the climax of *The Fountain*, where our Western distinctions between man and nature, youth and age, and life and death are exposed as illusions. The numerous circles in the symbolism and structure of that play reproduce the polar rhythms of Taoism as well. Depicting Ponce de Leon's quest for a "Western passage to the East," *The Fountain* indicates O'Neill's commencement on a similar journey, in which he seeks to reconcile Oriental faiths with the Christian love ethic. *"Marco Millions"* again travels East, following Marco Polo to China; and again, Taoism stands behind the play's rhythms, and its philosophy as well. But the healing monism of the Tao fails to bridge the enormous gap between East and West. The prevailing dualism of *"Marco Millions"* is, in fact, more typical of O'Neill's first phase than the impulse toward unity found in *The Fountain*. Tragedies like *The Hairy Ape*, *Diff'rent* and *Desire Under the Elms* imply that struggle is both inevitable and ennobling in a dualistic universe; but elements in the other plays discussed above indicate O'Neill's simultaneous desire to transcend the struggle and apprehend the mystical serenity sought by Oriental sages.

This Eastern impulse was repeatedly expressed, but ultimately repudiated, during the next four years of O'Neill's career. As he composed plays for a new "religious" theatre, he read widely in comparative religion, philosophy and psychology. Consequently, his Eastern and Western sources sometimes conflict, sometimes coalesce, in the four experimental plays of this period. The polarities of Taoism, as filtered through the psychology of Jung, provide the internal and external character conflicts of *The Great God Brown*; the play's cyclical conception of time is indebted to Nietzsche's concept of eternal recurrence as well as the Indian belief in transmigration. Jungian personality types and principles also determine the characterization of *Lazarus Laughed*, while Nietzsche's Zarathustra and Dionysus provide models for the protagonist. But Oriental mysticism contributes just as heavily to this, O'Neill's most Eastern play. The passivity and gnosticism of Buddha permeate the speeches of Lazarus; the Hindu belief that human personality is a form of *māyā* explains the play's elaborate masking; and the dynamic polarity of the Tao appears in the play's rhythmic alternation between life and death, comedy and tragedy. Again, in the subsequent *Strange Interlude*, all three mystical religions—especially Buddhism (partly via Schopenhauer)—shape the play's vision of human existence as a painful, mystifying illusion. Here, however, Nina Leeds' vacillation between serene, rhythmical mother god and interfering, judgmental father god duplicates O'Neill's own struggle between Eastern and Western thought. While East appears to prevail in the work's resigned conclusion, the influence of Freud overshadows all others, as O'Neill begins to return to his modern European roots. *Dynamo* completes that return. The Great God Electricity—another rhythmical mother god—explicitly stands for modern science, but is also associated with Oriental religions, and this force destroys the neurotic young man who turns to it for comfort.

O'Neill's repudiation of this deity signaled his implicit admission that his native Western viewpoint was inescapable. That admission governed O'Neill's art for the remainder of his life. *Mourning Becomes Electra* looks to an ancient Greek trilogy for its inspiration; *Ah, Wilderness!* and *Days Without End* returned to O'Neill's personal past; the plays of his ill-fated Cycle focused on American history. His final, autobiographical tragedies seem equally Western, with their realistic dramaturgy, dualistic visions, and obsession with time. But *The Iceman Cometh* and *Long Day's Journey Into Night* exhibit dynamic polarities that correspond to those of Taoism. Both plays also suggest that man's hopes and beliefs are a veil of *māyā* that obscures the void at the center of reality; both contain a pair of characters who seek peace in passive transcendence of the desires and struggles of existence. That escapist urge is scrutinized and ultimately found wanting by the mature O'Neill, who is now resigned to the twin Western burdens of ego and history, and believes that a Christian ethic of forgiveness and compassion is man's only hope. And O'Neill's penultimate effort, the one-act *Hughie*, likewise repudiates his Eastern impulses. As in *Iceman*, the Oriental abyss of non-being is dramatized, appearing at the very center of the play: "*the night recedes, too, until at last it must die and join all the other long nights in Nirvana, the big night of nights.*"[8] But neither of the two characters can long endure staring into the void, and they retreat from it into a small community based on illusion. For them, and finally for O'Neill, the void—which the Oriental mystic finds liberating—is too terrifying to embrace.

O'Neill's efforts to embrace Oriental approaches to reality, however, must not be lightly dismissed. His attempts to view man and nature as one, to move beyond the separate self, and to reconcile dualistic oppositions into a unified rhythmic process all connect him to contemporary Western culture. The sciences, arts and religions of America today ask many of the same questions O'Neill posed in the 1920s and 1930s about the "inscrutable forces behind life." Contemporary physics hypothesizes black holes, composed of anti-matter, floating in outer space. The ecology movement, field theory, kinetic sculpture, Gestalt psychology and quantum physics all assume a unity between perceiving individual and perceived environment that closely resembles the sense of unity sought by Oriental mystical religions. And millions of young Americans and Europeans turn to Buddhism, Transcendental Meditation and other Eastern practices to replace a Christian God that no longer answers their spiritual needs. O'Neill was perhaps too traditional, too much a New England Irish Catholic himself, to find a satisfying solution to his inner torments in Oriental thought. But the frequent tension in his drama between Eastern and Western approaches pertains to many of the conflicts, and possibilities, that exist in our world today.

8. *Hughie* (New Haven: Yale Univ. Pr., 1959), p. 19.

2

Journeys East

Eugene O'Neill's explorations of Oriental religion placed him in a long line of modern Western thinkers and artists. The *philosophes* in eighteenth century Europe idolized Confucius; the German romantics, Ralph Waldo Emerson and T. S. Eliot were intrigued by Hinduism. O'Neill, however, was more eclectic in his quest than most. He claimed in a 1929 letter that "off and on, of late years, I have studied the history and development of all religions with immense interest as being for me, at least, the most illuminating 'case histories' of the inner life of man."[1] His personal library bears witness to this claim. Among the fifty-three volumes dealing with religion are numerous books on Christianity, Frazer's *The Golden Bough*, Albert Churchward's *The Origin and Evolution of Religion*—and eight books on Oriental faiths, including studies of Zoroastrianism, Islam, and the mystical religions of Hinduism, Buddhism and Taoism. O'Neill admitted in 1932 to doing "considerable reading in Oriental philosophy and religion," though he claimed it was "many years ago."[2] Probably in the early 1920s, in fact, O'Neill began studying Eastern religion, with a dual motive: the immediate need to gather background for *The Fountain* and "*Marco Millions*," and the deeper desire to explore intellectual and spiritual systems that might illuminate his own mystical intuitions about reality.

1. Letter to Martha Carolyn Sparrow, 13 Oct. 1929; cited by her in "The Influence of Psychoanalytical Material on the Plays of Eugene O'Neill" (Diss., Northwestern Univ., 1931), p. 77.
2. Quoted in Carpenter, "Eugene O'Neill, the Orient and American Transcendentalism," p. 210.

Because of his isolated residences and reclusive nature, O'Neill's research in comparative religion was largely confined to his own books. Generally, he chose them carefully, and this is the case with the volumes on Oriental mystical religions that his library contained in the 1920s.[3] For Hinduism, he turned to *Six Systems of Indian Philosophy* by the eminent Sanskritist Max Müller, obtaining from it an accurate description of Vedanta, Samkhya, Yoga and the other branches of Hinduism. A. K. Coomaraswamy's *Buddha and the Gospel of Buddhism* provided a lengthy summary of Buddha's legendary life, an even more extensive analysis of Buddhist thought, history and art, and a comparison of Buddhism and Brahmanism. Finally, James Legge's *The Texts of Taoism* offered both a translation of and commentary upon Lao Tse's *Tao Te Ching* and half of his follower Chuang Tse's writings. All three books were produced by scholars acknowledged to be authorities on their subjects; and my discussion of these religions will examine these particular texts to determine (as far as possible) what O'Neill considered the essential teachings of Hinduism, Buddhism and Taoism.

The three mystical systems exhibit numerous similarities that distinguish them from most Western thought: all subordinate reason to intuition; all agree that the ultimate reality is impersonal, yet spiritually connected to man's essence; all aim to liberate man from his conventional view of a separate self, and thereby help him recognize his profound unity with the universe. Consequently, all emphasize the passive realization (through meditation) of the blissful presence of an immanent universal force. This ecstatic experience transports the believer to an inner realm where non-being dwells. Hinduism and Buddhism posit that void as the essence of reality; Taoism asserts that non-being and being participate in a unified rhythmic process that characterizes countless other oppositions, like male and female, life and death.

Despite their essential agreement, substantial distinctions separate the three systems. The Indian faiths focus on the mitigation of

---

3. O'Neill's signature style in all three indicates their purchase prior to 1929, when he wed Carlotta. (All books purchased after their marriage were either signed by Carlotta, or received a bookplate with both their names done in O'Neill's handwriting.) Internal evidence discussed in this and subsequent chapters points to the purchase of all three in the early 1920s, or earlier.

human suffering; Taoism seeks to lengthen life via harmony with the Tao. Metaphysically, Taoism assumes that *yin* and *yang* principles order all aspects of reality; the Indian religions are not so polaristic (though Hinduism also postulates a pervasive cosmic rhythm). Differences also exist between orthodox Hinduism and Buddhism. The latter denies reality to even a universal Self, proposing a Nirvana of absolute annihilation; Hinduism agrees in principle, but not in emphasis. These and other differences are important in understanding O'Neill's divided vision, which varied according to which system influenced him more at the time of a play's composition. *"Anna Christie"* and its sea god display affinities with Vedanta Hinduism, for example, while *"Marco Millions"* moves to the polar rhythms of Taoism. Hence, the following discussion will attend to that which distinguishes these systems from one another, as well as the major asumptions that unite them.

Hinduism

O'Neill's first indirect encounter with the wisdom of the East was with Hinduism, via Emerson, whose essays he read while still an adolescent. Years later, in Greenwich Village and Provincetown, he read the Theosophist pamphlet *Light on the Path* which (as we shall later see) drew heavily upon Hindu conceptions of *karma*, liberation, and transcendence of ego. The close friend who gave him that pamphlet, Terry Carlin, was himself intrigued by Indian mysticism. He associated with a young Indian anarchist, Dhan Gopal Mukerji, and many of Carlin's acquaintances saw in him (according to one O'Neill biographer) "the wisdom and beauty of a Hindu holy man." [4] Reinforcing O'Neill's mystical nature, Carlin also steered it in an Eastern direction. When the two moved into a Provincetown apartment in 1916, the aspiring young playwright painted on the rafters a mystical passage from *Light on the Path*: "Before the eye can see it must know blindness. Before the ear can hear it must be deaf to the noise of the world: before the heart can learn to love it

---

4. Alexander, *Tempering*, p. 211.

must have known the agony of emptiness."⁵ Not content with so superficial an understanding of Hinduism, however, O'Neill acquired Müller's *Six Systems of Indian Philosophy* within the next few years to deepen his knowledge.⁶

Müller's volume on Hinduism does not explore all aspects of this multifaceted religion. There is virtually no mention of the countless Hindu myths and deities, no treatment of popular texts like the Bhagavad-Gita, no discussion of developments in Hindu thought since the medieval period. Instead, after tracing the growth of primitive Hindu thought out of the Vedas and Upanishads (sacred texts written between 1500 and 500 b.c.), Müller examines the six traditional schools of Hindu esoteric philosophy. Only two points from the introductory chapters are pertinent here. First, Müller distinguishes between the mythological Prajapati and the metaphysical Brahman, and reveals his focus on the latter. "One Being, neither male nor female, a Being raised high above all the conditions and limitations of personality and of human nature," describes Brahman.⁷ And though this Being assumes various names in the different systems, Müller's argument directs itself toward describing how each defines this impersonal, neuter and transcendent entity. The second point concerns the unity that lies behind all Indian systems, including Buddhism. Müller identifies four ideas shared by Buddhism and the different Hindu schools. First is metempsychosis (*samsara*), the belief that at death our soul transmigrates into other

5. This is recorded by O'Neill's second wife, Agnes Boulton, in her *Part of a Long Story* (Garden City: Doubleday, 1958), p. 139. However, Doris Alexander, in *Tempering*, cites a slightly different quotation: "Before the eyes can see they must be incapable of tears. Before the ear can hear it must have lost its sensitiveness. Before the voice can speak . . . it must have lost the power to wound. Before the soul can stand . . . its feet must be washed in the blood of the heart" (p. 219: ellipses Alexander's). Professor Alexander's version is a verbatim duplication of one in *Light on the Path*; Ms. Boulton's involves a paraphrase. Whichever version is correct, O'Neill was obviously inspired by the Theosophist pamphlet, which will be examined in chapter three.

6. The exact date of purchase is indeterminable, for the "Eugene O'Neill" signature includes neither place nor date, and his correspondence sheds no light on the matter. Internal evidence from *The Fountain*, though, suggests O'Neill had acquired the volume by 1922.

7. Max Müller, *Six Systems of Indian Philosophy* (London: Longmans, 1919). This is the same edition as O'Neill's personal copy. Subsequent references are documented in the text.

bodies until it is sufficiently purified to escape the cycle. Consequently, Indians "fear rather than doubt a future life" (p. 106), due to their preoccupation with suffering—the second and third common features. Indeed, "the aim of all Indian philosophy was the removal of suffering, which was caused by nescience, and the attainment of the highest happiness, which was produced by knowledge" (p 107). Indian thought discovers the cause of suffering in our ignorance (*avidyā*) of reality, and in the consequent works and thoughts which perpetuate our misery in this and future existences. These works and thoughts operate according to *karma*, the final concept common to all Indian philosophies.

The moral law of *karma* dictates the "continuous working of every thought, word and deed through all the ages" (p. 109), guaranteeing that all human behavior has eternal consequences. But *karma* ceases for the liberated soul. Though we must undergo the cycles of *samsara* while under *karma*'s sway, *samsara* is ultimately unreal and non-eternal. This unreality also characterizes the broad metaphysical cycle that envelopes *samsara* and *karma*, whereby Brahman alternately creates and destroys the phenomenal world. At the end of each *kalpa* (an enormously long period best described as a temporal eternity), Brahman absorbs the cosmos into itself, leaving the universe in an undeveloped state of non-being. Subsequently, Brahman creates a new, material universe. However, as Müller notes, "what is truly eternal [the soul], is not affected by the cosmic illusion . . . and may recover at any moment its self-knowledge, that is, its self-being, and its freedom from all conditions and fetters" (p. 110). Thus, in a universe of cycles involving both one's *karma* and the entire material world, only the soul—which partakes of the larger Soul or Self, Brahman—remains eternal.

The remainder of the book delineates the contrasting features of the six systems. Three of them are treated cursorily because their orientation is not metaphysical; a fourth system, Yoga, gets only slightly more attention, because its metaphysical assumptions duplicate those of the Samkhya school. Müller makes apparent, then, his central interest in the original philosophical speculations of Indian philosophy. Nearly half the volume focuses on the major competing systems of Vedanta and Samkhya, the two schools most profound in their speculations on ultimate reality. As Müller points out, the orthodox mainstream of Indian religious philosophy lies in Vedanta, which emerged as a consistent system when formulated by Samkara in the eighth century A.D. Its central feature is the identification of the human and the divine. Not simply a transcendent force, Brahman also exists in each soul as the *Atman*, the deepest level of one's being. The identity of that self and the infinite, timeless Self is summarized by the Sanskrit phrase *Tat tvam asi*, literally "Thou art that." The subjective and objective realms are thus reconciled, for this identity unites man and all creation. As the Khandogya Upanishad puts it, "that which is the subtile [sic] essence, in it all that exists has its Self. It is the True. It is the Self, and thou, O Svetaketu, art it" (p. 130). That Self cannot be reached through the senses or reason. The Katha Upanishad proclaims that "beyond the senses there are the objects, beyond the objects there is the mind, beyond the mind there is the intellect, the Great Self is beyond the intellect" (p. 136). In fact, it transcends all categories. "Beyond the Great there is the Undeveloped, beyond the Undeveloped there is the Person. Beyond the Person there is nothing—this is the goal, the furthest road" (pp. 136–37). But paradoxically, Brahman is also *every*thing: "That Self is hidden in all beings and does not shine forth, but it is seen by subtle seers" (p. 137).

Resolving this apparent contradiction between pantheism and nihilism poses the central challenge of Vedantic metaphysical speculation. The explanation is ingenious. The phenomenal world, Vedantists claim, represents Brahman in a state of forgetfulness, dispersing itself into myriad forms and thereby obscuring the fundamental unity of all existence. This cosmic nescience—known as *māyā*—corresponds to the ignorance (*avidyā*) of one who mistakes those separate phenomenal forms for ultimate reality. As Müller expresses it, "Creation is not real in the highest sense in which Brahman is real, but it is real in so far as it is phenomenal" (p. 162). In other words, the material world has a *provisional* reality, and those under *māyā*'s spell err in mistaking the provisional for the ultimate. In this common state of ignorance, we believe in the reality of separate phenomena and (especially) the separate self. But the enlightened soul recognizes the spiritual unity of all existence in Brahman, the "tremendous synthesis of subject and object, the identification of cause and effect, of the I and the It" (p. 170).[8] Vedanta sees all existence as absorbed into the undifferentiated unity of Brahman, denying in particular the reality of the separate, perceiving ego so precious to Western thought.

The mystical realization of this unity liberates one from all desires concerning the phenomenal world, and hence from the suffering produced by those desires. This liberation (*moksha*) also frees the soul from the endless transmigrations caused by *karma*. The discovery of *tat tvam asi* places one in a sphere where the moral law no longer applies; "the Atman, which is above the distinctions of subject and object, of past and present, of cause and effect, is also by necessity above the distinction of good and evil" (p. 180). This does not grant one a license for evil. Presumably, the liberated soul will be so serene that any action will hold little appeal. As Müller puts it, the blissful *Atman* "cannot do anything, good or bad" (p. 180)—that is, the enlightened one will tend to refrain from action altogether, or at least not identify with the consequences of those actions.[9]

The pantheism and monism of Vedanta represent the native philosophy of India, so that the casual Western student tends to think all Hindu thought shares these features. The book's lengthy discussion of the dualistic Samkhya system of Hinduism demonstrates that such is not the case. But Müller's discussion of Samkhya is tangential to my concerns, for it is the orthodox system of Vedanta that appears in the drama of Eugene O'Neill. His treatment of the sea in "*Anna Christie*," for instance, demonstrates interesting parallels to the pantheistic monism of Vedanta. On the one hand exists

8. This sounds like Berkeley, but a crucial difference obtains between this approach and that of Western idealism. Systems like Platonism and Christianity similarly deny the reality of the world as our senses and intellects perceive it, Müller admits: "but no one has ventured to deny at the same time the reality of what we call the Ego, the senses and the mind, and their inherent forms" (p. 183).

9. As we shall see in chapter three, this doctrine differs from Nietzsche's apparently similar belief that the Superman is "beyond good and evil." The Western philosopher believes in the creative power of the individual ego and will, in a way that Vedanta Hinduism does not. Moreover, Nietzsche's position involves a romantic disdain for collective bourgeois morality, while the Vedantic stance derives from a belief that the moral law of *karma* has only provisional reality.

Anna's desire to merge with the ocean, which she regards as a deeper Self; on the other hand is Chris's unwillingness to trust "that ole davil," which has often worn the deceptive veil of *māyā*. Later, in *Lazarus Laughed*, the protagonist proclaims man's identity with a pantheistic God, but incites mobs who wear the multiplicitous masks of *māyā*. Thus, some of the key Hindu concepts discussed by Müller can be found in the symbols and situations of O'Neill's drama. For Vedanta Hinduism, if not exercising a direct and consistent influence on the playwright's vision, corresponded closely to O'Neill's own intuitions about man and reality at certain points in his career.

Buddhism

The same companion who interested O'Neill in Hinduism probably pointed him toward Buddhism. Terry Carlin was familiar with the teachings of this rival Indian system, which both resembles and deviates from the Hindu orthodox mainstream. Carlin once advised his friend Mukerji to return to India, with the words, "your ancestors found the truths you are seeking thousands of years ago; Buddha was the greatest of all anarchists." [10] On another, more somber occasion, he wrote that "even my own acts and thoughts take on the futility of nightmare, and Nirvana is very welcome, if I could be sure of it, but I had rather stay what I am than start life all over again in some other shape, with a possible creeping recollection of my former existence." [11] Whether Buddha was indeed a great anarchist is debatable; but Carlin's allusion to the concept of Nirvana suggests at least a basic acquaintance with Buddhist doctrine. By the early 1920s, O'Neill had also made that acquaintance, as an unpublished series of observations by Agnes Boulton makes clear. "Thoughts on Her Marriage," a five-page typescript dated "Probably 1920 or 20's" by its transcriber, contains remarks Agnes made (or perhaps wished she had made) to her husband, Eugene O'Neill.

10. Alexander, *Tempering*, pp. 213–14.
11. Ibid., p. 217.

"You speak of that sense of isolation," one section reads, "of feeling that no matter what life does to you, there is something apart, something that cannot be touched; you speak then of the Bhuddis-tic [sic] idea, of the feeling of lives lived, of lives to come, of the great slow inward spiral; a flash of the truth of this comes to one sometime, and brings spiritual realization with it." [12] O'Neill obviously knew enough of Buddhism to allude to its concepts (shared with Hinduism) of transmigration and detachment, articulating these sometime in the 1920s—definitely before 1927, when he deserted Agnes. In fact, he probably studied Buddhism between 1921 and 1925 when he wrote *The Fountain* and "*Marco Millions*," since scenes in both plays contain Buddhist priests.

The book on Buddhism in his library was A. K. Coomaraswamy's *Buddha and the Gospel of Buddhism*. Broader in scope and less scholarly than Müller's esoteric tome, Coomaraswamy's volume includes ninety pages on the life, legends and major pronouncements of Gautama Buddha, who lived in India in the sixth century B.C. Following this is an analysis of the central Buddhist doctrines, a comparison of Buddhism with the three contemporary Indian systems at its time of inception, brief observations on Mahayana and Zen Buddhism, and a closing survey of Buddhist art. The book thus manages to treat all the important points of Buddhist legend, philosophy and practice. One of its most enlightening arguments concerns the essential similarity of Buddhism and the Brahmanism (i.e., early orthodox Hinduism) against which it reacted in the fifth century B.C. Brahmanism (the precursor of Vedanta) and Buddhism are almost identical in their conception of the individual soul's unreality. The Brahman that Vedanta later termed *neti, neti*—"not so, not so," i.e., indefinable—resembles the Buddhistic Nirvana, "invisible, unutterable and unfathomable" and partaking of non-being. [13] Both systems further agreed that bondage to the illusory ego and phenomenal world produces suffering, preventable only through the cessation of desire; that liberation is possible in this life; and that the ultimate reality is impersonal. On one matter,

12. File Folder Za/O'Neill/215, O'Neill Collection, Beinecke Library, Yale Univ.
13. Ananda K. Coomaraswamy, *Buddha and the Gospel of Buddhism* (London: Harper, 1916), p. 202. Again, the edition cited is the same as that owned by O'Neill; again, all subsequent references will be documented in the text.

however, they disagreed totally. Brahmanism (and later, Vedanta) was monistic, orthodox Buddhism dualistic. Like Samkhya Hinduism, orthodox Buddhism teaches that the transitory world of matter and time cannot be reconciled with the spirit, which resides in a changeless eternity. Consequently, Buddhism is more emphatic in its renunciation of the self and world than Vedanta.

Buddhism was (and is) more democratic than Hinduism as well, since Buddha disregarded the caste system that the mother religion had instituted and perpetuated. The spiritual democracy of Buddhism helps account for its spread throughout the Orient. Like Christianity, it expanded because of its enormous appeal to the underprivileged of society. In fact, the largest school of Buddhism, known as Mahayana (literally, the "Great Raft"), resembles Christianity in numerous respects. But Coomaraswamy's treatment of Mahayana is brief. He concentrates instead on the gospel (*dharma*) of the Buddha, a rigid adherence to which characterizes the orthodox Hinayana ("Little Raft") school. Those teachings sharply contrast to Christian doctrine concerning the Christ. Hinayana followers regard Buddha as an exceptionally perceptive man, not a god. They conceive of Buddha's life as a human being's progress toward Nirvana, which (when attained) released him from the endless cycles of life and death. They prefer not to comment on whether the "soul" of Buddha survived in heaven after his death. Moreover, they preach liberation through knowledge, not love; and they pursue the monastic ideal of the Arahat, who reaches Nirvana and becomes indifferent to worldly sorrow, assuming as passive an attitude toward existence as possible. Since Hinayana doctrine receives Coomaraswamy's emphasis, my explanation of Buddhist teachings will focus on it.

Coomaraswamy recounts scrupulously the various legends that have accrued around the Buddha, but his major interest is the awakening Buddha achieved after seven years of spiritual discipline while meditating under the Bodhi tree. Buddha put his enlightened perceptions in the form of the Four Ariyan Truths: "that there is suffering (*Dukkha*), that it has a cause (*Samudaya*), that it can be suppressed (*Nirodha*), and that there is a way to accomplish this (*Magga*), the 'Path'" (p. 90). This "Eightfold Path" involves "Right Belief, Right Aspiration, Right Speech, Right Conduct, Right Living, Right Effort, Right Recollectedness, Right Rapture." Coomaraswamy concentrates on the first division of the Path, which constitutes the Gospel of Buddha and "is most tersely summarized in the triple formula of *Dukkha, Anicca, Anatta*—Suffering, Impermanence, Non-egoity" (p. 91).

The First Truth declares suffering the essence of individual existence, as witnessed in our birth, aging, illness and death. The Second Truth identifies the cause of this suffering: impermanence, "the fundamental and pitiless law of all existence" (p. 91). The world exists in an eternal state of becoming, without beginning or end, and never attains to a state of being. This applies to the individual personality as well. The doctrine of *Anatta* maintains that, "in place of an individual, there exists a succession of instants of consciousness" (p. 95). Anyone attempting to find permanence suffers from the same ignorance described by Hinduism, and Buddha likewise describes the illusion of stasis that existence offers as *māyā*. Buddha's emphasis, however, is not metaphysical but psychological. He analyzes the mental states that operate to produce suffering (the famous "Wheel of Causation") and concludes, in Coomaraswamy's paraphrase, that "from Ignorance arises the thought of entity, whereas there exists but a becoming; from the thought of self as entity, and from the desires of Me, arises life; life is inseparable from Evil [i.e., suffering]" (p. 97). The Third Truth logically follows: one ends suffering by annihilating all desires, even the desire for life itself. The Fourth Truth prescribes a systematic method for doing so, the Eightfold Path.

Probably the most startling of Buddha's doctrines is *Anatta*, for the absence of individual identity reflects the absence of any larger Self. A disciple inquired of Buddha, "What is meant, lord, by the phrase, the world is empty?" The Buddha responded, "that it is empty, Ananda, of a Self, or of anything of the nature of a Self" (p. 98). While Buddhists thus agree with Hindus on the non-reality of the ego, they proclaim the absence of Self (Brahman) as well. In other words, they identify being with void. Consequently, while borrowing many Hindu terms and concepts, Buddha often twists them in the direction of nothingness. For instance, the Buddhist wheel of *samsara* differs slightly from its Hindu counterpart. Instead of conceiving the soul animistically (as Brahmanists had done), Buddha teaches the transmigration of "character," of "personality without a person" (p. 106). The soul disappears altogether at death, even the non-liberated soul; and rebirth into a new life occurs when *karma* incorporates that moral "character" into a new knot of causes, and propels it into a new body. Buddha compares the transmigrating character to an insubstantial flame, transmitted from one candle to another. While the two religions essentially concur on *samsara*, then, Buddhism emphasizes the vacant nature of ultimate reality more than does Hinduism.

Nowhere is this more apparent than in the concept of Nirvana. Like the Hindu *moksha*, Nirvana represents the enlightened consciousness that follows one's intuition of ultimate reality. It similarly liberates one from *karma* into a constant feeling of bliss. But in the Upanishads, Coomaraswamy observes, Nirvana is presented as perfect self-realization; in Buddha's gospel, it instead involves a "dying out" of the self (p. 117). If transmigration transmits the "flame" of personality, Nirvana extinguishes it, thereby effecting a "cessation of becoming" and a "release from individuality" due to emancipation from "the conceit of self-reference" (pp. 118–19). A Sacred Buddhist text, the Suttanipata, makes this clear. "Who have crossed the flood of desire, / Who have entered upon the calm delight, / Of these no trace remain" (p. 121). Hence, to escape the suffering of a world in flux, one must enter "the Abyss, wherein all Becoming is not" (p. 122). Paradoxically, that non-being also comprises the essence of being. To the liberated soul, "the doors of perception being cleansed, he must continue to see all things as they are, infinite—or to revert to Buddhist phraseology, as void" (p. 125).

To be sure, the Hindu Brahman also represents void. As is usually the case with the two religions, the difference is one of emphasis. Moreover, the ethics of Buddhism and Hinduism scarcely differ at all, though Buddha is famous for proposing a "middle way" that avoids the ascetic excesses of Brahmanism. Like its mother religion, Buddhism proposes knowledge as the key to salvation. The Eightfold Path's middle sections, with their numerous moral injunctions, are designed to finally achieve "Right Recollectedness" and "Right Rapture," where ethical considerations are transcended along with the illusory ego. As Coomaraswamy states, "since the 'individual' does not exist, there can be no question of reward or punishment for the individual, and therefore there is no sanction for morality based on reward or punishment affecting the individual in the future" (p. 137). In fact, Buddhism—for all its apparently ethical doctrine—is ultimately just as passive and amoral as Hinduism. Buddha says of all efforts to obtain salvation, "it is not the effort itself which I blame, which flinging aside the base pursues a high path of its own; but the wise, by all this common toil, ought to attain that state in which nothing ever needs to be done again" (p. 146). In that state, Hinayana Buddhism preaches, no concern need exist for the welfare of others, for the goals of orthodox Buddhism and Hinduism are identical: to escape from suffering and attain release from this world.

The relationship of Buddhism and Hinduism is obviously not simple. Furthermore, the history of the two religions involves the splitting of each into various schools and sects that influenced one another, making their relationship even more tangled. Doubtless, the details of this multiplication and division held little interest for Eugene O'Neill, whose fascination with the Orient lay in its mystical speculations about man, God and reality; here, orthodox Hinduism and Buddhism reached nearly identical conclusions about the illusory phenomenal world, the unreal ego, the ensnarements of desire, the wandering soul, and the impersonal forces behind life. Certain O'Neill plays, however, display a Buddhist perspective on these questions. *Strange Interlude*'s picture of a world in flux, and a grasping heroine who finally moves beyond desire, clearly has Buddhist thought behind it; *The Iceman Cometh* presents two major characters who pretend to have liberated themselves by confronting the void behind existence; *Hughie* demonstrates the inability of Western man to face the abyss. But the Buddhist influence largely confines itself to O'Neill's later phases, from 1925 to 1928 and from 1939 to 1943. Unlike the Vedantic and Taoist concepts, the teachings of Buddha probably had to simmer several years in O'Neill's unconscious before achieving expression in his drama. His interest in Buddhism, however, apparently continued even after his career had ended. The last book on Eastern thought acquired by O'Neill, three years before his death, was C. T. Suzuki's *Introduction to Zen Buddhism*.

Taoism

In addition to the Indian religions, O'Neill studied Taoism during his period of "immense interest" in all religions in the early 1920s. No external evidence indicates precisely when he read the volume on Taoism his library contained at that time, James Legge's translation of the *Tao Te Ching* and the first half of the *Chuang Tse*. But various facts indicate that the playwright's involvement with Chinese religion and culture was deeper and broader than his interest in India. He acquired several books on Chinese poetry and art around 1922 and 1923 while researching his only play set in the Orient, "*Marco Millions.*" He recurrently toyed with the idea of writing a play about an ancient Chinese Emperor, Shih Huang Ti, and read books on Chinese history with this in mind.[14] He and Carlotta Monterey took a cruise to China at the end of 1928; more important, Carlotta was herself an avid student of Chinese culture, purchasing numerous books on Chinese history and art throughout her life, and maintaining friendships with Chinese who lived in America. Two such friends, the authors Mai-Mai Sze and Lin Yutang, presented copies of books on Chinese thought and art to the O'Neills when they moved into their new residence in California, Tao House, in 1937. Lin Yutang's two books, *My Country and My People* and *A Philosophy of Living*, repeatedly exposed his deep regard for the teachings of Chuang Tse. Mai-Mai Sze's two contributions focused more exclusively on Taoism. The first was Legge's translation of the complete writings of Lao Tse and Chuang Tse (which contained the volume O'Neill already owned plus a subsequent volume, bound together under one cover); the second, Dwight Goddard's *Lao-tzu's Tao and Wu Wei*, included a more modern translation of the *Tao Te Ching* and an informal essay on

14. The "Shih Huang Ti" idea is first mentioned in O'Neill's Work Diary on 3, 4, and 5 May 1929, where his notes indicate that he had read and taken notes for a proposed play about this third century B.C. ruler. Entries for 17 and 18 July 1929, 12 July 1932, and 5 and 8 Nov. 1934 indicate that he continued to be interested in the idea for over five years ("Work Diary," II, transcribed by Donald Gallup: File Folder Za/O'Neill/126x, O'Neill Collection, Beinecke Library, Yale Univ.). One of the books he consulted was A. E. Grantham's *Hills of Blue: A Picture Roll of Chinese History* (London: Methuen, 1927). O'Neill's personal copy contains marginal lines, marking certain passages on the pages that describe the reign of this emperor.

the Taoist principle of inaction. While no record exists of O'Neill's response to these gifts, he was presumably grateful. Five years earlier (in the previously cited letter to Carpenter), the playwright had indicated that "the mysticism of Lao-Tse and Chuang-Tzu probably interested me more than any other Oriental writings." [15]

Taoism was also, it appears, the only one of the three Eastern religions for which O'Neill read a translation of the sacred texts, not just a commentary on them. Legge's *The Texts of Taoism* offered one of the first translations (1891) of the *Tao Te Ching* and the writings of Chuang Tse. It also contained Legge's general introduction to Taoism, and his comments on each chapter (called "book") of the works of both authors. O'Neill's volume on Taoism, then, provided both a primary knowledge and a scholarly explanation of this philosophy, courtesy of an outstanding authority on Chinese religion.

Legge's introduction provides background for the layman, and briefly summarizes the lives of Lao Tse and Chuang Tse in the sixth and fourth centuries B.C., respectively. After discussing textual matters, Legge identifies the major features of the Taoist religion instituted by these two men. The word "Tao," translated "road," is a metaphor for something "not a positive being, but an immaterial mode of being" that is "the spontaneously operating cause of all movement in the phenomena of the universe." [16] As in Indian mysticism, this force is impersonal, for "the old Taoists had no idea of a personal God." It likewise defies our language and conceptions, for "the nameless Simplicity of the Tao" must "disappear before Knowledge" (pp. 18, 30). In summarizing the Taoist principles of conduct, which consist of imitating the spontaneous activities of the Tao, Legge quotes from Chuang Tse in describing those who succeeded:

15. Quoted in Carpenter, "Eugene O'Neill, the Orient and American Transcendentalism," p. 210.
16. *The Texts of Taoism*, trans. James Legge (1891; rpt. London: Oxford Univ. Pr., 1927), p. 15. This edition contains volumes 39 and 40 of the *Sacred Books of the East* series, edited by Max Müller, and is the same edition acquired by O'Neill in 1937. It completes the *Chuang Tse*, and appends various other Taoist tracts. My references documented in the text will be to this double volume, though the vast majority of citations refer to material in vol. 39, obtained separately by O'Neill in the early 1920s. All subsequent references to the *Tao Te Ching* refer to vol. 39, which contains that work in its entirety; references to the *Chuang Tse* also refer to vol. 39, unless otherwise indicated. Any parenthetical material in the quotations is Legge's, not mine.

" 'vacancy, stillness, placidity, tastelessness, quietude, silence and nonaction' would be found to be their characteristics" (p. 17). The importance of emptiness and passivity in the metaphysics and ethics of Taoism demonstrates two more correspondences to the Indian systems, particularly Buddhism. And Taoism's preaching of indifference to the world, renunciation of desire, and a balance between extremes of behavior strikes further resonances with Buddhist teachings. Due to its different origin, however, Taoism also contrasts with Buddhism. Little mention of spiritual discipline can be found in the writings of either Lao Tse or Chuang Tse. Something as systematic as the Eightfold Path would be anathema to a Taoist, whose principle of *wu wei* (spontaneous non-action) constitutes not just Taoism's goal, but its very essence.[17]

Another feature that distinguishes Taoism from Buddhism is the dynamic polarity of the Chinese system. Though Legge fails to discuss this, a cyclical quality informs all the operations of the Tao. Like Buddhism, Taoism finds the world a constant process of transformation; unlike Buddhism, Taoism sees these transformations operating according to the polar opposites *yin* and *yang*. Originally referring to the sunny and shady sides of a mountain, *yin* and *yang* had by Lao Tse's time come to represent the polarity of all nature. The *yin* is dark, receptive, female, intuitive and still, and associated with the earth; the *yang* is light, aggressive, male, rational and active, and associated with heaven. These two forces are not static, but constantly changing in their relationship with each other. As one expands, the other diminishes until the point is reached where the process is reversed, throughout eternity. *Yin* and *yang* also contain seeds of each other, so that these two opposites actually interpenetrate. Unified by interpenetration and involvement in the same cycle, *yin* and *yang* thus symbolize the hidden, rhythmic unity of countless phenomenal oppositions. Morally, the *yin/yang* implies that passivity may constitute the best approach to life, for whatever

17. A major reason for this radical passivism is historical. Unlike Buddhism, which closely resembles Hinduism, Taoism diametrically opposed the contemporary competing system in China, Confucianism. The Confucianist emphasis on correct social behavior, including respect for authority and kindness to others, was rejected by Taoism. Taoist sages not only refuse to strive after wisdom, benevolence and righteousness (the three cardinal virtues of Confucianism), they refuse to strive after *anything*, for striving contradicts the effortless activities of the Tao.

one does, it is bound to be reversed in time. Consequently, it is preferable to do as little as possible, since (as one student of Taoism has put it) "although one may not get very far this way, one is certain to go in the right direction." [18]

The *yin/yang* dynamic explains an essential theme of the *Tao Te Ching*, the operation of the Tao by contraries. As Legge translates, "The movement of the Tao / By contraries proceeds; / And weakness marks the course / Of Tao's mighty deeds" (p. 83). The same paradox obtains in the phenomenal world. "Some things are increased by being diminished, and others are diminished by being increased"; "the softest thing in the world dashes against and overcomes the hardest"; "constant action overcomes cold; being still overcomes heat" (pp. 85, 87, 88). But of action and stillness, the Taoist imitates the latter, for Taoism provides the counterbalancing *yin* in Chinese philosophy to the active Confucianist *yang*. As another passage concludes, "purity and stillness give the correct law to all under heaven" (p. 88).

Many of the seventy-eight brief books of the *Tao Te Ching* offer similar descriptions of the abstract qualities of the Tao. In addition, numerous images both symbolize the Tao and serve as models for those who would harmonize with it. The power of stillness, for instance, is illustrated by the female who "always overcomes the male by her stillness" (p. 104). Perhaps the most intriguing simile is that of the infant:

> He who has in himself abundantly the attributes (of the Tao) is like an infant. Poisonous insects will not sting him; fierce beasts will not seize him; birds of prey will not strike him.
>
> The infant's bones are weak and its sinews soft, but yet its grasp is firm. . . . All day long it will cry without its throat becoming hoarse;— showing the harmony (in its constitution).
>
> (p. 99)

Like other images, this declares the virtues of weakness and harmony. But the infant symbol also suggests several other key features

18. Fritjof Capra, *The Tao of Physics* (Berkeley: Shambhala Publications, 1976), pp. 95–96.

of the Tao: its repudiation of a systematic approach toward life, and celebration of the instinctive; its primitivism, which later causes Chuang Tse to invoke a past Golden Age when the human race was in its infancy; and its major value of spontaneity, freedom from the dictates of the intellect and will.

The Tao's spontaneity and simplicity form, with passivity, the central virtues of Taoism. That passivity assumes an extreme form in the counsels of Lao Tse, and is associated with the void contained within the Tao. "He who devotes himself to the Tao (seeks) from day to day to diminish (his doing). He diminishes it and again diminishes it, till he arrives at the point of doing nothing (on purpose). Having arrived at this point of non-action, there is nothing which he does not do" (p. 90). The stillness of the sage duplicates that of the cyclical Tao, which, "ceaseless in its action," always "returns and becomes nothing" (p. 57). Taoism thus acknowledges that activity and passivity are two poles of the Tao's eternal rhythm, but heavily emphasizes the latter. In a wheel image found also in Buddhist literature, this passivity is connected to emptiness. Lao Tse observes that "the thirty spokes unite in one nave; but it is on the empty space (of the axle) that the use of the wheel depends" (p. 55). The *Tao Te Ching* sees the void as something within man that he must cultivate, just as the Buddha enjoins man to find Nirvana in the inner emptiness.

Chuang Tse's writings reinforce and expand the *Tao Te Ching* in a whimsical and imaginative fashion. Mixing satire, beast fables, illustrative images, quotations (real and invented) from numerous other philosophers, and long passages of subtle reasoning, the *Chuang Tse* (as Sinologists call his untitled writings) is a remarkable work. Chuang Tse's central dictate duplicates that of his master: harmonize with the impersonal Tao by pursuing simplicity, spontaneity and passivity. But he seems more eager than Lao Tse to convince his reader of the freedom that passive harmony offers. His extravagant style, full of outlandish episodes and comparisons, demonstrates the workings of a spontaneous imagination committed to "Sauntering or Rambling at Ease" (the title of Book One). Submission to the Tao (called by Legge "the highest issue of Taoism") offers a bliss unobtainable through striving with purpose and deliberation after one's goals. An obvious parallel with Christianity presents itself here, since the Western faith exalts obedience to a ruler God whose service is perfect freedom. Christianity, however, views this obedience as a deliberate achievement of the moral will; Chuang Tse warns, "there is no weapon more deadly than the will" (40:84). "Repress the impulses of the will," he cries, "put away the entanglements to virtue; and clear away all that obstructs the free course of the Tao" (40:87).

The conjunction of passivity and spontaneity can best be found in the Taoist Golden Age, to which Chuang Tse alludes frequently. The ancients shared "the placid tranquility" because "at that time the Yin and Yang were harmonious and still; their resting and movement proceeded without any disturbance . . . Men might be possessed of the faculty of knowledge, but they had no occasion for its use. This was what is called the state of Perfect Unity. At this time, there was no action on the part of any one, but a constant manifestation of spontaneity" (pp. 369–70). In this "age of perfect virtue," man and all other creatures were on terms of equality, and "free from desire, they were in the state of pure simplicity. In that state of pure simplicity, the nature of the people was what it ought to be" (p. 278). Again, the harmony of all creatures recalls Christianity's Edenic myth; and knowledge (brought by "sages," not a serpent) subsequently destroys paradise, as in Genesis. Christianity, however, assumes man's nature to be sinful; Taoism (like Rousseau) assumes it to be good, and believes that obedience to one's tranquil and spontaneous nature will bring happiness and harmony.

Also unlike Christianity, Chuang Tse's philosophy distinguishes man's nature from his ego: "the Perfect Man has no (thought of) self" (p. 169). When men "have forgotten external things, and have also forgotten the heavenly element in them, they may be named men who have forgotten themselves. The man who has forgotten himself is he of whom it is said that he has become identified with Heaven" (pp. 317–18). In other words, identification with the Tao produces the same extinction of self as the Buddhist Nirvana. In a phenomenal universe where constant transformation is the law, identity is an illusion, as the *Chuang Tse's* most celebrated illustration makes clear: "Formerly, I, Kwang Kau, dreamt that I was a butterfly, a butterfly flying about, feeling that it was enjoying itself. I did not know that it was Kau. Suddenly I awoke, and was myself again, the veritable Kau. I did not know whether it had formerly been Kau dreaming that he was a butterfly, or it was now a butterfly dreaming that it was Kau. . . . This is a case of what is called the Transformation of Things" (p. 197).

Another passage describes life as an illusion, and death as "the great awaking, after which we shall know that this life was a great dream" (p. 195). Chuang Tse pays more attention than Lao Tse to death, presenting it as simply another transformation that no wise man need fear. The death of Lao Tse himself, for instance, occasions no grief in a true disciple, who informs the mourners, "when the Master came, it was at the proper time; when he went away, it was the simple sequence (of his coming). Quiet acquiescence in what happens at its proper time, and quietly submitting (to its ceasing) afford no occasion for grief or for joy" (p. 201). On another occasion, a skull appears to Chuang Tse in a dream, informing him that in death, "tranquil and at ease, our years are those of heaven and earth. No king in his court has greater enjoyment than we have" (40 : 6). But a final passage is more consistent with the cyclical Taoist approach: "death and life, their ending and beginning, are but as the succession of day and night, which cannot disturb their enjoyment" (40 : 48).

Life and death, then, represent two different states of reality, participating in "the constant flow of transformations and changes" that operate according to the pattern of *yin* and *yang*. Similarly, "decay and growth, fullness and emptiness, when they end, begin again"; all things "begin and end as in an unbroken ring, though how it is they do so be not apprehended" (p. 383; 40 : 144). That which transcends these smaller cycles is the Tao itself, which flows in a cosmic cycle between nothingness and fullness, non-being and existence. According to Chuang Tse, "all things come from non-existence. The (first) existences could not bring themselves into existence; they must have come from non-existence" (40 : 85). Evolving from nothing, the Tao behind the universe divided into *yin* and *yang* and created the material world; but the *yin* and *yang* also seem (paradoxically) to dictate the eternal patterns of the Tao. For "when the Nature has been cultivated, it returns to its proper character; and when that has been fully reached, there is the same condition as at the Beginning. That sameness is pure vacancy, and the vacancy is great" (pp. 315–16). Like the Vedantic Brahman, which alternates between states of phenomenal reality and void, the Tao moves in a vast metaphysical rhythm between being and emptiness. Again, however, Taoism's emphasis resembles Buddhism, since both stress vacancy more than fullness.

The features shared by Taoism and the Indian systems are those which appear most repeatedly in the drama of O'Neill: the mystical unity of man and spirit in a universe of flux; the passive resignation to destiny; the suspicion that the self and the objective world are illusions. Taoism, however, exerted its own unique—and ubiquitous—impact as well, by contributing to O'Neill's polaristic vision of reality. The playwright probably first discovered this concept in Emerson and Jung, but it permeates his thought in the same way it dominates Taoism, thereby explaining his preference of Taoism over other Oriental religions. Play after play discovers polar oppositions between settings, characters, emotions, and states of being. O'Neill vacillates between a Western acceptance of a tragically dualistic universe, and an Eastern suspicion that those dualities are part of a larger monistic rhythm. This is the central issue in "*Marco Millions*"; the same tension occurs, moreover, in *The Fountain*, *The Great God Brown*, *Lazarus Laughed*, *The Iceman Cometh* and *Long Day's Journey Into Night*.

O'Neill himself endeavored to mystically unite opposites in his life and work, suspecting that the rationalistic separation of self and nature lay behind his inner conflicts. He turned to Oriental religions to find a philosophy that accorded with his suspicion that life was one—that the ultimate reality was an amoral, immanent force which moved, like his beloved sea, in a unified, eternal rhythm. The Western man in him, however, constantly challenged that intuition. His Catholic upbringing and unhappy childhood plagued him with a guilty conscience that implicitly acknowledged a god of judgment. Furthermore, the Western intellectual tradition encouraged a philosophical dualism that glorified struggle, not inner peace. Some rivers of Occidental thought nevertheless contained Oriental currents. Christianity, romanticism and American culture—the three traditions that dominated O'Neill's intellectual background—had all felt the impact of Oriental thought. O'Neill's position in these traditions must be determined before we examine his plays. The playwright turned West long before he turned East; and the battle between mysticism and rationalism in his drama is anticipated in all his major Western sources.

3
Northwest Passages

Eugene O'Neill did not stand alone among modern dramatists in his interest in the Orient. The Nōh plays of W. B. Yeats, the alienation effects of Bertolt Brecht (derived partly from Chinese theatre), the revolutionary manifesto of Antonin Artaud that coalesced after he viewed the Balinese dancers—all demonstrate the impact of Eastern theatre on some of our most innovative drama theorists and playwrights. O'Neill differs from the above artists in that Eastern dramaturgy did not affect the form of his plays, which remained (for all his experimentation) essentially Western. But Oriental mystical approaches to time, personality and ultimate reality influenced his vision in deep and subtle ways. In this he resembles several great modern poets—notably Yeats and Eliot—who explored Eastern religion to escape the twin Western burdens of time and self, and to discover a God responsive to modern needs. As James Baird has observed, numerous modern poets have been "unable to discover in recent Western culture life symbols to answer the demands of feeling," and consequently have looked to the Orient, "perhaps fully hopeful of rebirth, but at least intent upon finding substitutions for what has been lost in the West."[1] O'Neill shared their despair and desires. Unable to respond to a Christian God declared dead by his favorite philosopher, Nietzsche, he sought sustenance in Indian and Chinese mystical systems, hoping to satisfy his spiritual yearnings through discovery of a timeless and self-less Nirvana.

1. "Critical Problems in the Orientalism of Western Poetry," in *Asia and the Humanities*; Papers presented at the Second Conference on Oriental-Western Literary

His search, however, did not confine itself to the ancient East. The ideas of Emerson, Schopenhauer and Nietzsche, the new psychological theories of Freud and Jung, and the philosophies and religions of the ancient Greek and early Christian eras also received his intense scrutiny during his adult life. Nietzsche and Jung, in particular, strongly influenced numerous plays, including *The Emperor Jones*, *The Great God Brown*, *Desire Under the Elms*, and *Lazarus Laughed*. But many Western thinkers (particularly modern ones) are surprisingly "Eastern" in their concepts and values. In fact, the European intellectual tradition has always contained a mystical stream, leading A. K. Coomaraswamy to remark once that "nothing is more usual than for an Oriental to say to a European that there is little or nothing in his culture or sacred books that the latter does not already possess, if he would but remember it."[2] Differences between East and West almost invariably involve emphasis, not absolute opposition. We should not be surprised, then, that many notions associated with the mysterious East—the unreality of ego and world, the impersonality of God, the inadequacy of reason, and the rhythmic nature of reality—appear frequently in Western philosophies. I term these ideas "Eastern" only because they stand outside the *central* tradition of Western thought, which tends toward rationalism, dualism, and (in religion) theism.

The above qualifications suggest that O'Neill absorbed Eastern ideas from thinkers like Christ, Plato, Emerson and Schopenhauer, as well as from Nietzsche and Jung. Indeed, his intellectual passages to India and China were initially indirect. As a child at Catholic boarding schools, he worshipped a very Western God, the product of rationalistic Thomist theology. The mystical element in Catholicism, though, paralleled the more emphatic mysticism of Oriental faiths; and the Christian instruction O'Neill received acquainted him (however superficially) with theology, laying a foundation for his later studies in comparative religion. A second major Western tradition, modern romanticism, also offered a circuitous route to the East. O'Neill responded as a young man to the works of Scho-

and Cultural Relations, ed. Horst Frenz (Danville, Ill.: Interstate Printers and Publishers, 1959), p. 47.

2. "Understanding and Reunion: An Oriental Perspective," in *The Asian Legacy and American Life*, ed. Arthur E. Christy (New York: Day, 1945), p. 226.

penhauer and Nietzsche, for he shared their romantic intuition of a
visionary and transcendent dimension to experience. This intuitive
apprehension of reality forms the bedrock of Eastern mystical systems, and these German philosophers—along with Strindberg in
drama and Jung in psychology—familiarized O'Neill with assumptions he rediscovered in Hinduism, Buddhism and Taoism. Finally,
the young O'Neill was propelled toward Eastern philosophy by his
native culture. The mysticism and pantheism of heterodox Puritans
and rebellious Transcendentalists received their most eloquent expression in Emerson (himself an Orientalist), whom O'Neill read as
an adolescent and adult. And a surge of popular American interest
in India coincided with O'Neill's most productive years as a playwright, in the 1920s.

The following discussion of the East/West mixture in the Catholic, romantic and American traditions examines O'Neill's response
to the particular sources that appealed to him within each. Not surprisingly, O'Neill's divided vision frequently duplicated the mixed
mode of his sources. Various plays pit the Western emphasis on reason, ego, will and morality against the Eastern view that mystical
intuition liberates the soul into a realm that transcends these entities. Beneath this field of battle lies a more profound one, involving contrasting visions of ultimate reality. The Western universe is a
dualistic and conflictive one, in which man struggles against himself, nature, history and a personal God. The Oriental cosmos is
unified and timeless, where apparent dualities reveal themselves to
be contraries that interpenetrate each other in a divine rhythmic
movement. Drawn to the Eastern view, O'Neill was nonetheless
bound to the Western one. The result in numerous plays is an
intriguing tension: the Western imperative expresses itself in the
tragic personal conflicts depicted; the Eastern impulse appears in
the rhythmic structure and mystical overtones of the work. Only
rarely, as in *Lazarus Laughed*, do West and East merge. In nearly
all the other plays they conflict or uncomfortably coexist—and
thereby parallel the unresolved personal tensions of the playwright
himself.

Broad differences between Eastern and Western thought have been
outlined in previous chapters, but that outline must be filled in

somewhat before we turn to O'Neill's Occidental sources. As suggested earlier, the central opposition between the dominant traditions of Eastern and Western philosophy is the mystical monism of the former, and the rationalistic dualism of the latter. Oriental mystical faiths regard all distinctions (sensory or rational) as illusions;[3] the European tradition gives more credence to individual differences, and categorizes them. The fundamental Western distinction lies between subject and object, or self and world, and this dualism informs numerous other relationships: transcendent God and fallen man, good and evil, life and death, man and nature. The East generally views these oppositions as provisional at best, with Taoism regarding them as dynamic polarities. Thus, to the mystical Oriental eye, man is *in* nature (and vice-versa), not her conqueror or victim; life and death are two contrasting phases in the rhythm of being; good and evil are relative to each other, and ultimately unreal; God's immanence matters more than his transcendence.

The dualistic Western view of life is reflected in its psychology and art. The radical split of self and world implies the empirical reality of "self" as apart from "world"; and the supreme importance of this separate self provides the cornerstone of both Greek philosophy and Christian theology. The psychological self that obsesses us today embodies cultural assumptions expressed since the Renaissance by Western art's love of individual portraiture, and our drama's skill at individual characterization. Eastern art and theatre, on the contrary, persist in more generalized and abstract imitations of reality, because the ego does not preoccupy the Eastern mind. In Indian thought, the self possesses no fundamental reality; Taoism ignores psychological questions, focusing instead on the Tao that pervades existence. Non-egoism accounts for the passiveness of Hindus and Buddhists, and the *wu wei* of Taoists. Their main goal is abandonment of self to the undifferentiated unity of being—or non-being—rather than development of self in the mundane world.

Believing in a self distinct from environment, Western man feels compelled to master that environment, and pictures life in terms of struggle. Greek tragedians dramatize the battle between man and

3. It should be noted that orthodox Buddhism is dualistic, unlike Vedanta Hinduism and Taoism; nonetheless, it places no credence in phenomenal distinctions, regarding them as *māyā*.

fate; Christian myth describes the eternal opposition of God and Satan in all of us. The outcome of these cosmic tests depends upon the will, our most vital moral concept.[4] In Eastern mystical faiths, however, will is subordinate to knowledge. Through seeing the world correctly as an illusion, or unified play of forces, the Oriental mystic reaches a plane of existence where action becomes unnecessary. Will power may initially be required to prepare oneself (via Yoga, e.g.) for the liberating knowledge, but that knowledge is the agent of transformation, not the will. And the basis of morality—"willed" good and evil—appears irrelevant to the enlightened soul, who has achieved release from any moral law. To the East, the process of liberation is less a struggle against an opposing force than a descent into one's own depths, where Being resides.

That Being resembles the Christian God in one major respect: it lies beyond time. But the Judeo-Christian deity condescends (through grace) to enter history, finally becoming finite in the historical person of Jesus Christ. This concept and its corollary, that history evolves toward Christ's second coming, represent the main contribution of the Christian tradition to Western thought. They lead to our conception of history as linear and progressive, and place a premium upon man's moral activities in the historical world. By contrast, a Hindu or Buddhist sees history as circular, an eternal pattern of life, death and rebirth until the soul's liberation. After liberation, time—like all other human concepts—becomes meaningless. Ultimate reality is spaceless as well as timeless. While it may pantheistically pervade all space (as in Vedantic metaphysics), it also dwells in the void of non-being; and the mystical apprehension of non-being provides, paradoxically, the most blissful experience of pure being. This doctrine has obvious parallels in the lives of Christian mystics as well. Orthodox Christianity nonetheless skirts the attribution of non-being to God, and views God only as essential Being. By including both plenitude and emptiness in their ultimate reality, the Eastern religions go beyond traditional Western thought, and the Hindu and Taoist belief that Being and

4. And not just moral. As Arthur Danto has observed, "the agony over freedom of the will" is "the paradigmatic philosophical concern in the Western tradition." *Mysticism and Morality: Oriental Thought and Moral Philosophy* (New York: Basic, 1972), p. 17.

non-being interpenetrate each other in an eternal rhythm points up the dynamism of the Oriental world view, despite its ultimate goal of serenity.

Any definition of "Western" and "Eastern" thought must concede the relativity of such distinctions, particularly when the generalizations are as sweeping as those above. Moreover, O'Neill himself may not have fully understood the differences between the two traditions. When applied to his drama, however, these distinctions illuminate his tragic tensions. While affirming the full development of one's unique self, he longed to lose himself in a higher force. Though celebratory of man's ennobling struggle against fate or himself, O'Neill often (especially in the later plays) questioned the value of will and action, and suspected that human existence might be a mere illusion. And play after play offers apparently irreconcilable oppositions that O'Neill struggles to unify by viewing them as rhythmic contraries. Such issues, however, are matter for later discussion. We must now turn to the Western sources of his divided vision.

Christianity East and West

Any treatment of O'Neill's relationship to Oriental mysticism must begin with the Catholic faith in which he was raised and confirmed. In some respects, after all, Roman Catholicism is an "Eastern" faith, going against the grain of the rationalistic Western intellectual tradition. As William Ernest Hocking has observed, Christianity "still seems strange to us—otherworldly, remote, extravagant, impractical—in short, 'Oriental.'"[5] Hence, O'Neill's indoctrination as a boy in the dominant religion in the Western world inadvertently prepared him for his interest as a man in Oriental mystical faiths. From its inception, however, Christianity has leaned heavily toward the West, since it represents the confluence of Greek, Jewish and Roman traditions. As it developed, it became even more Westernized in its theology and dogma. The Baltimore Catechism

5. "Living Religions and a World Faith," in Christy, *Asian Legacy*, p. 195.

from which young Eugene O'Neill learned the faith, for instance, was very rationalistic in its content and structure. Thus, the Catholic Church can be regarded as the first battleground between Eastern and Western approaches in O'Neill's background; and its enormous influence over his mind and soul is partly reflected in his divided vision.[6]

We must first consider the causes of O'Neill's disillusion with the Church, because his rejection of it is partially a reaction to its Western features. Admittedly, O'Neill's reasons for abandoning Catholicism two years after his confirmation were personal as well as philosophical. The circumstances surrounding his attendance at two Catholic boarding schools were unfortunate. He considered the first a "rigid Christian exile," and vividly recalled "the outbursts of hysterical loneliness" that overtook him on his returns to Mount Saint Vincent Academy in Riverdale, New York.[7] He frequently spent Christmas there (his parents being on tour at the time), redoubling his loneliness and feelings of abandonment during a major Christian holiday. (Throughout his life, one biographer has recorded, the approach of Christmas brought on depression for O'Neill.)[8] Moreover, life at the school was generally unpleasant, due to its austerity—no central heating or indoor plumbing—and rigid discipline. O'Neill nevertheless strived to be devout, hoping to find in the love of Jesus a substitute for the love of his family; but his devotion failed to console him for the absence of his parents. Later, while attending De La Salle Institute in Manhattan from ages twelve to

---

6. Three points must be clarified concerning the subsequent discussion. First, I use the terms "Catholicism" and "Christianity" interchangeably, since the teachings of the Roman Catholic Church are what O'Neill himself understood to be Christianity. Second, I rarely compare the teaching of Christ *himself* to Eastern thought, but rather the teachings of His church. O'Neill saw Christ's gospel through the refractive lenses of nearly two millennia of Catholic theology, which de-emphasized much that was Eastern in Jesus's preachments. Finally, my concern lies with esoteric doctrine. While O'Neill himself received the exoteric instruction of the Baltimore Catechism, my primary interest is in the theology behind that catechism. In this, I follow in O'Neill's own footsteps: when he studied religion as an adult, he did not purchase popular tracts designed for mass consumption, but scholarly studies of religious thought—some of which will figure in my discussion.

7. Elizabeth Sergeant, "Eugene O'Neill: The Man with a Mask," *New Republic*, 16 Mar. 1927, p. 92.

8. Louis Sheaffer, *O'Neill: Son and Playwright* (Boston: Little, 1968), p. 71.

fourteen, he prayed for the cure of his mother from her morphine addiction.[9] Again, his prayers were futile, helping precipitate his final loss of belief in the benevolent Christian God. At fourteen, he refused further religious education, and entered the non-sectarian Betts Academy in Connecticut. A year later, he stopped attending church, and never returned.

The unhappy connection between Catholic schooling and his neglectful parents may have prompted O'Neill's remark to a Mount Saint Vincent classmate that "religion is so cold."[10] But chilliness characterized his religious instruction as well. Rigid Thomistic orthodoxy prevailed in the American Church at this time, along with a harsh Jansenism that emphasized how sin alienated man from God. It is understandable that the boy found little solace in a Christ who seemed more transcendent savior than immanent, loving presence. The Baltimore Catechism of 1885 that he learned was not very comforting. It drew largely upon the teachings of Aquinas, the central figure in Catholic theology following Pope Leo XIII's Encyclical of 1870 "On the Restoration of Christian Philosophy." Thus, it emphasized God's otherness more than His loving presence. While God was "infinitely perfect," man had inherited the "sin and punishment" caused by the disobedience of Adam and Eve.[11] The continuation of that sin, the Catechism warned, "shuts us out of heaven and condemns us to the eternal pains of hell" (p. 21). God was not only a distant punisher, of course, for he became Christ to redeem sinful man and offer the promise of salvation. But the only way to attain God's grace was to follow the teachings of the Holy Roman Catholic Church, not to rely upon the intuitions of the heart. The cold emphasis on dogma was reinforced, moreover, by the Catechism's scholastic form of question and answer, which left little room for the emotions of the catechumen.

9. O'Neill discovered his mother's drug habit when he came home early from school one day. He was living at home at the time, but the discovery caused his parents to board him at the school; again, the church was connected with exile, even punishment, in his mind.

10. Sheaffer, *Playwright*, p. 68.

11. *A Catechism of Christian Doctrine, Prepared and Enjoined by Order of the Third Plenary Council of Baltimore* (Baltimore: J. L. Spalding, 1895), pp. 6, 9. Subsequent references documented in the text.

A book that Mount Saint Vincent Academy gave O'Neill as a prize not long after his first communion suggests the school's emphasis upon the more forbidding aspects of Catholic dogma. Entitled *The Great Day: A Souvenir of First Communion*,[12] the anonymously written 124-page book made clear to the new communicant the dangers of spiritual complacency. The first paragraph of the introductory material proclaims the difficulty of salvation: "There are multitudes of unhappy souls burning in everlasting flames, who approached the holy table with as good disposition as yours. They had commenced well; but for want of courage and vigilance, ended ill" (p. [13]). The section following the introduction offers twenty pages on the terrible effects of sin, under headings like "Folly of those who render themselves unfaithful to God" and "Dangers to which we expose ourselves in abandoning the service of God" (pp. 34, 40). The author admonishes the new Church member that "you were, by your birth, the vile slave of the demon" (p. [25]); that "God has no need of us" (p. 34); that a confirmed child who offends God is "criminal and ungrateful," his sin "inexcusable" (p. 27). Indeed, "the first mortal sin that you commit will deprive you of all your merits, and open anew the gates of hell beneath your feet" (p. 41). Appropriately, the section concludes with an exemplum about a young man induced by a libertine friend to commit a great sin. "Scarcely was the sin committed, when the young man met with an accident and was instantaneously killed, without having time to confess his fault" (p. 45). While the remainder of the book is less apocalyptic in tone, it is frightening to consider the effect of these passages on a lonely, sensitive boy already prone to guilt.

The comfortlessness of his Catholic instruction indirectly prompted O'Neill's later interest in Eastern thought, which offered less morality and hence less guilt. Ironically, however, that interest manifested a curiosity about theology that might never have existed without his Catholic school background. Moreover, O'Neill discovered mystical elements in Catholicism which demonstrated that intuitive impulses had a place in organized religion. Upon his first communion,

12. Trans. J. Sadier (New York: Excelsior Catholic Publishing House, 1895). Subsequent references documented in the text.

he received a copy of Thomas à Kempis's *Imitation of Christ*. The boy studied carefully the teachings of a contemplative who believed that man's chief endeavors were to meditate on the life of Christ and conform one's life to His, achieving union with God through an unconditional surrender of the heart. This emphasis on contemplation and transcendent union helped prepare the way for O'Neill's later interest in Oriental religion, where mystical contemplation is the primary aim.

Twenty-five years later, the mysticism and theological bent encouraged by his Catholic education led O'Neill to peruse several volumes on the religions of the early Christian era. At that time, in 1926, O'Neill needed historical background for *Lazarus Laughed*, which is set around the time of Christ's death. But an interesting common thread ran through several of the books. O'Neill's readings revealed that early Christianity and other contemporary systems—Platonism, Neoplatonism, the mystery religions and Gnosticism—all exhibited the impact of certain Hindu and Buddhist ideas. Of course, Christianity from the outset had displayed affinities to Indian religions in its values of passiveness and renunciation, and in its belief in an afterlife. Moreover, as the young religion's theoreticians debated with Neoplatonists and Gnostics, they made some subtle compromises in an Eastern direction. In these affinities and compromises, with which O'Neill became familiar, we find revealed the most intriguing Oriental features of Christian thought.

A remote source of early Christianity's Eastern leanings was Greek philosophy, one of the foundations of Catholic theology. Much Greek thought of the pre-Socratic and Socratic periods has—possibly due to an Indian influence—a pronounced mystical element that appealed to early Christian thinkers. Unquestionably their most admired philosopher was Plato, whose vision of a realm of Ideas influenced the Christian doctrine of the Trinity. Both concepts involve a transcendent, yet immanent, eternal force; both perceive multiplicity in unity, since the Ideas form a hierarchy, with the Idea of the Good, or Perfection, at the apex. However, Platonic philosophy also contains Eastern features, like an impersonal god and a belief in transmigration. And its most Oriental idea—that of a living, pantheistic World Soul that (like Brahman) causes the motion of the world—influenced early Christian thought via the Neoplatonism of Plotinus, a third century Alexandrian philosopher. Neoplatonism affected O'Neill directly as a consequence of his reading the Thomas Taylor translation of the works of Plotinus. Interestingly, the editor of O'Neill's edition, G. R. S. Mead of the London Theosophical Society, insisted upon the correspondences between Neoplatonism and Vedantic Hinduism. The opening paragraph of his fifteen-page commentary on Plotinus points out that his philosophy "bears a remarkable similarity to the great Vedantic system of Indian philosophy. Deity, spirit, soul, body, macrocosmic and microcosmic, and the essential identity of the divine in man with the divine in the universe—. . . or of the Jivatman with the Paramatman—are the main subjects of his system." The next sentence identifies the supreme principle of Neoplatonism, the One, with "the All-self of the Upanishads, Brahman or Paramatman"; and Mead quotes from the *Upanishads* frequently throughout the preface, concluding with a discussion of the Eastern quality of Plotinus's mysticism.[13]

While Mead may interpret Neoplatonism from an Oriental perspective because of his Theosophical beliefs, it is nonetheless true that major assumptions in Plotinus's *Enneads* correspond to Indian mysticism. To Plotinus, all reality was spiritual, emanating from an ineffable One through various lower degrees of being. The two highest degrees were the Divine Mind and the Soul, the latter penetrating the phenomenal universe (though it is "asleep" in matter). Man can participate in the Soul, or achieve a direct mystical union with the ineffable One. This immediate experience of union with an impersonal god that stands beyond being (yet *is* pure being) demonstrates obvious parallels with Hinduism. In addition, the pantheistic aspects of Neoplatonism, and its rhythm of emanation and return from one to many, recall the movement of the omnipresent Brahman in a cosmic cycle. Some of these Oriental elements probably influenced St. Augustine, the fifth century Christian theologian

13. G. R. S. Mead, Introduction to *Select Works of Plotinus*, trans. Thomas Taylor (London: Bell and Sons, 1912), pp. xviii, xx. That O'Neill read the book is indicated by a passage he copied from it into his notes for *Lazarus Laughed* (File Folder Za/O'Neill/33x, O'Neill Collection, Beinecke Library, Yale Univ.).

who emphasized the mystical and intuitive faculties in his insistence that theology was faith seeking understanding. Neoplatonism also affected other early formulators of Christian dogma. As David Knowles observes, its tendency toward pantheism was felt (albeit usually resisted) by various Christian theologians. Furthermore, it provided a theological formulation for Christian mysticism that originated ultimately in the East.[14] Thus, the Oriental tendencies of Neoplatonism touched O'Neill twice: directly, in his readings of Plotinus as an adult; and indirectly, in the mystical elements of the Catholicism of his childhood.

Other books acquired in 1926 by O'Neill provided more explicit discussion of the Orient's impact on Christian thought. One such volume, T. R. Glover's *The Conflict of Religions in the Early Roman Empire*, notes how various mystical cults from Egypt and Asia Minor "orientalized every religion of the West."[15] Another, Samuel Angus's *The Mystery Religions and Christianity*, outlines an early Christian era "into which Oriental cults rushed like an irresistible tide," causing "the dissemination of Oriental mysticism and with it a world-renouncing ethic in the West." Angus further observes the "prevalence for half a millenium of the *Gnosis* conception of religion which left its indelible mark on Christian theology," and he links Gnosticism to the Middle Eastern mystical religions that form the prime subject of his book.[16] According to Angus, the mystery religions anticipated Gnosticism in emphasizing a *gnosis* of God, a knowledge gained through an ineffable mystical experience and passivity of soul. Calling this approach "an Oriental reaction against the epistemology of the West"—which stressed the logical, rational apprehension of existence—he claims that Christian revelation theories result from an era in which "Orient and Occident

---

14. *The Evolution of Medieval Thought* (Baltimore: Helicon, 1962), p. 31. As Knowles also notes, Plotinus is not (strictly speaking) a pantheist, because his system developed higher and lower degrees of being, and the One, the ultimate cause of being, lies outside the realm of being (p. 25).
15. London: Methuen, 1909, p. 24.
16. *The Mystery Religions and Christianity: A Study in the Religious Background of Early Christianity* (London: Scribners, 1925), pp. 10, 2. O'Neill's notes on *Lazarus Laughed*, cited in n. 10, copy Angus's definition of a mystery religion, proving that he read at least part of the book.

gradually approached in their thinking until the Occident adopted the point of view of the Orient."[17] Again, we find the mystical elements of O'Neill's childhood faith traced to Eastern religion, though he came to understand this only in later years.

Another volume O'Neill owned and read focuses exclusively on Gnosticism, seeing it as another influence of East on West in the early centuries of the first millenium. Henry Longueville Mansel's *The Gnostic Heresies of the First and Second Centuries* identifies Buddhism as a principal source of the Gnostic sects that both opposed and modified Christian teachings. Mansel concedes that Gnosticism never advocated (like Buddhism) the total annihilation of the self. He does contend, however, that Buddhism's "influence in a diluted form may undoubtedly be traced in the antagonism which [the Gnostics] maintained to exist between matter and spirit, in the deliverance of spirit by asceticism, and in the contrast between ignorance and knowledge, the one the source of illusion and misery, the other the sole means of obtaining deliverance and repose."[18] Mansel also notes that Gnosticism shared with both Hinduism and Buddhism the doctrines of the unreality of matter and the "emanation of the world from the one absolute existence, and of its final reabsorption into that existence."[19] But Gnosticism's impact on Christian dogma mainly concerned the pursuit through knowledge of a mystical unity with God. In a passage marked by O'Neill in his personal copy, Mansel asserts that Paul's Epistles to the Corinthians are the earliest apostolic writings "in which we can with any probability recognize an allusion to the germs of a teaching which afterwards developed itself in the Gnostic schools."[20] Paul, of course, was hardly a Gnostic enthusiast himself. The scripture cited by Mansel, in fact, speaks of this embryonic Gnostic teaching in a deprecatory fashion. But Paul's teachings nonetheless made room for the mystical absorption into God which constitutes the backbone of Gnostic dogma: it was he who asserted that all

17. Angus, *Mystery Religions*, p. 2.
18. *The Gnostic Heresies of the First and Second Centuries*, ed. J. B. Lightfoot (London: John Murray, 1875), p. 31.
19. Mansel, *Gnostic Heresies*, pp. 29–30.
20. Ibid., pp. 48–49.

Christians "are the mystical body of Christ, member for member" (1 Corinthians 12:27).

Though such assertions are clearly subordinate to numerous other Pauline dictates concerning the daily faith of the Christian, this subtle Gnostic impact on early Christianity demonstrates another area where Western faith exhibits an indirect Eastern influence. As such, it helped develop the mystical attitude toward God and reality that O'Neill shared with Oriental religions. And O'Neill's fascination as an adult with the competing creeds of the early Christian era suggests an additional conclusion: at the time of *Lazarus Laughed*, at any rate, he appeared to find in this historical epoch a reflection of his own inner conflict between Western and Oriental approaches toward ultimate questions.

The mysticism O'Neill encountered in his childhood faith may have originated in the Orient, but it assumed a different form and role in Catholic teachings. For as noted, Christian thought generally developed in a Western direction. The overt Western aspects of Roman Catholicism overshadowed the covert Eastern ones in their impact on O'Neill. The conception of a god that provokes man's guilt over his sins figures in numerous plays, like *The Emperor Jones*, *All God's Chillun Got Wings*, *Strange Interlude*, *Days Without End* and *Long Day's Journey Into Night*. The fundamental principle of Christian theology—that God, through grace, became Christ to save man—is equally ubiquitous in O'Neill's drama. We see it in the fall from grace of Yank the stoker, and the return to grace of John Loving; the self-sacrificing love of Eben Cabot; the Christ symbolism attached to the salesman Hickey; and the father gods of Ephraim Cabot, Nina Leeds and Reuben Bright. But mother gods also appear in the plays, corresponding to the Oriental mystical religions that subordinated will and morality, and offered liberation from guilt and suffering. This theology informs *The Fountain*, *Lazarus Laughed*, and *Strange Interlude*. These faiths and Christianity, then, pulled O'Neill's work in contrary directions.

In both Judaism and Greek philosophy (the twin pillars on which

Christian theology was erected), a concern with morality and the individual will is paramount. From Judaism came a personal God, from Greece came the rational interest in expressing the infinite in finite terms; the result is the Christian doctrine of incarnation, of God made man. And the two great figures in medieval Catholic theology, St. Augustine and St. Thomas Aquinas, reinforced the Western bases of early Christian thought. Their systems agreed on the importance of the personal and historical Christ, the centrality of God's grace and man's free will, and the vital place of human reason in the cosmic scheme. Augustine, writing during the early Christian era, is more mystical (especially in his *Confessions*). But his Western bias announces itself in his insistence that will is man's essence; that man's will depends on God's grace; that Christ has freed the citizens of God into a progressive history that marches steadily toward the Second Coming; and that reason and will are inseparable, so philosophy and religion belong together. Aquinas, writing eight centuries later, asserts that philosophy employs reason to attain natural knowledge, while religion depends on faith in the Scriptures (revelation) to reach a higher form of knowledge. But reason's role is hardly denied. The scriptural wisdom obtained through God's grace does not contradict natural knowledge, but rather perfects it. The existence of the Thomist God can be proven by man's reason in five different ways; and His will, though unchangeable, always operates rationally. It is man's will that often abides by erring reason, thereby leading him into sin. As with Augustine, reason and man's free will constitute the main emphases of his argument, along with divine grace as man's redeemer. But with Augustine, faith *precedes* reason, whereas faith *supplements* reason in Aquinas. The Thomist God is thus more rationalistic than the Augustinian, and considerably less approachable as well. Throughout the *Summa Theologica*, Aquinas reiterates the otherness of God. God creates and rules all things without commingling with them, so His nature remains very different from man's; and because human faculties cannot achieve direct access to the divine, our knowledge of God must be imperfect in this life, with full knowledge possible only after death.

The distant God revealed to O'Neill in his Catholic instruction—the remote father god of *Desire Under the Elms*, *The Great God*

Brown, Strange Interlude and *Dynamo*—was largely that of Aquinas, a major contributor to the Westernization of Christianity. For the mystical, Oriental elements in early Roman Catholicism consistently gave way to the more Western elements. This is apparent even in regard to the central feature they seem to share—mysticism itself.

Though the mystical experience remains central today in Hinduism, Buddhism and Taoism, Christianity has always made mysticism peripheral to its dogmatic concerns. Though Christ himself was a mystic, and St. Paul's conversion on the road to Damascus was mystical, Paul subordinated mysticism to the more normal experiences of Christian life in his preaching. He emphasized the love of God and neighbor, and the endurance of suffering—a position maintained by the Church over the centuries. Moreover, Paul's version of a mystical experience differs from that of Eastern mystics, for it originates in response to the "mystical body of Christ." As Samuel Angus interprets Paul's teachings, "the Christian who is 'in Christ' finds himself in fellowship with a person, and is not lost . . . in the ocean of the Absolute, nor, as in the Mysteries, does he undergo divinization. He becomes like Christ, but never Christ."[21] This applies equally to subsequent mystics, martyrs, and saints. As another student of this subject observes, "Santa Teresa is alone on a cloud, individuated at the moment of unity."[22] The Christian mystic, then, retains a sense of self during the ecstatic experience, and feels kinship—but not identification—with God. God's love and grace elevate the worshipper, but do not annihilate his separate personality.

The Eastern mystic's experience differs from this. Not believing in a personal and historical god, he seeks not loving fellowship, but oneness with the universe; and rather than retain a sense of self during the mystical experience, he desires absorption into pure being. Unlike the Christian, the Oriental mystic perceives no difference between man and ultimate reality—and he descends (rather than ascends) to an immanent plane where the fiction of "self" evaporates.[23]

21. Angus, *Mystery Religions*, p. 297.
22. Danto, *Mysticism and Morality*, p. 56.
23. The contrast between Eastern descent and Western ascent of the soul was first proposed by a prominent student of Eastern religion, Carl Jung. See Baird, "Critical

Since Hinduism, Buddhism and Taoism ascribe no metaphysical reality to the ego, there exists no "self" to lose; and grace, so indispensable to the Christian, does not matter to the Oriental seer. If God is not just within you, but *is* you, then a change of perspective—enlightenment—is all that is required to reach pure being.

As we shall see, O'Neill's mysticism leaned East. When Edmund Tyrone recalls his mystical absorptions into the sea, he remembers a loss of all sense of self. The same is true of Lazarus, who understands "there is no death" because individual identity is an illusion. Desirous to free himself from the ego, Lazarus seeks liberation rather than salvation, for Christian salvation stipulates the continuance through eternity of one unique individual self. (Hence, the Nicene Creed postulates the resurrection of the body, indicating that the total self will ascend into heaven after death and remain individuated.) Hinduism and Buddhism agree with Christianity on the continuation of life after death, and the effect of one's moral behavior (*karma*) on that future life. However, they differ in three important respects: first, they hold that future life involves a return of the soul to earth in a different body; second, that this continues only until liberation from *karma*, at which point the individual soul vanishes into Brahman or Nirvana; and third, that liberation is available now, not just after death.

The philosophical differences described above create contrasting ethical systems. Christianity believes in the moral necessity of self-sacrifice, but assumes the self's reality; Indian religions and Taoism deny the self's very existence, making the moral behavior of that self secondary. Existential realization of the self's emptiness—achieved by the protagonists of *The Fountain* and *Lazarus Laughed*—thus lifts one beyond the moral laws, whose distinctions between good and evil now seem anthropocentric and artificial. This liberation through knowledge directly opposes the Catholic doctrine of salvation by works. Believing that our wills are free to choose between good and evil, Catholic dogma emphasizes the necessity of actively seeking to do good to earn redemption. The individual should be prepared to suffer in that struggle against evil,

---

Problems," who quotes Jung's contention that "the European seeks to raise himself above this world, while the Indian likes to turn back into the maternal depths of nature" (p. 51).

for Christianity regards suffering as a real aspect of existence that can be turned to good purposes, producing awareness and compassion. This is the viewpoint behind such O'Neill plays as *All God's Chillun Got Wings* and *Desire Under the Elms*. But other works—*Lazarus* and *Interlude*—regard suffering as an illusion to be transcended, reproducing the approach of Oriental mystical faiths. The compassion of the Buddhist Bodhisattvas, and of O'Neill's Lazarus, is directed toward lifting others above the plane of suffering, rather than toward helping them endure it.

The differences between Catholicism and the Oriental faiths derive, finally from the dualism of the former, the monism of the latter. The impersonal Being of Hinduism and Taoism contains fullness and goodness, but also emptiness and evil, for it dwells in a realm where such distinctions are transcended. The personal God of the West, however, epitomizes goodness and perfection, and consigns evil to Satan, who tempts man's free will toward sin. The symbol of the trinity, as Harvey Cox has noted, likewise indicates that the Christian God recognizes genuine distinctions in existence[24]—between good and evil, man and God, self and others—and the devout Christian must struggle to love those who differ from himself. The Oriental mystic has no such burden, for the ultimate reality he recognizes absorbs all existence into a unity that denies any fundamental differences. Hence, such concepts as loving one's enemy, or choosing to do good, are ultimately meaningless to him. Again, we find O'Neill caught between the two views. Split characters like Dion Anthony and John Loving suggest O'Neill's belief in genuine moral distinctions, as do his frequently melodramatic plots; his regard for individual personalities is evident in his sharply drawn characters. But *The Fountain*, "*Marco Millions*," *Lazarus Laughed* and *Strange Interlude* imply that moral distinctions can be misleading, even meaningless; and "*Anna Christie*" and *Lazarus* blur the lines between characters through doubling and parallelism.

The mysticism of the Catholic faith O'Neill rejected thus helped direct him to Indian and Chinese mystical systems that resembled Catholicism in some respects, and differed profoundly in others. Those differences reflect many of the deepest inner conflicts of O'Neill's own soul, and those of many modern Western artists and

24. *Turning East* (New York: Simon, 1977), p. 88.

thinkers. Unable to accept the rationalistic, historical and personal God of Catholicism, O'Neill sought sustenance from the mystical, timeless and impersonal being described in Oriental mysticism. But as a Western man, he could not totally embrace Eastern teachings either, and he vacillated between Christ and Nirvana. Throughout the 1920s he mingled Eastern and Western conceptions of God in the same plays ("*Anna Christie*," *The Fountain*, "*Marco Millions*," *Lazarus Laughed*), or pictured characters who were themselves caught between the two (*Strange Interlude, Dynamo*). The late tragedies repudiated the mysticism he associated with the Orient. But *Journey, Iceman* and *Hughie* demonstrate O'Neill's inability to exorcise his Oriental impulses completely—though they are outweighed in these plays by a profoundly Christian belief in forgiveness and compassion.

Western Roads to Xanadu

Those who describe O'Neill's drama as religious are outnumbered only by those who term it romantic. It was both, of course, since modern romanticism emphasizes spiritual values and concerns. Asserting the central place of man in an organic universe, the romantic writers and thinkers of nineteenth-century Europe praised the emotions and intuition, and directed attention to the sublime and visionary aspects of existence. They concentrated on man's yearnings toward the infinite, his intense encounters with nature, and his lonely confrontations with himself. And, whatever their individual differences, nearly all the romantics possessed strongly religious tempers that believed in a higher spirit operating in the universe.

Not surprisingly, numerous romantics (particularly in Germany) were intrigued by Oriental religions. This was partly an accident of history. Hindu sacred writings first became available to Europeans during the early 1800s, with philologists like the Schlegels providing translations and interpretations of the ancient texts.[25] But the

25. In the eyes of one unsympathetic literary historian, the close connection between romanticism and Oriental thought began long before the modern age. The

German interest in the Orient was motivated also by the mystical bent of German romanticism; and numerous Germanic thinkers displayed varying degrees of enthusiasm about Oriental mystical systems, continuing into the early years of this century. Arthur Schopenhauer admitted the impact of Indian sacred texts upon his philosophy, and was severely criticized for his "Buddhistic" pessimism. The young Friedrich Nietzsche fell under Schopenhauer's influence, giving an Eastern bias to his early speculations. Even after his break with Schopenhauer, however, Nietzsche (while overtly disdaining Orientalism) offered ideas on time and morality that resemble Indian mystical concepts. In addition, Carl Jung, a Swiss, avidly studied Oriental religions and folklore throughout his career. Not only did he illustrate his ideas with Eastern myths and symbols, but he reflected Oriental metaphysics in his theories about the human psyche.

Not coincidentally, these three men were O'Neill's favorite philosophers (along with another romantic, Emerson). Schopenhauer's ideas excited him as a young man; Nietzsche (whom he idolized) affected O'Neill's vision in countless ways; Jung he found "extraordinarily illuminating" and more compatible with his outlook than Freud.[26] To these three romantics must be added a fourth, August Strindberg. Influencing not only O'Neill but much of modern drama in ways that are still being discovered, the Swedish writer shared with the others an interest in Buddhism and Hinduism, and could in addition read Chinese. His impact on O'Neill was mo-

---

Neo-humanist Paul Elmer More proclaimed that the romantic attitude toward existence originated in ancient Alexandria, where Neoplatonism and Gnosticism contended with (and influenced) early Christianity. These movements introduced to Western thought the Oriental sense of infinity as "vague unlimited forces forever striving for expansion," lamented More. When this combined with the Occidental notion of the ego as an active emotional entity, the result was "the birth of our sense of an infinite, insatiable personality" which More designates as the prime feature of romanticism. More regretted that these romantic features modified Christian teaching somewhat, but rejoiced that orthodox Christianity managed to maintain uncorrupted the more restrained Greek idea of the infinite for many centuries—until modern romanticism arose in the latter part of the eighteenth century. (*The Drift of Romanticism*, Shelburne Essays, Eighth Series [1913; rpt. New York: Phaeton, 1967], pp. 22, 26.)

26. O'Neill to Sparrow, 13 Oct. 1929; quoted in Sparrow, "Psychoanalytical Material," p. 77.

mentous, both in vision and technique; and those expressionistic plays produced by O'Neill's own Provincetown Players were among Strindberg's most Oriental works in their symbolism and world view. In Strindberg and the others, then, O'Neill discovered reinforcement for his own intuitive drift toward Eastern mystical avenues. As kindred romantic spirits, they shared his disillusion with the Western tradition, and looked to the Orient for inspiration. Each of them, however—particularly Nietzsche—remained Western in the fundamental features of his thought or art. As a consequence, their divided visions offer numerous parallels to that of their devoted American admirer.

Before the modern romantic movement, European interest in the Orient had largely confined itself to China, particularly the rationalistic philosophy of Confucius. But while Enlightenment *philosophes* like Voltaire were reverencing the Chinese sage, British colonial officials in India were providing English translations and analyses of the Bhagavad-Gita and other Indian sacred texts. As early as 1797, Europeans could study Hindu philosophy, literature and religion translated from primary Sanskrit sources.[27] Some English romantic poets, such as Blake, Coleridge and Shelley, familiarized themselves with Hindu philosophy and mythology; but ironically, the British in general did not respond deeply to the Indian culture made available by their own officials. Such was not the case with German thinkers and writers, who had been primed for Indian mysticism by the idealistic philosophy of Immanuel Kant. His *Critique of Pure Reason* directed German intellectual attention to a noumenal realm of the mind that differs from the phenomenal world of the senses, and to a God who could be apprehended only by intuition. Johann Fichte's subsequent emphasis on the unity of man and universe in the moral realm also contributed to a developing idealistic intellectual climate in which the spirit, and man's participation in it, were viewed as the essence of reality. Hence, when Friedrich Schlegel published *Language and Wisdom of the Indians* in 1808, he addressed a receptive audience. Schlegel (and his

27. Kenneth R. Stunkel, "Indian Ideas and Western Thought During the Romantic Age: A Critical Study" (Diss., Univ. of Maryland, 1966), pp. 2–3.

brother, Auguste Wilhelm) had studied Hindu religion, philosophy and mythology in the original Sanskrit; and this volume placed romanticism's imprimatur on Indian mysticism, helping lead to the establishment of Oriental studies at numerous German universities like Jena, where Georg Wilhelm Friedrich Hegel lectured on Hinduism and Buddhism. Hegel himself was not sympathetic to Indian thought, condemning its denial of self-consciousness and the consequent absence in it of a "true" definition of spirit. But to Arthur Schopenhauer, who repudiated Hegel and built on Kant's foundation, that lack of consciousness was precisely what made spirit— renamed Will in Schopenhauer's system—the moving force behind existence. That Will demonstrates numerous and deliberate parallels with the Brahman and Nirvana of Indian philosophy.

The concepts offered by Schopenhauer in *The World as Will and Idea* fascinated the young Eugene O'Neill. In 1906, at the age of eighteen, O'Neill first discovered the German thinker; by 1908, according to one biographer, he was "reading him with almost as much enthusiasm as he had felt when he first explored Nietzsche."[28] In his courtship with a young woman four years later, he showed his esteem by giving her a copy of Schopenhauer. O'Neill obviously sensed a kinship with this mystical and pessimistic philosopher during his youth, those years when he was groping toward his own tragic vision of life. It is thus not altogether surprising that he reread *The World as Will and Idea* years later before composing one of his most ambitious and challenging plays, *Strange Interlude*.[29] And in his encounters with Schopenhauer's monumental work, O'Neill discovered a system that frankly admitted its indebtedness to Oriental thought. In the preface to the first edition, after conceding his dependence upon Kant and Plato, Schopenhauer called his era's access to the Vedas and Upanishads "the greatest advantage this still young century enjoys over previous ones"; and if "the reader has also already received and assimilated the sacred, primitive Indian wisdom, then he is best of all prepared to hear what I

28. Alexander, *Tempering*, p. 128.
29. Arthur and Barbara Gelb, *O'Neill* (New York: Harper, 1962), pp. 209–10; Travis Bogard, *Contour in Time: The Plays of Eugene O'Neill* (New York: Oxford Univ. Pr., 1972), p. 303n. The Gelb biography is hereafter cited as "Gelbs."

have to say to him." [30] Conversant with the entire range of English and German scholarship on India, even given to frequent use of Hindu terms in his work (particularly *māyā*), the German philosopher presented the young O'Neill with explicit formulations of Eastern mystical concepts that struck a sympathetic chord in the latter's soul.

Schopenhauer's prime correspondence with Eastern thinkers is in his monistic idealism. The world represents (as Kant had argued) one's idea, with no reality apart from the perceiver, and that which connects perceiving subject to objective world in both is the Will. The Will in fact resembles Brahman, pure being that unites mind and matter. "The whole world, with all its phenomena," he asserts, "is the objectivity of the one indivisible Will, the Idea, which is related to all other ideas as harmony is related to the single voice" (1: 206). This leads Schopenhauer to a Vedantic disregard for distinctions between individual phenomena, since "the individual is only the phenomenon, not the thing-in-itself" (1: 357); and space and time throw a "veil of Maya" over existence, concealing the hidden unity of things. Referring to the central Vedantic precept of *tat tvam asi* (that art thou), he observes that "whoever is able to say this to himself, with regard to every being with whom he comes in contact is certain of all virtue and blessedness, and is on the direct road to salvation" (1: 483). Like Hindu mystics, Schopenhauer denies the self's separate reality, and urges his reader to suspect the counsels of our intellect, which is "only designed to know things so far as they afford motives for the will, but not to fathom them or to comprehend their true being" (2: 326).

The most noticeable Eastern aspects of Schopenhauer's thought are more prominent in Buddhism than in Hinduism. Schopenhauer, like Buddha, perceives human suffering as the product of consciousness and desire. Man experiences the most pain of any creature, for "as consciousness ascends, pain also increases, and reaches its highest degree in man" (1: 400). As a selfish creature, man also is victimized by Will, the "blind, purposeless, directionless urge to live" which germinates desires that usually are frustrated. The only

---

30. *The World as Will and Idea*, trans. R. B. Haldane and J. Kemp, 7th ed. (London: K. Paul, Trench, Trubner, 1887), 1: xiv. Hereafter documented in the text.

solution lies in transcending desire, for "so long as we are given up to the throng of desires with their constant hopes and fears, so long as we are subject to willing, we can never have lasting happiness or peace" (1: 253). Schopenhauer admired Buddhism because it seemed to make the destruction of the will its prime purpose, and the Buddhist ethic (as Schopenhauer understood it) of first identifying with the world's suffering in order eventually to renounce all action also exerted enormous appeal to him. Hence, the final volume of *The World as Will and Idea*, concentrating on life as a tragic phenomenon, advises the Buddhist stance of denial and renunciation.

While Schopenhauer seems to be a disciple of the East, though, two very Western assumptions operate in his thought. First, his proclamation of the Will as the essence of reality indicates his participation in the Greco-Christian tradition, where will is paramount. To Indian philosophers, happiness is life's goal, and the will is a barrier to attainment of *moksha* or Nirvana, the ultimate reality; to Schopenhauer, the Will *is* ultimate reality, though he wants to escape it. His pessimism consequently runs much deeper than that of Eastern sages, for the passiveness he advises only constitutes a holding pattern against the misery of existence caused by blind Will. The world as Will is one of Darwinian strife, in which "the will to live everywhere preys upon itself, and in different forms is its own nourishment," where "even the human race . . . reveals in itself with most terrible distinctness this conflict, this variance of the Will with itself" (1: 191). This points to the second fundamentally Western aspect of his thought, his obsession with the struggle of existence; even his monistic ruling principle is in conflict with itself. Only death provides final release from pain—a position different from Oriental mysticism, which preaches the possibility of serenity in this life via union with a higher force.

For all his Eastern leanings, then, Schopenhauer remains Western in his focus on will and struggle. The terms of his inner division between East and West can also be applied to his American admirer. *Strange Interlude*, in particular, depicts a prolonged battle between will and fatalism, struggle and passiveness. But one can perceive the same ambivalence in other O'Neill plays like "*Anna Christie*" and *The Great God Brown*; and the playwright's entire career seems to move from the affirmation of tragic struggle in the early plays to fatalistic resignation in the late ones. Of course, Schopenhauer's importance goes well beyond his impact on O'Neill. As a thinker whose blind Will anticipates the Darwinian survival instinct and the Freudian id, he plays a prophetic role in Western thought. Moreover, he helped confer on Oriental ideas a philosophical respectability in the West, and thus hastened the arrival of the future he predicted: an age when "Indian philosophy streaks back to Europe, and will produce a fundamental change in our knowledge and thought" (1: 460–61).

Not all subsequent German philosophers were so enchanted by the prospect of the West's Orientalization. In 1873, Friedrich Nietzsche proclaimed that "the world has been Orientalized long enough; and men now yearn to be Hellenized." [31] Ironically, Nietzsche had been "Orientalized" himself by his youthful admiration of Schopenhauer and his own reading of Eastern philosophy. Early works like *The Birth of Tragedy* consequently embrace Indian mystical precepts. Later books like *Thus Spake Zarathustra*, however, explicitly repudiate Oriental passivity and egolessness. Indeed, the value Nietzsche places on creative struggle, the will, the ego, and the material world would seem to mark him as a quintessential Western thinker. But actually, Nietzsche offers a reverse image of Schopenhauer; where his predecessor proves more Western than is apparent, Nietzsche—even in *Zarathustra*—proves more Eastern.

In his reluctance to acknowledge any indebtedness to Eastern thought, Nietzsche paralleled his American worshipper O'Neill. O'Neill resembles Nietzsche in many other ways as well, as countless articles, books and dissertations have testified. No philosopher was so admired by the playwright, and none affected his thought so profoundly. "Zarathustra," O'Neill wrote a friend in 1928, "has influenced me more than any book I've ever read," and he was still rereading it annually and copying out excerpts as late as 1936.[32]

31. From *Thoughts out of Season* (1873); quoted in Will Durant, *The Story of Philosophy* (1926; rpt. New York: Washington Square Pr., 1962), p. 411.
32. 1928 letter to Benjamin de Casseres; quoted in Gelbs, p. 121.

O'Neill's admiration of Nietzsche was not gained solely from *Zarathustra*, though; in 1925 he read *The Birth of Tragedy*, which influenced *Lazarus Laughed* and subsequent dramas.[33]

The Birth of Tragedy from the Spirit of Music was published in 1872, seven years after Nietzsche's discovery of Schopenhauer had led him to declare the pessimistic philosopher a mirror of himself.[34] The naturalism and aesthetic justification of existence that the book contains have their obvious roots in Schopenhauer, and the work refers to the earlier philosopher's ideas frequently, quoting him on several occasions. In three instances, Nietzsche invokes his predecessor's favorite Hindu word—*māyā*—and these (and other) overt Oriental references point to the work's deeper correspondences with Eastern mysticism. It exhibits, for example, great scepticism about the power of reason. Nietzsche theorizes that Socrates, the exemplar of Western "theoretical man," helped (with Euripides) to destroy the revitalizing view of life presented in the tragic drama of Aeschylus and Sophocles. The elimination of the primitive Dionysian spirit by the Socratic belief that "whatever is to be beautiful must also be sensible" has led Western man (so the argument runs) to his current dispirited state. Fortunately, the modern music of Beethoven, Brahms and Wagner, by engendering a new tragic myth that transcends reason, has provided "hope for the rejuvenation and purification of the German spirit."[35] In the mystery of a revived Dionysian spirit, claims Nietzsche, lies salvation; and that spirit recalls Eastern philosophy in an additional respect. The impulse symbolized by Dionysus resembles Brahman in its cosmic playfulness, whereby it "playfully shatters and rebuilds the teeming world of individuals" (p. 143). Indeed, at one point Nietzsche explicitly identifies the tragic and Brahmanic views of existence, since both offer the "metaphysical solace that life flows on, indestructible, beneath the whirlpool of appearances" (p. 107).

The phrase "whirlpool of appearances" points up the young

33. O'Neill also read *The Joyful Wisdom*, as Louis Sheaffer indicates in *O'Neill: Son and Artist* (Boston: Little, 1972), p. 174. However, the major ideas covered there are also covered in *Thus Spake Zarathustra*, so I have in the interest of brevity chosen not to treat *Joyful Wisdom*.

34. Durant, *Story of Philosophy*, p. 404.

35. *The Birth of Tragedy and the Genealogy of Morals*, trans. Francis Golffing (New York: Doubleday, 1956), pp. 79, 94, 123. Hereafter documented in the text.

Nietzsche's indebtedness to Schopenhauer, and ultimately to Indian thought. Like them, he sharply contrasts the whirling phenomenal world with the thing-in-itself, and he quotes Schopenhauer at length on the power of music to penetrate the phenomena and represent "'the metaphysics of everything physical in the world'" (p. 99). The phenomenal world is one of appearance, of illusion, of, in a word, *māyā*: behind it lies the primordial oneness to which all need to return to refresh their souls. Like Buddha, Nietzsche identifies individuation as "the source of all suffering" and "the root of all evil" (pp. 66–67). Ancient Greek tragedy offered temporary fusion with that original oneness, he asserts, while in modern life "music alone allows us to understand the delight felt at the annihilation of the individual" (p. 101). A major feature of the Dionysian spirit, then, is its power to destroy all self-consciousness. And if the pagan, communal manner in which this is accomplished differs markedly from the solitary ascetic meditation of the Eastern sage, the goal seems nearly identical.

However, *The Birth of Tragedy* does not propose a consistently ecstatic approach toward existence. The unifying Dionysian spirit must be balanced by the individuating Apollonian principle, and this to Nietzsche was the triumph of pre-Socratic Greek culture. Where Indian religion renounces life, Greek tragic art effects reconciliation with it, bringing the spectator back to his individual self following the mystical experience. While thus desiring the rebirth of the ego-annihilating Dionysian spirit, Nietzsche affirms a dialectical relationship between this and the ego-affirming Apollonian principle. Interestingly, however, Nietzsche's dialectic suggests another Eastern dimension to his argument. While the attributes of the terms differ, the relationship of Dionysian and Apollonian recalls the *yin/yang* dynamic that presumes the secret unity of opposites. The Dionysian force delights in feeling, paroxysm, and the violent destruction of the individual; the Apollonian concentrates on images, ideas and illusions, aiming at "a tranquil delight in individual forms" (p. 141). The two forces achieve union in tragic drama, where "the eternal goal of the original Oneness, namely its redemption through illusion, accomplishes itself" (p. 33). Moreover, unlike Hegel—but like Taoism—Nietzsche does not regard their synthesis as the beginning of a new dialectic. Rather, the two principles are eternally contrary, yet eternally striving to unite—a non-progressive, cyclical approach that anticipates the later concept of the eternal recurrence.

The eternal recurrence is the doctrine Zarathustra hesitates to preach, because of its frightening depiction of time and the soul. Moreover, its cyclical Eastern conception of time seems incongruous in a book emphasizing Western values. *Thus Spake Zarathustra* (1885) deliberately embraces this world, and the prophet condemns his previous renunciation of it as an act of weakness. Zarathustra confesses that the world formerly seemed the creation of a suffering God who desired escape from pain via self-annihilation. "A dream the world then seemed to me," he admits, a dream *The Birth of Tragedy* represented as the *māyā*-like phenomenal world.[36] Now, however, he regards his former desire to escape from life as hypocritical and sick, and he ridicules the "immaculate perception" of all men who (Buddha-like) try to observe life without desire or will. Now he is ready to celebrate the material world, to be faithful to the earth and to his body; and given this fundamental naturalism, other Western values do not seem surprising. Zarathustra affirms, like the ancient Greeks, the "creating, willing, valuing ego, which is the measure and value of all things" (p. 144). Later he cautions his followers, "this is my way; where is yours? . . . For *the* way—that does not exist" (p. 307). This modern existential focus on the subjective creation of meaning continues a long Western tradition of individualism that directly contradicts the Eastern denial of the reality of the ego. Zarathustra's will to power also draws on Western sources (including Schopenhauer and the Greek Promethean myth) in its praise of "the unexhausted procreative will of life" and its assertion that life is "that which must always overcome itself"—a psychological internalization of the Western progressive view of history (pp. 225, 227). Finally, that will to power involves another Occidental assumption, the virtue of struggle. "Let your work be a struggle," Zarathustra exults, "let us strive against one another like

---

36. *The Portable Nietzsche*, ed. Walter Kaufmann (New York: Viking, 1954), p. 142. Hereafter documented in the text.

gods (pp. 159, 214). This even applies to the fruits of the individual's progress, for "whatever I create and however much I love it—soon I must oppose it and my love" (p. 227).

Unquestionably, *Zarathustra*'s argument is more stridently Western than that of *The Birth of Tragedy*, but the prophet nevertheless slips in an occasional Oriental idea. Foremost among them looms the eternal recurrence, whose conception of time and immortality resembles that of Eastern mystical systems. Zarathustra proclaims that each person will be reborn into exactly the same personality and situation, in an eternal rhythm. Nietzsche himself regarded the idea as a synthesis of the dynamic and static views of Heraclitus and Parmenides, but this scarcely denies its similarity to Oriental thought—especially since the pre-Socratic Greek philosophers exhibit numerous analogies to their contemporary Indian religious thinkers. The pantheistic Brahman of Vedanta Hinduism (and the Tao as well) also reconciles a world of becoming to one of being. Another aspect of the eternal recurrence recalls Buddhism. Buddha gave no credence to the notion of an eternal, individual soul that journeys intact from one life to the next. Rather, the phenomenal "self" vanishes at death, to be reconstituted when the nexus of causes in the universe brings about its reincarnation. Nietzsche likewise proposes that the self evaporates at the body's demise, until the knot of causes propels it (eternally) into identical existence. The word "identical" is crucial, of course, because Nietzsche does not recognize any moral law of *karma* that rewards or punishes the soul by changing its state in the next life. Nevertheless, Nietzsche resembles Buddha in his implicit nihilism, which continues to frighten more traditional Western thinkers.

Zarathustra's doctrine of the relativity of morals—which greatly intrigued O'Neill[37]—also has an Oriental flavor. The prophet announces that "men gave themselves all their good and evil," for "only man placed values in things to preserve himself—he alone created a meaning for things, a human meaning" (p. 177). The view

---

37. O'Neill's papers contain nine pages of notes on *Thus Spake Zarathustra*, written in the playwright's tiny handwriting, with eighty-four separate entries; thirteen discuss the relativity of values. File Folder Za/O'Neill/153x, O'Neill Collection, Beinecke Library, Yale Univ.

that moral distinctions lack any transcendent sanction corresponds to Taoist and Indian thinking. Nietzsche's Superman, asserting that "the highest evil belongs to the highest good," finally arrives at a plateau where the "good" and "evil" defined by society are irrelevant (p. 228). The Oriental faiths would concur that "good" and "evil" actually interpenetrate each other, and would also agree with Nietzsche's basic assumption that no God stands behind these moral labels. Though the Indian concept of *karma* pays heed to moral behavior, the more important act of *moksha* liberates one from *karma*; and Taoism sees all human distinctions, moral or otherwise, as irrelevant to the Tao.

Thus, Zarathustra's dynamic message corresponds in some of its concepts to the Eastern religions whose renunciation ethic it intends to refute. In this ambivalence, Nietzsche resembles O'Neill. They also display a similar ebb and flow of Orientalism in their visions as they change over the years. Sensing the bankruptcy of post-Socratic Greek and Christian approaches to life, the young Nietzsche found temporary solutions in the mystical notions of Schopenhauer, which led him to explore the period in ancient Greece previous to the deification of Reason. The altar to Dionysus he subsequently erected resembled an Oriental shrine, for there one could celebrate the ecstatic annihilation of the individual self, and view the phenomenal world as a deceptive illusion—ideas that deeply influenced O'Neill's religious theatre half a century later. Furthermore, Nietzsche's recognition that Dionysus needed Apollo to produce great tragic art implied a polar interpretation of reality not unlike that of Taoism. Nietzsche retained the dialectical approach, though its terms were to change to "good" and "evil" in *Thus Spake Zarathustra*. But by the time he composed his masterpiece, Nietzsche had discarded Schopenhauer, and become more fundamentally Western in his radical assertion of ego, will, the body, and the glory of struggle. Eastern elements remained, such as the eternal recurrence, but Nietzsche was predominantly Occidental in this central philosophical work. O'Neill's career displays some interesting parallels. *The Fountain* and the plays following *Desire Under the Elms* (including *Brown, Lazarus, Interlude* and *Dynamo*) exhibit a strong Oriental desire to annihilate the self and mystically abandon the material world. Following *Dynamo's* failure, however, O'Neill became disillusioned with Eastern mysticism, and his drama remained fundamentally Western for the remainder of his career. Oriental elements reappear in his mature tragedies, *Iceman, Journey* and *Hughie*: but they are subordinated to a much stronger Western vision that asserts the primacy of self and history, and the necessity of pity and forgiveness.

Nietzsche's vision of an amoral and atheistic universe influenced the early naturalistic drama of his correspondent, August Strindberg. But following the "Inferno" period of 1894–98, when he suffered a series of nervous breakdowns, Strindberg emerged with a moral and theistic conception of God, as well as a revolutionary expressionistic aesthetic. The method of these post-Inferno experimental plays affected O'Neill's expressionistic works of the 1920s, as the American playwright frankly confessed. "All that is enduring in what we loosely call 'Expressionism,'" he asserted in a playbill for the Provincetown Players' production of *The Spook Sonata*, "all that is artistically valid and sound theatre—can be clearly traced back through Wedekind to Strindberg's *The Dream Play, There Are Crimes and Crimes, The Spook Sonata*, etc."[38] *The Spook Sonata* (entitled *The Ghost Sonata* by most translators) and *A Dream Play* were particular O'Neill favorites, produced by his own theatre company in 1924 and 1925; and these plays manifest Strindberg's sporadic, yet characteristically intense, interest in Oriental mystical thought. Thus, they furnished yet another Western source for the Orientalism of Eugene O'Neill.

Strindberg's turn toward the East strongly resembled that of his American admirer. A deeply spiritual man, Strindberg could find no comfort (nor even a satisfactory explanation of his misery) in the conventional Christian God. Like O'Neill, he consequently ex-

---

38. Playbill for the Provincetown Players production of *The Spook Sonata*, 3 January 1924; reprinted in Oscar Cargill, N. Bryllion Fagin, and William S. Fisher, eds., *O'Neill and His Plays: Four Decades of Criticism* (New York: New York Univ. Pr., 1961), pp. 108–9.

plored an incredible variety of spiritual systems, including Theosophy, Swedenborgianism, occultism, Manicheism—and Indian mysticism. He never escaped his harsh Lutheran upbringing, however, so the vision that finally emerged in his post-Inferno work imposed Eastern (and other) religious insights on a Christian foundation. Moreover, his expressionistic methods betray the divided vision of one who—again like O'Neill—gravitated toward Oriental conceptions of reality while remaining in the Western theatrical tradition. In fact, Strindberg's technical innovations helped O'Neill dramatize his own Eastern intuitions to Western audiences. For a playwright "only too proud of my debt to Strindberg," the greatest indebtedness may have derived from the model provided by the Swedish master in devising Western vehicles to carry Eastern mystical insights.[39]

Strindberg's interest in Oriental thought had existed for some time before it surfaced in his drama. Working with Far Eastern manuscripts at the Royal Library in Stockholm, he was so intrigued by the Orient that he learned Chinese in 1874, and possibly read Taoist and Buddhist philosophy in this language.[40] His preoccupation with the Orient also manifested itself in his research on Sweden's relationship to China, his learning Japanese in 1880, the bust of Buddha he kept in his home, and his readings in Oriental philosophy and religion.[41] When he became acquainted with Theosophy in the early 1890s, he naturally recognized its origin, noting that in the 1880s "Vedanta, Buddhism, penetrated into Europe and religion returned under the designations of Theosophy and Occultism."[42] Later, during his agonizing Inferno period, he frequently turned to Buddhism as an avenue of escape from his misery. He often called himself "Buddha" in his letters of 1894, and expressed his longing for Nirvana in repetitive outbursts similar to Buddhist chants. An 1895 essay, "In the cemetery," found him speaking of

39. O'Neill, Nobel Prize acceptance speech, 10 Dec. 1936; quoted in Gelbs, p. 814.
40. See Leta Jane Lewis, "Alchemy and the Orient in Strindberg's *Dream Play*," *Scandinavian Studies*, 35 (1963): 208–22.
41. Lewis, "Alchemy," p. 210.
42. Quoted in ibid., p. 212.

flowers as "superior beings that have realized Buddha's dream of coveting nothing, of enduring all things, of descending into the self, even to the point of unconsciousness." [43] Later, he wrote about this period that "a Buddhist work makes a stronger impression on me than all the other sacred books, since it places positive suffering above incontinence." [44]

Buddhism was not the only system that appealed to Strindberg during the Inferno period, of course. But by the time he composed *A Dream Play* in late 1901, both Buddhism and Hinduism were on his mind. He decorated his home with Indian draperies, and wrote the following in his diary: "Am reading about the teachings of Indian religion.—The whole world purely an illusion . . . The divine archpower . . . let itself be seduced by Maja [sic] or the urge of procreation. The divine archmatter thereby committed a sin against itself. . . . The world thus exists purely because of a sin, if indeed it does exist—for it is merely a vision seen in a dream (thus my *Dream Play*, a vision of life), a phantom whose destruction is the task of asceticism." [45] Though Strindberg slants his account of the Hindu creation myth in the direction of Genesis (emphasizing seduction and sin), he designates the central idea of his play as Oriental. The same diary entry concludes, "now the 'Indian religion' has given me the explanation of my dream play, and of the meaning of Indra's daughter. The Secret of the Door = Nothingness. All day I read about Buddhism." [46] Strindberg does not proceed to explicate the meaning of the play and its protagonist, but Buddhism had obviously provided him a key to both. The door appears toward the beginning and at the end of *A Dream Play*, and is supposed to contain the secret of life. When it finally opens, however, nothing stands behind it; and to the playwright himself, that nothingness represents Nirvana.

If Buddhism illuminates this image, Hinduism helps explain the

43. Quoted in Gunnar Brandell, *Strindberg in Inferno*, trans. Barry Jacobs (Cambridge: Harvard Univ. Pr., 1974), p. 101.
44. Quoted in ibid., p. 102.
45. Quoted in Gunnar Ollen, *August Strindberg*, trans. Peter Turner (New York: Ungar, 1972), p. 89.
46. Quoted in ibid., pp. 89–90.

plot and characterization. All that happens after Indra's Daughter descends to earth is unreal, *māyā*, because it occurs outside the heavenly realm where reality lies. Moreover, though Indra's Daughter strongly resembles Christ—she descends to earth to experience human life, suffers, and carries the supplications of tormented mankind to her father upon her resurrection—she also behaves like the Vedantic mythical deity. The protagonist assumes many different identities during the play, and those transmutations reflect the shifting forms of the divine Brahman in the phenomenal world. Indeed, this flux operates in all the characters. As Strindberg's famous preface proclaims, "the characters split, double and multiply; they evaporate, crystallise, scatter and converge."[47] This expressionistic technique, blurring the lines between separate identities, corresponds to the Indian belief in the insubstantiality of the separate self. Like Oriental mystics, Strindberg also ignores the limits dictated by reason. "Anything can happen," the preface argues, "everything is possible and probable. Time and space do not exist; on a slight groundwork of reality, imagination spins and weaves new patterns made up of memories, experiences, unfettered fancies, absurdities and improvisations."[48] In addition, the play's ambition to reproduce the flow of a dream—the movement of our inner lives and hence (to Strindberg) of life itself—corresponds to the Indian aim of alerting believers to the flux of the material world. The play's closing symbol reiterates these Oriental themes. The castle is burning, destroyed by the flames that in Buddhism symbolize life's pain and transience; and "the flower-bud on the roof bursts into a giant chrysanthemum," the flower of peace and spirit in Indian mythology.[49]

The Ghost Sonata was written six years after *A Dream Play*, but Strindberg juxtaposed the later work's composition with rehearsals

47. "Author's Note" to *A Dream Play*, trans. Elizabeth Sprigge, in *Modern Drama: A Norton Critical Edition*, ed. Anthony Caputi (New York: Norton, 1966), p. 425.
48. Strindberg, "Author's Note," p. 425.
49. Strindberg, *A Dream Play*, p. 224. Leta Jane Lewis perceives a possible Taoist symbolism here as well: in a Chinese alchemical text Strindberg had access to, *The Secret of the Golden Flowers*, flowers represent a return to the Tao via liberation from the earth ("Alchemy," p. 219).

for a production of the earlier play. The similarities of the two are hence not surprising. Once again, Strindberg treats an Oriental theme: the essence of life as suffering and illusion. Once again, he dramatizes this with Eastern effects: the Japanese death screen, the "exotic and Oriental" Hyacinth Room, the large statue of a seated Buddha with flowers rising from his lap. The flowers and Buddha express future salvation, as the visionary Arkenholz informs the dying girl in the final scene: "It is an image of the Cosmos. This is why Buddha sits holding the earth-bulb, his eyes brooding as he watches it grow, outward and upward, transforming itself into a heaven. This poor earth will become a heaven. It is for this that Buddha waits." [50] As with the Hindu cosmogony in *A Dream Play*, however, Strindberg distorts Eastern teachings in a Western direction. In Buddhist scripture, Buddha does not wait for earth to become heaven; rather, his teachings enable the believer to quickly transcend suffering in this life. More than in *A Dream Play*, Strindberg's stance is that of a morbid Lutheran who desires death to liberate him from earthly life, and hopes for a second coming. Hence, the student invokes Christ in addition to Buddha, and the play's concluding line reads "may the Lord of Heaven be merciful to you upon your journey."

The immediately preceding line also points up the mingling of Buddhism and Christianity in *Ghost Sonata*. "You poor little child," Arkenholz addresses the dying girl, "child of this world of illusion, guilt, suffering and death, this world of endless change, disappointment and pain." [51] The themes of guilt and death, grotesquely embodied in Hummel and the guests at the ghost supper, are primarily Christian; but the play's world of illusion and endless changes directs us once again to Eastern sources. The deceptive appearances of everyone perplex the innocent Arkenholz: his benefactor Hummel is actually a villain, the beautiful girl is nearly a corpse, the respectable Colonel is a fraud. The apparently all-powerful Hummel perishes in the closet previously inhabited by the Mummy; the Mummy suddenly drops her parrot-like way of talking when she exposes Hummel; Bengtsson relates that he and Hummel have

50. Strindberg, *The Ghost Sonata*, trans. Elizabeth Sprigge, in *Classics of the Modern Theatre*, ed. Alvin Kernan (New York: Harcourt, 1965), p. 295.
51. *Ghost Sonata*, p. 301.

alternated being servant and master in the past. In this transient, illusory world, the best solution is an Oriental one: put no faith in appearances, but concentrate solely on one's soul. This, of course, resembles the Christian goal of laying up treasures in heaven, not earth. And Christian themes of sin and death overshadow the Buddhistic ones, as communal guilt provokes Arkenholz to lament, "the curse lies over the whole of creation, over life itself." [52]

The two Strindberg plays known best by O'Neill, then, evidence the same mingling of East and West seen in Schopenhauer and Nietzsche. Their assumption of the instability and suffering inherent in human existence corresponds to Buddhism and Hinduism. Breaking down the normal distinctions between events and objects, Strindberg also repudiates the Western notion of a clearly definable, unique identity. Personalities split and merge, particularly in *A Dream Play*, thereby communicating an Oriental sense of the artificiality of all distinctions. Behind these dramas lurks a man yearning desperately for a monistic vision, and devising new expressionistic methods to both attain and express that unity. Mocking his monistic dream, however, is the tragic, dualistic cosmos of the European tradition, where good and evil engage in mortal combat. This in turn explains other Western features: a theology of sin, guilt and redemption; a world where man struggles constantly, often with inner demons; a universe where final happiness must wait until the afterlife, but where human suffering has expiatory value.

Empathizing with Strindberg in all these areas, O'Neill similarly sought to reconcile Western attitudes with Eastern mystical approaches that might afford relief from his torment. More important, the expressionistic machinery he borrowed from Strindberg labored (sometimes clumsily) to express Oriental attitudes toward personality and reality. Like *A Dream Play*, *The Great God Brown* splits and multiplies personalities, thereby questioning the notion of individual egohood; like *Ghost Sonata*, *Lazarus Laughed*'s bewildering variety of masked figures suggest that life is *māyā*. Strindberg's example, furthermore, helped convince O'Neill that mystical insights could be dramatized on a Western stage geared toward realism and naturalism. The Swede's expressionism was thus crucial

52. Ibid., p. 300.

in regard to the American's Orientalism. For without Strindberg's pioneering theatrical innovations, the young O'Neill might never have devised an aesthetic appropriate to his Eastern side.

O'Neill's vision in both *Brown* and *Lazarus* was also influenced by the Swiss psychologist Carl G. Jung, whose theories O'Neill found "extraordinarily illuminating in the light of my own experience with hidden motives." [53] O'Neill's praise can be related to the interest Jung, like Strindberg, took in Oriental philosophy. More than any European thinker of our century, Jung made Eastern insights available to the Western mind, due partly to his belief in their superior wisdom. In *Psychological Types* (1921), he decried our "more primitive, Western forms of religion—primitive because lacking insight," and praised the Eastern "psychological doctrine of salvation which brings the way of deliverance within man's ken and capacity." [54] Not surprisingly, Jung's own "psychological doctrine of salvation" displays deep indebtedness to the Oriental systems he studied.

O'Neill was particularly intrigued by an early Jung book that set forth his psycho-religious doctrine. In a 1929 letter, O'Neill remarked that "the book that interested me the most of all those of the Freudian school is Jung's 'Psychology of the Unconscious,' which I read many years ago. If I have been influenced unconsciously it must have been by this book more than any other psychological work." [55] But while no documentary proof exists that O'Neill read other Jung works, internal evidence suggests a familiarity with *Psychological Types*. Oscar Cargill, terming *Lazarus Laughed* "the fusion point of Jung and Nietzsche," argues persuasively that this volume stands behind the play's schematic classification of personality types.[56] My emphasis will mirror the evi-

53. 1929 letter to Sparrow; quoted in "Psychoanalytical Material," p. 77.
54. Trans. H. Godwin Baynes, rev. R. F. C. Hull (Princeton: Princeton Univ. Pr., 1971), p. 194.
55. Letter to Sparrow, quoted in "Psychoanalytical Material," p. 77.
56. Cargill, "Fusion Point of Jung and Nietzsche," in Cargill, Fagin and Fisher, *Criticism*, pp. 410–11.

dence: *Psychology of the Unconscious* will be explored in some detail, while comments on *Psychological Types* will be briefer and more general. Both volumes discover yet another O'Neill source mingling East and West in his thought; but the large role Oriental religion plays in Jung's theories makes him of particular importance to this study.

Psychology of the Unconscious, first published in 1912, demonstrates Jung's wide knowledge of Oriental myth, folklore and metaphysics. Countless examples from Eastern sources are marshalled to support his contention that a universal psychological conflict between life and death takes place within the libido (rather than between libido and thanatos, as Freud asserts). Despite these examples, however, Jung's goals and methods are quintessentially Western. First, his illustrations prove the universality of the neurosis of a patient whose case history structures the book. The reader is hardly asked to accept mystical assertions on faith, since he is offered a carefully reasoned, abundantly documented argument. Second and more important, Jung is thoroughly Western in his basic intention: the desire to rationally integrate the individual ego to allow for a fulfilling, active life. Jung argues that the adolescent must sacrifice the childish self, thereby clearing the way for authentic integration and individuation. This, however, is a delicate process because the shaper of the childish self—the mother—is also the source of life. In fact, the mother is the prime representative (and chief archetype) of the libido, the force that both nourishes and threatens our identity; and the secure individual draws upon the energies of the libido while resisting domination by it. This is only possible through willed introversion, a descent into depths of the libido to derive strength. "This is the dangerous moment," warns Jung. If one remains in the libido, the result is psychological paralysis; if one emerges back into the upper world, "this journey to the underworld has been a fountain of youth, and new fertility springs from his apparent death." [57] Thus, the introverting process serves traditional Western goals in its design to nourish the individual ego, not—as in Eastern religion—to obliterate it.

57. *Psychology of the Unconscious*, trans. Beatrice Hinkle (New York, 1919; rpt. London: Kegan Paul, Trench, Trubner, 1922), pp. 181–82. Hereafter documented in the text.

The death/rebirth process central to Jung's theories is also central to Christian dogma, and Jung likewise agrees with Christian thinkers on the value of self. But another Western feature of Jung's argument is antithetical to the Church. Jung proposes rationalistic liberation from the religious myths that disguise and repress our primitive Oedipal urges. The alternative he proposes is "conscious recognition," whereby "man could without compulsion will that which he must do . . . without delusion through belief in the religious symbols." Though he admires the beauty of religious symbolism, he sees it as necessary only to an "infantile mental state," and emphasizes that "*belief should be replaced by understanding*" (pp. 144–45; Jung's italics). While he would later open himself more to mysticism, Jung here demonstrates a reverence for reason that betrays his indebtedness to both Freud and the European philosophical tradition. Equally Western is his fear of excessive introversion. Terming the instinctive attraction to libido "a deadly longing for the depths within," he cautions that "this death is no external enemy, but a deep personal longing for quiet and for the profound peace of non-existence, for a dreamless sleep in the ebb and flow of the sea of life." The state he describes duplicates the goal of the Oriental mystic; but Jung views it as a desire to return to the womb, and believes the individual "must fight and sacrifice his longing for the past, in order to rise to his own heights" (p. 215).

Activism, rationalism and egoism, then, constitute the Western foundations of *Psychology of the Unconscious*. But Jung's version of the libido demonstrates the impact of his Eastern examples. As the Hindu believes that all souls contain Brahman at their deepest level, Jung believes that every ego emerges from a libido that provides energy and meaning for each life. Admittedly, this immanent universal force (an early version of Jung's "collective unconscious") parallels Christianity's Holy Spirit as well as the Vedantic Brahman. Christian theology, however, has emphasized the transcendent (God the Father) and personal (Jesus Christ) aspects of the triune Godhead; Jung and Oriental thought stress its immanent, impersonal nature. Hence, the individualized libido "sinks into its 'own depths,'" according to Jung, and "finds there below, in the shadows of the unconscious, the substitute for the upper world" (p. 181). Not surprisingly, many of his illustrations from Hindu folklore point up exactly this aspect of the libido, which is to the ego as Brahman is to *Atman*.

The resemblance of the libido to Oriental conceptions of ultimate reality by no means ends here. Jung asserts that the libido (like the amoral Brahman and Tao) "obeys no human moral law"; his conviction that the "unhappy combination of religion and morality . . . must be overcome" repudiates Judeo-Christian assumptions. Second, the libido is monistic, uniting man and world, subject and object. Indeed, Jung argues that our monistic conceptions actually spring from the libido, since we transfer our infantile erotic yearning for a parent into a spiritual longing for a God—a God not metaphysical but "metapsychological," who unites the inner and outer worlds and colors all "objective" reality. Third, the libido is dynamic. Beatrice Hinkle, in her introduction to the-translation of *Psychology of the Unconscious* read by O'Neill, observes that Jung argues for a "dynamic theory of life; the conception that life is in a state of flux—movement—leading either to construction or destruction" (p. xxiii). The flux of existence is likewise emphasized in Hinduism and Taoism. Last and most important, the libido resembles Brahman and the Tao in its ambivalence: it unites good and evil, creation and destruction, male and female, life and death. Jung works repeated variations on his assertions that the libido is "power which beautifies everything, and which under other circumstances destroys everything"; it is both "God and Devil," offering in the "terrible mother" both death and renewal (p. 63). The Hindu scriptures cited by Jung illustrate this ambivalence. Observing that the "ambitendency" of the human will is its normal state, he theorizes that the incest wish "frees the pair of opposites, which are normally most intimately united, and causes their manifestation in the form of separate tendencies; it is only thus that they become willingness and unwillingness, which interfere with each other. The Bhagavad-Gita says, 'Be thou free of the pair of opposites'" (pp. 107–08); Jung similarly says opposites within the soul must be reconciled, and their actual unity recognized.

As the preceding quotation suggests, the libido resolves our conflicting impulses in much the same way the Tao harmonizes *yin* and *yang*. This harmonization constitutes a central theme of *Psychological Types* (first published in 1923), which argues for the necessary reconciliation of opposites. Jung becomes most fervent when he discusses the teachings of Hinduism and Taoism that closely approximate his own. Criticizing the "childishness" of the Western God who heals our inner divisions "as and when it suits him and for reasons we are not fitted to understand," he lauds the Oriental proposal of a deliverance "attainable by means of a conscious attitude" that effects "release from the pairs of opposites in order to reach the path of redemption." [58] When he discusses the Brahmanic version of the uniting symbol, he notes the close similarity of Brahman to the dynamic, creative libido. Both effect an "irrational union of opposites," and both participate in a polar process resembling "those processes of nature which always remain constant and arouse the idea of regular recurrence." [59] In a subsequent section on the *yin/yang* symbolism of Taoism, Jung points out that Chinese philosophy counsels avoiding the conflict of opposites by living in harmony with the Tao—which is, like Brahman, an irrational, mystical force.

As is evident, a large difference between *Psychological Types* and *Psychology of the Unconscious* is Jung's increased sympathy toward the mysticism of the Eastern approaches. Jung in fact became ever more attracted to Oriental thought as he grew older: he eventually wrote numerous essays comparing Eastern and Western religions, and contributed forewords to D. T. Suzuki's *Introduction to Zen Buddhism* and the *I Ching*. [60] Eugene O'Neill offers an interesting contrast in his development. Unlike Jung, his mysticism announces itself from his first works, peaks in the religious plays of his middle period, and then almost disappears until *The Iceman Cometh* and *Long Day's Journey* introduce it again. Not surprisingly, the middle plays represent the zenith of the influence of both Jung and Orientalism. *The Fountain*'s title symbol, for instance, exhibits many of the mystical features shared by the Jungian libido, the Vedantic Brahman, and the Tao. *Lazarus Laughed*, so Jungian in its categorization of psychological types, is the most Oriental of

58. *Psychological Types*, p. 104.
59. Ibid., pp. 199, 212.
60. These essays are collected in C. G. Jung, *Psychology and Religion: East and West*, trans. R. F. C. Hull (Princeton: Princeton Univ. Pr., 1958).

O'Neill's plays, particularly in the dynamic polarities it discovers everywhere in existence. That polar dynamic—one of the most consistent features of O'Neill's vision—is also the point of greatest correspondence between Jung's theories and Eastern mystical concepts. It was thus inevitable that O'Neill discovered an affinity between his world and that of Jung. Both the artist and the psychologist (each a mystic of sorts) had turned East in search of systems that discovered a profound unity underlying all conflicts. Indeed, the deepest correspondence between the two men may be their common fascination with Oriental mystical philosophy.

All the romantic thinkers and artists we have examined, of course, were vitally interested in the Orient at one time or another. Like Jung, they combined Eastern and Western approaches in a manner that reinforced those opposing tendencies in their student O'Neill. As heirs of the European tradition, all considered the will the primary component of human nature, and believed it needed to struggle for survival or dominance. But on other matters, they differed according to how "Eastern" they were. Nietzsche and Jung thus placed a traditionally high Western value on the creative individual ego; Schopenhauer and Strindberg, like Oriental thinkers, suspected the reality of the self. Whatever their differences, however, all urged the self to escape (at least occasionally) into a transcendent realm, whether called the libido, Nirvana, Dionysian ecstasy, or a painless condition beyond Will. This transcendentalism allied them with Oriental religions, as did their dynamic organicism. Nietzsche's Zarathustra concluded that both universe and individual were perpetually becoming. Strindberg intuited disturbing implications to this: a universe and identity in flux caused tragic uncertainty. Jung made flux (in the form of a Tao-like rhythm) a primary attribute of the libido; Schopenhauer resembles Buddha in seeking a state free from desire, ego, will and the fluid uncertainty of existence. Nearly all these ideas and responses appear somewhere in the plays of Eugene O'Neill—a true romantic with the same ambivalence toward Eastern thought as his major Western predecessors and sources.

The Orient on Native Grounds

To a large degree, American society represents the product of the Christian and romantic traditions discussed above. Founded mainly by Puritans in the north and Anglicans or Catholics in the south, it has always been shaped by Christian beliefs. Particularly in New England, it has tended to perceive reality as a moral contest between good and evil, and concerned itself with the spiritual state of the individual soul. The soul's condition obsesses modern romanticism as well, a movement whose birth coincided with the founding of the nation in the late eighteenth century. The early years of the republic, influenced by European romanticism, witnessed a growing belief in the individual, and a deepening conviction that God (and a return to Edenic innocence) lay in the undisturbed wilderness. The young O'Neill absorbed these and other native values that corresponded to his Christian upbringing and naturally romantic temper. As a result, his American background contributed, both indirectly and directly, to his interest in Oriental thought. For O'Neill's mysticism, pantheism and Orientalism have numerous antecedents in American culture. From the start, American thought betrayed an intriguing correspondence with Oriental philosophy in the latent mysticism of the Puritan mind. These affinities became most apparent in Emerson and Thoreau; but even after the Transcendentalist moment passed, American artists and writers continued to be drawn to the Orient, as is evident in the work of such figures as James Whistler, Lafcadio Hearn and Ezra Pound. Pound's friend T. S. Eliot (who had studied Sanskrit at Harvard) felt a sympathy with Indian mystical religions that "The Waste Land" made explicit. Moreover, the decade in which Eliot's masterpiece was published found America unusually interested in India. It was no coincidence, then, that the same decade responded to the mystical drama of O'Neill, himself an amateur student of Oriental religion.

O'Neill's New England ancestors, Emerson and Thoreau, were also students of the East, especially well versed in Hindu thought. But some of their most "Eastern" notions had been expressed long before they were born by Puritans with no knowledge of Oriental thought. Orthodox Puritan doctrine may have been rigidly Western in its emphasis on "right reason," and its distrust of mysticism. As Perry Miller has written about Puritanism, however, "the sense of an inward communication and of the divine symbolism of nature" co-existed uncomfortably with these mainstream teachings.[61] These mystical and pantheistic tendencies originated in the Protestant Reformation, which emphasized justification by faith rather than works. The consequent shift of focus from the objective behavioral world to the mysterious realm of the emotions—a realm known only to the individual believer—opened the door to the radical subjectivism of the Puritan rebels. Anne Hutchinson insisted (like the neighboring Quakers) that the individual might receive heavenly instruction through emotions and intuitions; and Jonathan Edwards, in his *Dissertation Concerning the End for which God Created the World* (1765), came close to discovering a pantheistic God in nature. In the mysticism and pantheism of these iconoclasts can be detected a spiritual impulse parallel to that of Oriental mystical thinkers.

The Eastern-leaning Transcendentalism of Ralph Waldo Emerson thus involved (in Miller's words) "restatements of a native disposition," not simply borrowings from German idealism and Hinduism.[62] Whatever the actual source, those restatements intrigued young Eugene O'Neill, who read Emerson's works in his father's library during his early adolescence. There, he encountered the musings of a man knowledgeable in the mysteries of Vedantic Hinduism. This may partially explain why, as an adult, O'Neill returned to Emerson, buying a six-volume edition of his *Complete Works*. In addition, he purchased and made marginal marks in Bliss Perry's *The Heart of Emerson's Journals* and Van Wyck Brooks' *The Life of Emerson*, taking notes on the latter and another Brooks work, *The Flowering of New England*. Thus, O'Neill's fascination with Emerson occurred twice in his life, and a large part of Emerson's appeal undoubtedly lay in his Eastern intuitions.

Frederic Carpenter has demonstrated in *Emerson and Asia* that the Concord sage's acquaintance with Hindu thought developed

61. Perry Miller, "From Edwards to Emerson," *New England Quarterly*, 13 (1940): 589–617; reprinted in *Interpretations of American Literature*, ed. Charles Fiedelson (New York: Oxford Univ. Pr., 1959), p. 123.
62. Miller, "Edwards to Emerson," p. 116.

gradually after initial resistance.[63] But like O'Neill, Emerson had already drifted toward the East through Western sources, especially Neoplatonism. The central feature of Emerson's system, the Oversoul, corresponds in its pantheistic emanations to Plotinus's conception of life's source as "a fountain possessing no other principles, but imparting itself to all rivers, without being exhausted by any of them, and abiding quietly in itself."[64] Also like Plotinus's World Soul, the Oversoul strongly resembles the Vedantic Brahman, flowing in and out of the material world and providing its movement; Emerson's subordination of the cognitive faculties to the mystical ones again parallels both Neoplatonism and Hinduism.

Directed by Neoplatonism toward Hinduism, Emerson read the translations of the Bhagavad-Gita and the Upanishads by the British Orientalists. In July of 1842, he contributed an essay on Hinduism to *The Dial*; by the 1850s, he was keeping a separate journal called "The Orientalist." Not surprisingly, then, the biographical essays collected in *Representative Men* in 1850 discovered Oriental elements in Swedenborg, Goethe and Plato. In the essay "Plato," in fact, Emerson perceived "the fundamental Unity" of existence as finding "its highest expression in the religious writings of the East, and chiefly in the Indian scriptures, in the Vedas, the Bhagavat Geeta, and the Vishnu Purana."[65] Ten years later, the "Illusions" essay in *The Conduct of Life* implicitly discussed *māyā*, and that essay's assertion that "we live amid hallucinations" was explicitly related to *māyā* in two other pieces in the volume, "Works and Days" and "Poetry and Imagination."[66] Hindu thought also informed the essays "Fate" and "Immortality," the latter concluding with a paraphrase of the Katha Upanishad. Finally, Hinduism provided titles for three Emerson Poems: "Hamatreya," "Brahma," and "Maya."

Detailing overt Oriental references only touches on Emerson's involvement with the East, however. From "Nature" through the es-

63. *Emerson and Asia* (1930; rpt. New York: Haskell House, 1968), p. 10.

64. Thomas Taylor, trans., *Five Books of Plotinus* (New York: n.p., 1914), p. 237; quoted in Carpenter, *Emerson*, pp. 75–76.

65. *The Selected Writings of Emerson*, ed. Brooks Atkinson (New York: Random, 1950), pp. 476, 478–79.

66. *Major Writers of America*, ed. Perry Miller et al. (New York: Harcourt, 1962), 1: 567.

says in the 1840s that included "Compensation" and "The Oversoul" to his later meditations on *māyā*, Emerson's philosophy has a heavy Hindu flavor. Primary among his Eastern ideas are his fundamental convictions of man's unity with nature and God, and the soul's importance in effecting this unity. This Vedantic conception of *tat tvam asi* receives its most cogent expression in "The Oversoul": "Within man is the soul of the whole; the wise silence; the universal beauty, to which every part and particle is equally related; the eternal One. . . . The act of seeing and the thing seen, the seer and the spectacle, the subject and the object, are one. We see the world piece by piece, as the sun, the moon, the animal, the tree; but the whole, of which these are the shining parts, is the soul." [67] This Oversoul is dynamic, as "Brahma" reveals: the ignorant, proclaims the divine Hindu persona, "know not well the subtle ways / I keep, and pass, and turn again." [68] Furthermore, this god of process renders all oppositions provisional, for Emerson and Hinduism agree that actions, thoughts and causes are all bipolar, that all is one: "Polarity, or action and reaction, we meet in every part of nature; in darkness and light; in heat and cold, in the ebb and flow of waters. . . . An inevitable dualism bisects nature, so that each thing is a half and suggests another thing to make it whole." [69] Though a spiritual wholeness underlies all dualisms, it must express itself in the inferior realm of matter—making the material world misleading and illusory, an idea emphasized in Emerson's later work. The essay "Illusions," as suggested, finds life "a kingdom of illusions" where "all is riddle, and the key to a riddle is another riddle," where "we wake from one dream into another dream." [70] This idea is repeated in the poem "Maya." But behind these illusions lies an impersonal law of compensation that duplicates the Indian concept of *karma*. "All things are moral," asserts the essay "Compensation," and "thou shalt be paid exactly for what thou hast done, no more, no less." [71] While Emerson's Yankee soul will not permit ultimate liberation from *karma*, however, he does allow immediate access to spiritual

67. *Selected Writings*, p. 262.
68. Ibid., p. 809.
69. Ibid., p. 172.
70. *Major Writers*, 1: 569, 567.
71. *Selected Writings*, pp. 175, 179.

forces through intuitive mystical experiences. In "Nature," he speaks of retreating to the woods and becoming a "transparent eyeball"; "I am nothing; I see all; the currents of the Universal Being circulate through me; I am part or parcel of God." [72]

As we might expect, various Western assumptions counterbalance Emerson's Orientalism. "Self-Reliance," for example, enunciates a very Occidental individualism, indicating Emerson's disregard for the Eastern repudiation of the ego. Moreover, his core concept of the Oversoul, while Oriental in essence, receives Western humanistic applications. It stands, for instance, behind the justification of love and friendship, qualities of little concern to a Hindu sage. Nor does Emerson discount the ethical will, as an Oriental might. Moral earnestness informs every aspect of his vision—hence his essays on "Prudence," "Heroism," "Character," and "Manners." Finally, as Arthur Christy has observed, the Hindu desires to turn away from the artificial distinctions between "good" and "evil," while Emerson sees the world itself as good. [73] This optimism does not absolutely distinguish his thought from Hinduism, but it contrasts dramatically with the attention paid by Indian mystical religions to suffering. Accordingly, Buddhism, which more emphatically focuses on suffering as life's essence, exercised no appeal to Emerson, and he glided over those aspects of Hinduism that recognize the pain of existence.

The admixture of Occident and Orient we find in Emerson is also evident in O'Neill, who likewise sought mystical union with an impersonal being while simultaneously reflecting Christian morality. *Lazarus Laughed*, the radical expression of the mystical impulse, must be weighed against drama like *Desire Under the Elms* (with its self-sacrificing ethic) and *The Great God Brown* (whose hero has the soul of a Christian martyr). O'Neill, however, differs from Emerson in a major respect: like the Indian thinkers, the tragic playwright was obsessed with human suffering. In this, O'Neill also differs from Henry David Thoreau, whose work O'Neill examined while working on *A Touch of the Poet*, when he purchased three

72. Ibid., p. 6.
73. *The Orient in American Transcendentalism: A Study of Emerson, Thoreau, and Alcott* (1932; rpt. New York: Octagon, 1969), p. 85.

books by Thoreau.[74] He discovered in Thoreau what he found in
Emerson: a Western individualism and moral sense co-existing with
an Eastern pantheism and mysticism. Like Emerson, Thoreau had
also read the Bhagavad-Gita and other Hindu sacred texts, and
contributed columns to *The Dial* on Hinduism and Buddha. Emerson, Thoreau and other Transcendentalists injected Indian philosophy into American cultural currents, which had immediate impact
upon Walt Whitman (whose own passage to India was prompted by
reading Hindu Scriptures). Their work also helped precipitate an
Oriental vogue in American literature that influenced Hawthorne,
Poe and Melville, and pointed the way for later native thinkers and
artists. The 1880s and 1890s discovered various cultured Americans turning even farther East. Henry Adams and John La Farge
journeyed to Japan in 1886, and reflected that journey in their lives
and work. Adams often referred to the Saint-Gaudens statue of his
wife in Washington, D.C., as "Nirvana"; La Farge used Japanese
backgrounds for his mural in the Church of the Ascension in New
York, and made Confucius the central figure in works done in Baltimore and Minneapolis.[75] Two other painters, the impressionists
James M. Whistler and Mary Cassatt, were influenced by their
studies of Japanese prints, and the impressionistic literary style of
Lafcadio Hearn took its aesthetic justification from Buddhism.
Hearn settled in Japan, but his stories and essays were quite popu-
lar back in his homeland—where he was read by, among others,
Eugene O'Neill.[76]

The American interest in the East continued into the twentieth
century, where it exercised an impact on modernist poetry in particular. Ernest Fenollosa's translations of Far Eastern poetry and
Nōh plays were edited and published by Ezra Pound; and Pound's
own theories and poems, influenced by Oriental aesthetics, helped

74. O'Neill's Thoreau volumes included *Life without Principle* (New York: W. E.
Scott, 1936); *Walden* (New York: The Heritage Club, 1939); and *The Writings of
Henry David Thoreau*, ed. H. G. O. Blake, vol. 3: *Winter, from the Journal of Henry
David Thoreau* (Boston: Houghton, 1877). O'Neill's library also included a copy of
Henry Seidel Canby's *Thoreau* (Boston: Houghton Mifflin, 1939).
75. See Christy, "The Sense of the Past," in *Asian Legacy*, p. 45.
76. O'Neill's library contained a copy of Hearn's *Karma* (1918), purchased some-
time during the 1920s.

shape the verse and drama of numerous Western poets. Pound's indebtedness to the Orient was more formal than spiritual, for his own quasiscientific rationalism remained impervious to Oriental mysticism; his Penelope was Confucius, not Lao Tse. But his friend T. S. Eliot possessed a sensibility sympathetic to the non-rational side of Eastern thought, and he diligently studied Indian philosophy. "The Waste Land," which reflects Eliot's despair over the spiritual aridity of the modern West, alludes prominently to redemptive approaches in the sacred texts of Buddhism and Hinduism. The title of the third section, "The Fire Sermon," refers to the Buddha's central teaching about the ravages of fleshly desires; the concluding section, "What the Thunder Said," takes its title from a passage in the Upanishads, which counsels "Datta, Dayadhvam, Damyatta"— "give, sympathize, control." The poem concludes with these Sanskrit terms, followed by "Shantih shantih shantih"—the Upanishadic equivalent for "the peace which passeth understanding," Eliot notes.[77] Not coincidentally, Eliot's note points up the parallel with Christian scripture, for Eastern thought helped lead him back to orthodox Western religion, where he found numerous similar teachings. The obscure ruminations of *The Four Quartets*, however, offer convincing proof that Eliot's vision throughout his career remained more compatible with the mystical East than the rationalistic West.

Pound's and Eliot's disenchantment with contemporary Western culture paralleled O'Neill's, and the two poets provided modern precedents for the playwright in his turn toward China and India. America's flirtation with the Orient did not confine itself to intellectuals and artists, however. During the late nineteenth century, the Theosophical Society established chapters in the United States, and this strange amalgam of Oriental mysticism and Western evangelism directly affected O'Neill. As Doris Alexander has indicated, O'Neill became acquainted with this movement courtesy of Terry

77. T. S. Eliot, "The Waste Land," in *The American Tradition in Literature*, ed. Sculley Bradley et al. (New York: Norton, 1974), pp. 1193, 1202–4.

Carlin, who gave him a pamphlet entitled *Light on the Path* in 1916.[78] This twenty-eight page booklet probably constituted O'Neill's first encounter with some of the key terms and tenets of Indian religion. The subtitle clearly indicates its purpose: "A Treatise, Written for the Personal Use of those who are ignorant of the Eastern Wisdom, and who desire to enter within its influence."[79] The young playwright's enthusiastic response to it (painting one passage from it on the beams of his Provincetown flat) demonstrates that he fell under the influence of its "Eastern wisdom" himself.

Written by Mabel Collins in 1885, the tract's language and counsels are geared toward an Occidental audience. Its first section advises that one must "kill out desire of life" (the central teaching of Buddhism) and "kill out all sense of separateness" (the fundamental concept of Hinduism); but it displays a typically Western recognition of the struggle necessary to accomplish this. "The heart will bleed, and the whole life of the man seem to be utterly dissolved" (pp. 4–5). Moreover, all victories over desire and separateness will be only temporary, since "again and again the battle must be fought and won. It is only for an interval that nature can be still" (p. 13). While the goals are Eastern, then, the necessity of prolonged and painful battle seems Western. Furthermore, the language subtly keys itself to Western values. It advises the reader, for example, to "desire possessions above all," quickly adding that "those possessions must belong to the pure soul only" (p. 8); but Indian mystical systems repudiate the very *concept* of possession. The Theosophists may wish their followers to ultimately realize that "possession" possesses no reality; but their diction implicitly respects an idea an Indian mystic would reject.

Perhaps these Western elements represent the Society's pragmatic attempt to present their spiritual package in familiar wrappings, for their message is fundamentally Oriental. The primary objective is

78. See chap. two, n. five.
79. M[abel] C[ollins], *Light on the Path* (London: Theosophical Society, 1885). While it is not certain that O'Neill read this particular edition (hereafter documented in the text), subsequent editions altered nothing in the original pamphlet, but simply added more chapters. Also see Alexander, *Tempering*, pp. 216–18, and "*Light on the Path* and *The Fountain*," *Modern Drama*, 3 (Dec. 1960): 260–67.

knowledge (not faith), obtained through meditation on the immanent, impersonal God. "Within you is the light of the world—the
only light that can be shed upon the path"; once this light is perceived through "the use of the inner senses," you see that "you are
part of the harmony of life," since "your soul has become one with
all pure souls and with the inmost" (pp. 7, 18, 19, 21). The unity
with being enables the believer to pass mystically beyond material
distinctions. The "Final Rules" admonish the reader to "Hold fast
to that which has neither substance nor existence. Listen only to
that which is soundless. Look only at that which is invisible alike to
the inner and the outer sense" (p. 22). This withdrawal from the
sensory realm necessarily precedes attainment of the penultimate
knowledge: that of *karma* (the title of the pamphlet's concluding
section). *Light on the Path* recognizes with Hinduism and Buddhism that "the whole of the future is in unbroken continuity with
the present, as the present is with the past," so that a person's entire
spiritual history ordinarily determines his future (p. 25). But if one
chooses the proper path, liberation will follow, whereby one "simply lifts himself out of the region in which karma operates" (p. 27).
This is accomplished through karma yoga (though it is not identified as such), in renunciation of the consequences of personal actions and a resolution to "desire to sow no seeds for your own har-
vesting" (p. 28). Implicitly drawing on the Bhagavad-Gita (in which
Krishna warns Arjuna not to identify his eternal soul with his sol-
dierly activities), the pamphlet advises the reader to "stand aside in
the coming battle, and though thou fightest be not thou the warrior." Only then, when your desires "are fixed only on that state
wherein there is neither reward nor punishment, good nor evil"—
the state sought by all three Oriental mystical religions—can release be obtained from *karma* (p. 15).

O'Neill never became a Theosophist, but this pamphlet's Eastern
teachings inform the liberated protagonists of *The Fountain* and
Lazarus Laughed, and perhaps *The Great God Brown* as well.
O'Neill's Orientalism was further encouraged by another phenomenon gaining momentum at this time, the "Hindu invasion." At the
end of the 1920s, Waldo Frank commented on the contemporary
interest in India. He labelled the spreading Oriental ideas "nefari-
ous doctrines" subscribed to because, "as the Mediterranean dog-

mas grow worn with use, the peace and power hungering soul looks farther afield. America, moving West, comes to the East. So India sends patches of her glorious truth to be woven into modern comforters."[80] Statistics indicate the reasons for Frank's concern. The Vedanta Society, founded by the swami Vivekananda at the turn of the century, added two chapters in 1926 and 1929, and had eight swamis in America in 1929—the largest number for the society up to that time. 1920 saw the founding of the Yogoda Sat-Sanga Society in Boston; by 1930, there were twelve centers, a journal and a correspondence university. Moreover, several Hindu cultural movements began during the decade, and various popular and academic lecturers (including A. K. Coomaraswamy) addressed large numbers of people on Hinduism.[81] A corresponding interest was apparent on the literary scene. The number of books on India rose dramatically, from 51 in the 1917–21 period, to 69 between 1922 and 1926, to 123 between 1927 and 1931.[82] At the top of the sales charts was *Mother India*, a 1928 best seller that pandered to the public's fantasies about the exotic East; topping the critics' lists was *A Passage to India*, E. M. Forster's masterpiece detailing the cultural conflicts between East and West under the British Raj. Like Forster and others, O'Neill pursued an interest in Oriental culture at this time; and (though he would have denied this vehemently) part of his motive may have been its popular appeal.

O'Neill did not live to see the renewed American interest in the Orient today, but he would have understood its causes. The current fascination with the *I Ching* and Transcendental Meditation, and the presence on college campuses of Hare Krishna sects, expresses a disillusion with traditional Western values similar to that of the 1920s. The contemporary quest for rebirth in the East may be quixotic, based on a misunderstanding of Oriental teachings,[83] but its very presence symbolizes a widespread dissatisfaction, and a suspicion that Western religion forms part of the problem. That dissatis-

80. *The Re-discovery of America* (New York: Scribners, 1929), p. 187.

81. See Wendall Thomas, *Hinduism Invades America* (New York: Beacon, 1930), pp. 103–230.

82. The statistics are from charts compiled by Charles S. Braden in "The Novelist Discovers the Orient," *Far Eastern Quarterly*, 7 (Nov. 1947): 165–68.

83. See Cox, *Turning East*, pp. 137–38 and Bibliography.

faction and suspicion have, as we have observed, a long history in American culture. Heterodox Puritans like Anne Hutchinson felt similar frustration with a religion that implicitly encouraged, while overtly condemning, one's deeper intuitions; later, the New England Transcendentalists drew heavily on Hinduism in their depiction of an impersonal, pantheistic Oversoul that followed the law of *karma*, not grace. Subsequent American artists and intellectuals went even further East, falling under Japanese and Chinese influences in their theories and their art, but the popular interest shifted back to India following World War One, when O'Neill emerged as a playwright. O'Neill also explored the Orient, in his drama and in his life. "*Marco Millions*" explicitly describes the clash of Eastern and Western values; *Strange Interlude* and *Dynamo* implicitly contrast Orient and Occident in their characters and symbols. The playwright and his then-mistress, Carlotta Monterey, also journeyed to China in 1928. Most important, O'Neill read numerous volumes on Oriental religion and culture during this period, including the books on Hinduism, Buddhism, and Taoism discussed in the preceding chapter.

Like many Americans today, Eugene O'Neill experienced a deep alienation from his native culture. Like them, he turned East, travelling on the same path as the early Christian Church and the modern romantic philosophers and artists. Like them, he could not unreservedly embrace the philosophy of life he discovered there, for he remained a Western man. But his mind and soul were deepened by the encounter, as is apparent in the eclectic and complex art we turn to next.

4

A Western Passage to the East

From 1916 to 1925, O'Neill's Eastern dimension developed from a scarcely visible seed to a deliberate part of his art. His early plays of the sea, which view the ocean as a mystical, amoral presence that shapes human destiny, exhibit his Orientalism in its embryonic state. Nearly all these one-act works, however, portray this sea god as an "ironic life force" (in O'Neill's famous words) that frustrates the characters; in that defeat of man by sea, O'Neill expresses the time-honored Western assumption of antagonism between man and larger forces. Only one of these plays—*The Moon of the Caribbees*—hints that the sea may also provide serenity if approached with wise passiveness. This Oriental attitude is highlighted in the full-length *"Anna Christie,"* where the title character finds peace through symbolic absorption into the sea she worships. Admittedly, O'Neill's Western dualism remains prominent here, manifesting itself in Chris's distrust of "dat ole davil, sea"; but even that distrust displays Eastern shadings, for the sea god Chris fears resembles the Vedantic Brahman, weaving webs of illusion while impartially dispensing good and evil.

Not coincidentally, O'Neill initiated his studies in Oriental philosophy around the time he completed *"Anna Christie."* This research was reflected in two subsequent plays, which found the playwright journeying East in his imagination. *The Fountain* concerns the desire of the Spanish explorer Ponce de Leon to discover a "Western passage to the East" and thereby locate the fountain of youth (rumored to be in China). While never reaching the Orient, Juan experiences a mystical vision that merges the Christian god of love with the rhythmical force pictured by Hinduism and Taoism.

The Fountain optimistically implies the spiritual unity of East and West; "*Marco Millions*," however, pessimistically delineates their differences. The play contrasts the materialism of Marco Polo with the spiritualism of China, dramatizing Marco's journey to the medieval empire of Kublai Khan. O'Neill's satirical portrait of Marco Polo as a vulgar (and very American) businessman shows the playwright's sympathies with Eastern cultural values. O'Neill's deeper affinities with Oriental mystical thought appear in the structure and character relationships, some of which operate according to the polar rhythms of the Tao. But West ultimately conquers East as Polo returns to Venice a wealthy and complacent man, having caused the death (through his insensitivity) of the Chinese Princess Kukachin. West also vanquishes East in the vision of O'Neill; in presenting an irreconcilable opposition between Occidental and Oriental cultures, he implies that dualism rules the universe.

Traditional Western dualism, in fact, dominates O'Neill's vision during this first phase. However much the serenity of a life free from struggle appealed to him, he was too troubled to embrace consistently the mystical monism he preached occasionally. Thus, all his sea plays except *The Moon of the Caribbees* and "*Anna Christie*" depict man struggling *against* the sea, not seeking union with it. Moreover, in the five years following "*Anna Christie*," O'Neill usually sought to affirm struggle rather than to transcend it. In a 1922 interview, he observed that "life is struggle, often, if not usually, unsuccessful struggle; for most of us have something within us which prevents us from accomplishing what we dream and desire." [1] This conviction stands behind the tragic sense of life so evident in *Beyond the Horizon*, *The Emperor Jones*, *The Hairy Ape*, *Diff'rent*, *All God's Chillun Got Wings* and *Desire Under the Elms*. Yank, Brutus Jones, Emma and the others dramatize O'Neill's 1921 assertion that "the tragic alone has that significant beauty which is truth." [2] Like traditional tragedies, the plays of this period—the "Eastern" as well as the "Western" ones—also assume the reality of individual personality, reflecting our belief in the unique, separate

1. January 1922 interview with Oliver Sayler, *Century Magazine*; rpt. in Cargill, Fagin, and Fisher, *Criticism*, p. 107.
2. *New York Tribune*, 13 Feb. 1921; reprinted in Cargill, Fagin, and Fisher, *Criticism*, p. 104.

ego. Whatever forces they may symbolize, Smitty, Anna, Chris, Ponce de Leon and Marco Polo exhibit the playwright's primary interest in realistic psychological portraiture. Finally, the transcendent forces that baffle O'Neill's protagonists in the more mystical plays frequently express Christian as well as Oriental assumptions.

Though the dramatist's Western nature subordinated his Eastern impulses at this time, the four plays this chapter considers make apparent O'Neill's growing affinity with Oriental thought. *The Moon of the Caribbees* and "*Anna Christie*" offer early evidence that part of him leaned East. The placidity of the Donkeyman and Anna, and the beguiling nature of the god Anna serves, align the playwright with mystical approaches toward man and God. When O'Neill subsequently delved into Indian philosophy (seeking perhaps to clarify his mystical intuitions), Vedanta Hinduism emerged as a source of *The Fountain*. But more important was his discovery of Taoism, which informs not only *The Fountain* and "*Marco Millions*" but all his subsequent religious drama. In the mystical rhythms of the Tao lay the potential unifier of the oppositions that dominated O'Neill's personality as well as his drama. Hence, while it failed to unite East and West in "*Marco Millions*," the Tao provided O'Neill with the dynamic aesthetic that characterized his subsequent Eastern plays. The polar rhythms of *The Great God Brown*, *Lazarus Laughed*, *Strange Interlude* and *Dynamo*, and the later cycles of *The Iceman Cometh*, *Long Day's Journey Into Night* and *Hughie*, developed partially from O'Neill's study of Chinese religion in the early 1920s. The two final works of the first phase thus reveal an Eastern structural principle that became central in O'Neill's art; moreover, all three full length works considered here toy with other aspects of Orientalism that receive more extensive development later. We may consequently regard these early dramas as O'Neill's apprentice pieces in Oriental philosophy, important largely for their foreshadowing of the more profound Orientalism of the later phases. They are also, however, significant in their own right, for the tension between Eastern and Western impulses invests these plays with the complexity of imaginative and ambitious—if not yet great—dramatic art.

Two Plays of the Sea

The second volume of Louis Sheaffer's monumental biography of
O'Neill opens with a startling photograph. O'Neill, in full profile
on a beach, stares toward the ocean, his body draped with massive
ropes of seaweed that form tentacles emerging from his shoulders
and upper arms. Sheaffer appropriately captions the picture with
the title of O'Neill's projected autobiographical drama: "Sea-
Mother's Son."[3] The photo captures O'Neill's intense feeling for
the eternal mystery and calm of the ocean. Several pages later, another picture discovers O'Neill in a different mood, running up the
beach, arms spread like wings, head thrown back in glee.[4] O'Neill
had just learned, the caption indicates, of the cash award that ac-
companied the Pulitzer Prize for *Beyond the Horizon*; but in this
period, as Agnes Boulton has written, his daily routine included "a
run up the beach, his head thrown back, full of exuberance and
joy."[5] The sea apparently appealed to both the quietly spiritual and
joyfully primitive sides of his complex spirit, as Ms. Boulton confirms in her subsequent description of her former husband's behavior: "Gene would remove his swimming trunks and lie naked in the
sun (which warmed his closed eyes) his face turned upward, his eyes
closed, at peace at last with the sun, the sea and the earth. Sometimes he would get up and do a strange jungle dance, and then
plunge, laughing, into the sea. This laugh—for it seems to me I saw
it more than I heard it—was a half-pagan, half-ecstatic cry of himself to God."[6]

That O'Neill would plunge into the ocean, crying to God, sur-
prises no one familiar with his primitivistic adoration of the sea.
This side of O'Neill, drawn to the vitalism of Nietzsche, affirmed
man's glorious participation in the battles of existence. But in contrast to this quintessentially Western approach is the passive behavior of the "Sea-Mother's Son," lying on the beach "at peace at last
with the sun, the sea and the earth." It is the latter, much quieter
response that connects O'Neill's sea god to his Eastern impulses.

3. Sheaffer, *Artist*, frontispiece.
4. Ibid., ff. p. 17.
5. Boulton, *Part of a Long Story*, p. 317.
6. Ibid., p. 318.

O'Neill saw in the sea (and the natural world it stood for) a possible escape from the self into a pantheistic, meaningful whole. As he wrote to Pierre Loving in 1921, he loved his Provincetown beach house because, surrounded by "the sand and sun and sea and wind," you "merge into them and become as meaningless and full of meaning as they are." [7] The passive merging into nature promised the submersion of the ego into a larger "meaningless" presence that paradoxically made life "full of meaning." An identical paradox is prominent in the pantheism of Vedanta Hinduism: not coincidentally, Vedantic descriptions of Brahman help illuminate "*Anna Christie*," O'Neill's finest sea play.

"*Anna Christie*" concludes O'Neill's studies of the sea, which began with *Fog* in 1914. Between 1914 and 1921, he wrote a dozen plays in which the sea played a central thematic role. As suggested, however, the majority of these plays view the sea as an "ironic life force" that defeats man's desires. *The Long Voyage Home*, from the *S.S. Glencairn* quartet, is typical. The protagonist Olson prepares to return to his Swedish farm and escape the sea he has served for years. At the conclusion, though, having been drugged into unconsciousness in a London bar, he is about to be shanghaied into service on a ship bound around Cape Horn. Olson's immediate antagonists are the bartender and his cohorts, who are in the pay of the ship's captain; his ultimate antagonist is the sea itself, against which he struggles in vain for his liberty. O'Neill here works a modern, ironic variation on an ancient Greek theme, pitting man's hopes and dreams against the destiny decreed for him by a larger fate. Nearly all the other sea plays, like *Bound East for Cardiff*—in which a sailor dies at sea, yearning for his home on land—similarly picture men as fated victims of the sea, battling against both nature and destiny.

By the early 1920s, O'Neill had come to view these battles as man's "glorious, self-destructive struggle to make the Force [behind life] express him." [8] In the sea plays, however, he seemed content to objectively (and fatalistically) describe the struggle. But one of these one-acts hints at another response to man's ironic fate. On the

---

7. Quoted in Loving, "Eugene O'Neill," *The Bookman*, 53 (Aug. 1921): 516.
8. O'Neill to Arthur Hobson Quinn, ca. 1925; reprinted in Cargill, Fagin, and Fisher, *Criticism*, p. 125.

surface, *The Moon of the Caribbees* depicts once again the fated frustration of desire. A crew of sailors on board a ship at anchor, having arranged for sex and rum from some native Caribbean women, are denied fulfillment when their violent behavior causes the banishment of both liquor and women. The women are symbolically associated with the sea, which they travel across to board the ship. Once again, the ocean embodies man's ironic relationship to his fate, which (in this instance) grants his wishes only to later deny them. However, the sea accrues more positive meanings as well. O'Neill told Barrett Clark in 1919 that "the spirit of the sea— a big thing—is the hero. . . . I consider 'The Moon' an attempt to achieve a higher plane of bigger, finer values."[9] The spirit of the sea deliberately contrasts with the behavior of the rowdy sailors: only the sentimental Smitty and the passive, peaceful Donkeyman respond to its beauty. And in these characters and the simple action that involves them lies an implicit conflict between the active "Western" and passive "Eastern" sides of the playwright.

The plot alternates O'Neill's conflicting impulses. The opening scene's dialogue establishes the sailors' violence and lust. When the ladies and liquor come on board and quickly disappear into the cabins below, the second, passive movement commences. Alone with the Donkeyman on deck, Smitty softly and sadly recalls the lost love that drove him to sea. After Smitty rejects a native woman's advances, she reemerges with another sailor, and the drunken mob that follows initiates another active movement that culminates in a brawl and the knifing of Paddy. Following this climax, the action recedes again. Discovering Paddy and the rum, the Mate banishes the women; the rowdy sailors exit, leaving Smitty and the Donkeyman to converse briefly on deck; they finally leave, abandoning the stage to the moonlight and the "melancholy negro chant" from the shore which has punctuated the action.

In fact, the play offers two separate plots: an active one, following the hopes and disappointment of the boisterous sailors, and a passive (almost inert) one involving Smitty and the Donkeyman. The rowdy crew moves from expectation to brief fulfillment to loss,

9. O'Neill to J. B. Clark, 8 May 1919; File Folder Za/O'Neill/to Clark, O'Neill Collection, Beinecke Library, Yale Univ.

while the Donkeyman remains placid and Smitty broods ceaselessly over his lost love. Their stasis corresponds to the motionless ship and the unchanging moonlight, which is explicitly linked to the brooding chant, "*faint and far-off, like the mood of the moonlight made audible.*"[10] In the chant is embodied the mysterious spirit of the sea. Like the sea, the chant peacefully ebbs and flows during the play, emerging most clearly during the second movement and again at the end. Also like the sea, it encompasses the activities on board ship, since we hear it before anyone speaks and after all have departed. The chant and the sea combine with the moonlight, the ship, the Donkeyman and Smitty to form a quiet spiritual nexus of character and environment in vivid contrast to the animalistic sailors. The subdued nature of this nexus possesses an almost mystical serenity; the violence of the sailors exhibits the vigor of a naturalistic story by London or Crane.

The play's sources partially explain the mixture of tones. Behind the active plot lie naturalistic fiction (Jack London was in fact an O'Neill favorite) and theatrical melodrama; behind the passive plot are Conrad's fiction and Symbolist theatre. Maeterlinck, Synge and Yeats (all of whom O'Neill had read by this time) often subordinated plot to a poetic atmosphere created through theatrical effects. That atmosphere portrayed supernatural forces, a feature also found in Japanese Nōh plays, the highly stylized form that influenced Yeats. Thus, an indirect Oriental influence may help account for the passive plot of *Caribbees*. The ultimate source of any art, however, is the personality of the artist, and an intriguing similarity exists between the play's contrasting tones and O'Neill's own ambivalent response to the sea. On the Provincetown coast, we recall, O'Neill seemed at one moment "at peace at last" with his environment, then broke into a "strange jungle dance" and raised a "half-pagan, half-ecstatic cry of himself to God." The dreamy, mystical, vaguely Oriental side of his personality appears in the chant, the moonlight, the haunted Smitty, the detached Donkeyman; the primitive, pagan, Western side finds expression in the drunken, rabble-rousing sailors.

10. *The Plays of Eugene O'Neill* (New York: Random, 1954), 1: 474. Hereafter documented in the text.

O'Neill at this time preferred the pagan to the dreamer, as his previously cited letter to Barrett Clark reveals: "Posed against a background of that beauty, sad because it is eternal, which is one of the revealing moods of the sea's truth," he observed, "Smitty's silhouetted gestures of self-pity are reduced to their proper insignificance, his thin whine of weakness is lost in the silence which it was mean enough to disturb." O'Neill declared Smitty's "sentimental posing" to be "much more out of harmony with truth, much less in tune with beauty, than the honest vulgarity of his mates." [11] Certainly, Smitty is self-pitying, snobbish (priding himself on being a "gentleman") and generally unappealing. The sailors, however, can hardly be declared "in tune with beauty" or "in harmony with truth" themselves. They try to cheat the women, pick fights with each other, and behave so foolishly that the ship's authorities seize their rum and banish their women. Indulgence of their instincts brings no more satisfaction than the whining of Smitty.

Only one character, in fact, understands the sea: the Donkeyman, through whom O'Neill dimly foreshadows his later attraction to Oriental thought. Compare his response to the Negro chant to that of the sailors and Smitty. The rowdy sailors react negatively. Driscoll, the crew's leader, mutters "I wonder now, do they call that keenin' a song?" and later complains, "it's enough to give a man the jigs listenin' to 'em" (pp. 456, 457). Driscoll and the crew later drown out the chant with a boisterous sea chanty, "Blow the Man Down," which (appropriately) deals with a sailor's sexual encounter. By contrast, Smitty reacts by saying "(*with a trace of melancholy*) 'I wish they'd stop that song. It makes you think of—well— things you ought to forget'" (p. 459). Nonetheless, he remains with the Donkeyman on deck so he can hear the song and indulge in mournful memories, playing the part of the *sensitif* victimized by lost love. But the Donkeyman's response to the chant tentatively hints at a religious and aesthetic sensibility: "sounds kinder pretty to me—low and mournful—same as listening to the organ outside o' church of a Sunday" (p. 466). Indeed, the Donkeyman's spiritual

11. O'Neill to J. B. Clark, 8 May 1919; File Folder Za/O'Neill/to Clark, O'Neill Collection, Beinecke Library, Yale Univ.

quality, the product of years on the sea, has enabled him to transcend the lustful desires of the sailors and the maudlin ghosts of Smitty. He no longer drinks nor pursues women, and "ain't ever been bothered much" by memories (p. 467). The vain Smitty reacts "*with quiet scorn*" to the Donkeyman, since the latter's advice on women involves "a whack on the ear" whenever they act up (p. 467). The stage directions, however, repeatedly make clear that the Donkeyman possesses an enviable inner calm lacked by the others: he speaks "*quietly*," "*placidly*" and "*philosophically*," and recurrently spits "*contentedly*" and "*tranquilly*" (pp. 466, 467, 468, 473).

The Donkeyman constitutes the first, faintly etched portrait of a recurrent O'Neill type: the character who achieves a calm state beyond desire. In this, he resembles both Christian saint and Eastern sage. Like the saint, he shows compassion, persuading Smitty in a "kindly" manner to leave the deck and escape the chant at the end. Like the sage, he tolerantly accepts both Smitty's insults and the men's casual sex and drinking. While not perfect, he possesses the wisdom of one who has learned from the sea god he serves. He even embodies that sea on stage. Just as "*the sea is calm*" throughout (p. 455), so is he; as the sea has taught him, he tries to teach Smitty; as the sea accepts all behavior without passing judgment, so does he. In harmony with the sea, he acts as her priest and comprehends her message: place no faith in desires, whether vulgar or refined, because they will inevitably be frustrated by the constant flux of existence. This typically Oriental lesson is supported by the play's action. The sensitive Smitty mourns his vanished happiness; the sailors are briefly exuberant, but the interlude ends in pain and loss. To become like the Donkeyman and the sea, flowing patiently and passively with nature's rhythms and desirous of nothing, offers the only escape from misery.

In its passive subplot, *The Moon of the Caribbees* presents the renunciatory view of life that both Christianity and Oriental mysticism preach. Though O'Neill had largely moved beyond Christian dogma at this time, he still found part of himself attracted to the world-denying plane where Eastern and Western faiths meet. Another part of O'Neill lies in the main plot that depicts the futile struggle of man against nature; this part develops into the tragic playwright of *Beyond the Horizon*. But the spirit of the sea was pulling him East—in the direction of a Brahmanic being that pantheistically pervades nature, but plays tricks on ignorant man. This was to be the God of his most famous sea play, and a reformed prostitute would serve as its unsuspecting priestess.

"*Anna Christie*" resembles *The Moon of the Caribbees* in two major respects. First, while it exhibits some naturalistic sensationalism—drunkenness, violence, and prostitution—its meaning is fundamentally religious. O'Neill declared "the big underlying idea of the sea" as central to the dramatic action, so the spirit of the sea once again emerges as the true protagonist.[12] The second similarity involves the subordination of plot to other dramatic elements. In *Caribbees*, atmosphere prevails; in "*Anna Christie*," characterization is paramount. Writing to his agent about cuts in the Philadelphia production of *Chris Christopherson* (which later was revised into "*Anna Christie*"), O'Neill complained that "you can't cut a play in which the whole plot is a study in character built up bit by bit down to bare essentials of story without losing your play in the process." Nine days later, he reluctantly conceded that "such cutting might have been justified," but still lamented that "my character sketch [of Chris] must have gone to hell in the process."[13] Ironically, though, when he reworked the play, the main character was no longer the barge captain Chris, but his daughter—the young woman nicknamed "Anna Christie."

How had Anna—originally a respectable typist with a subordinate role—been transformed into a sentimentalized prostitute who stole the spotlight from her father? The answer lies in the play's focus on the sea. "The sea is a woman to me," O'Neill once wrote Carlotta,[14] and this notion eventually advanced to center stage in

12. O'Neill to George Tyler, 17 Mar. 1920; O'Neill Collection, Firestone Library, Princeton Univ.

13. O'Neill to Tyler, 17 Mar. 1920 and 26 Mar. 1920; O'Neill Collection, Firestone Library, Princeton Univ.

14. O'Neill to Carlotta Monterey, 29 Dec. 1926; File Folder Za/O'Neill/to Carlotta Monterey, O'Neill Collection, Beinecke Library, Yale Univ.

the person of Anna, worshipper and representative of the sea. As in *Caribbees*, then, one character reproduces the sea on stage. But the sea god of "*Anna Christie*" contains more facets than the mysterious force behind *Caribbees*. While *Anna* perceives an ironic life force shaping man's destiny, its plot draws more heavily on Greek tragedy than do the earlier sea plays. Christianity also looms larger in *Anna*, for the sea symbolically baptizes and redeems the heroine. Most important, the play's god is more Oriental in detail than that of *Caribbees*. Enveloping the characters in its fog, the sea unifies reality and blurs distinctions between personalities; and like Brahman in the state of *māyā* it also misleads everyone, and defies our relativistic notions of good and evil.

Perhaps the most obvious source of *Anna* is classical Greek tragedy, with its sense of antagonism between man and the gods. A family curse, emanating from the sea, seems to lie on the Christopherson clan. Chris's father, brothers and son have all left home to become sailors and nearly all have died on the water. Consequently, Anna finds herself (like young Oedipus) growing up in another land, a Minnesota farm where Chris believes "she don't know dat ole davil, sea."[15] Also like Oedipus, however, Anna rejoins her remaining parent and discovers her identity—as a daughter of the sea. As she tells Chris on his barge, "it's like I'd come home after a long visit away some place. It all seems like I'd been here before lots of times—on boats—in this same fog" (p. 28). By marrying the sailor Matt Burke, she becomes the sea's bride as well, destined to wait upon it until death. Anna welcomes this destiny. She had been treated like a servant on the farm, where her cousin's rape of her also caused a hatred of men that eventuated in her prostitution, but she feels cleansed by the sea and her love of a sailor. Her father, though, views all this as one more ironic trick of "dat ole davil," which dooms Anna to the same misery as everyone else in his family. His fears are quickly confirmed. In a final twist of fate, Chris and his detested prospective son-in-law are scheduled to sail off together on the *Londonderry* for a year, thereby deserting Anna— and subjecting her to the same loneliness suffered by all the Christopherson women.

15. *The Plays of Eugene O'Neill*, 3: 9. Hereafter documented in the text.

Curiously, the play treats Chris's fatalism ambiguously. Anna considers him a weakling who rationalizes his past unwillingness to care for her by pointing his finger at the sea. She reacts *"with a trace of scorn in her voice"* to his excuses, asking skeptically, "then you think the sea's to blame for everything, eh?" (p. 21). Moreover, the traditionally comic denouement—two lovers about to marry over a father's objections—makes the old man's gloom seem out of place. O'Neill himself, however, implicitly sided with Chris, in a letter to the *New York Times* about the misinterpretation of the conclusion as a contrived happy ending: "I wanted to have the audience leave with a deep feeling of life flowing on, of the past which is never the past—but always the birth of the future—of a problem solved for the moment but by the very nature of its solution involving new problems."[16] As he observes, in the final scene all three characters intuit a mysterious fate at work. Burke has *"superstitious premonitions"* about shipping out with Chris; Anna is heard *"forcing a laugh"* to try to break the spell; Chris's final words call our attention to the "fog, fog, fog, all bloody time! You can't see vhere you vas going, no. Only dat ole davil, sea—she knows!" (p. 78). The dialogue and setting thus dramatize the helpless subjection of all three to a larger force. And in its dominance the sea both parallels the fate of Greek tragedy, and more broadly expresses the dualistic Western distrust of nature.

The sea's portrait is also informed by another Western tradition, Christianity. Anna washes away her sins and feels reborn: "I seem to have forgot—everything that's happened—like it didn't matter no more. And I feel clean, somehow—like you feel yust after you've took a bath" (p. 28). The sea soon washes up Matt, providing Anna an opportunity for love that purifies her even more. "Will you believe it if I tell you that loving you has made me—clean?" she asks him, referring to her past prostitution (pp. 59–60). Burke's behavior provides another Christian lesson, on pride. Surviving a shipwreck, he crows "isn't it myself the sea has nearly drowned, . . . and never a groan out of me till the sea gave up and it seeing the great strength and guts of a man was in me?" (p. 48). His vanity

16. *New York Times*, 18 Dec. 1921, sec. 6, p. 1.

diminishes after he discovers his beloved is a prostitute, and he considers himself made "the fool of the world" by Anna—a woman he met because of the sea (p. 69). Hence, when Chris somberly comments on the sea's "dirty trick" in placing Burke and himself on the *Londonderry*, the young sailor, "*nodding his head in gloomy acquiescence*," concedes, "I'm fearing maybe you have the right of it for once, divil take you" (p. 78). Like the Christian God of providence, the sea teaches the boastful Burke a moral lesson, and he responds with new humility.

The sea's most intriguing religious dimension, however, is Eastern rather than Christian. Possibly O'Neill had read Müller's *Six Systems of Indian Philosophy* by the time he finished "*Anna Christie*," since the publication date of O'Neill's edition (1919) predates the play's revision. Or perhaps the dramatist independently developed an outlook akin to Vedantic thought by responding to intuitions the sea evoked in him. Wherever it originated, the sea god of "*Anna Christie*" resembles the Brahman described by Vedanta. Secretly unifying the world of time and space, it nonetheless appears as *māyā*, beguiling man into various false assumptions about reality. In Vedantic philosophy, this deception involves the spurious distinctions between the objects and events of the phenomenal world. However, O'Neill wrote not epistemological treatises, but plays about characters. Consequently, "*Anna Christie*" reveals *māyā* operating within and between human personalities, and the sea god's tricks point up our human illusions about our independence from each other, nature, and fate.

Like Brahman, the sea god exerts a unifying force that blurs character distinctions. Whatever their differences—and they are many—all three major characters respond to the sea's immanent spell: below the level of personality, all are *Atman* and part of Brahman. Anna dreamily capitulates to the sea in the second act, and later finds herself unable to leave her sailor lover; Burke is due to rejoin the sea in act four, having signed on board the *Londonderry* after his argument with Anna; even Chris, who has spent years half-resisting the sea by piloting a coal barge rather than sailing, finally gives in. Moreover, the antagonistic personalities of Burke and Chris subtly merge at the conclusion. They prepare to ship out, enlisted for the same stretch on the same boat; and both (as noted) recognize their kinship as victims of "dat ole davil." Finally, the setting reinforces the monism of the sea god. The last three acts take place on a boat, with the characters floating on water, the symbolic "ground" of their being. In acts two and four, fog surrounds them totally, symbolizing their mystical unity with each other and nature. In words echoed by Edmund in *Long Day's Journey Into Night*, Anna articulates her recognition of the escape this provides from the world and the self. Speaking "*with a trace of strange exultation*," she proclaims, "I love this fog! Honest! It's so—funny and still. I feel as if I was—out of things altogether" (p. 25).

The appeal of Eastern mysticism to O'Neill corresponds to the sea's seduction of Anna: both playwright and character yearn to transcend the suffering and guilt of the separate ego through absorption into a larger unity. In some ways, Anna's character *has* been absorbed into the sea, in fact, for she performs as its unwitting agent. After all, it is Anna who brings about the sea's reclamation of Burke and Chris. Had she not revealed the truth about her past, neither would have signed on to the *Londonderry*. More important, Anna heretofore has tricked both of them by not revealing her past. However understandable this may be, lover and father have been misled concerning Anna's recent life, with traumatic consequences for Burke in particular. That delusion resembles the tricks ascribed to the sea she unconsciously serves.

Anna's deception seems minor, of course, compared to the pranks played by that "davil" itself. Like Brahman as *māyā*, the sea fools everyone. But while the Hindu *māyā* refers to misconceptions about the phenomenal world, "*Anna Christie*" emphasizes our illusions about actions and their consequences. Chris, for instance, thinks he can render Anna immune to the sea's spell by sending her inland. When that fails, his desire to remain with her makes him take her on his barge, where she experiences the romance of sea and fog. The fog, he warns Anna, is the "vorst one of [the sea's] dirty tricks," blinding one to the sea's harsh reality (p. 28). On cue, Matt Burke emerges from that fog and sets in motion the plot that takes Anna from Chris, and eventually takes Chris far away from Anna. Burke's momentary victory over the sea deceives him into thinking he has conquered it, and been rewarded by the beautiful woman he meets in the fog. Later, he discovers that woman's wicked past, but cannot leave her. Feeling foolish, he will marry her but ironically sail off with her father—revealing Burke to be another victim of the sea, his true beloved. The sea god even deceives its own hand-maiden, by offering her a sense of liberation. While escaping her recent past, she falls victim to the family curse, and duplicates her mother's fate of wedding a sailor who abandons her for the sea.

The plot, then, reveals the sea to be monistic, *māyā*-like, and—again like Brahman—amoral. This is particularly true for Anna. If the sea cleanses her, it also causes her initial pollution, since fear of the sea's lure motivated Chris to place her in a situation that led to prostitution. If the sea provides her with a lover (thereby helping overcome her hatred of men), it takes away both her men at the end. Finally, if it furnishes her with her first moments of happiness, it promises misery ahead. Anna drinks and laughs with "*a determined gaiety*" at the finish, but Chris utters the play's last words about the deceitful sea, followed by "*the muffled mournful wail of steamers' whistles*" (p. 78). The sea distributes good and bad fortune indiscriminately to its subjects because (like Brahman) it mysteriously transcends our moral conceptions. But unlike Brahman, it is not reachable through knowledge. The experienced seer of its illusory ways—the wise fool, Chris—cannot find peace through his knowledge. O'Neill's conception of God reverts to his Greek tragic models in a final, crucial respect: the strong sense of relentless combat between this force and man. Despite the pull toward Eastern monism, the play's recognition of man's separation from God and nature finally prevails.

As we have seen, "*Anna Christie*" is in fact predominantly Western. Its characterization reflects Western individualism; its baptism motif and love story represent Christian beliefs; its themes of identity and destiny betray indebtedness to ancient Greek models. Its sea god nevertheless contains some intriguing Vedantic features, some of which characterize the god pictured in O'Neill's next mystical play. But O'Neill's acquaintance in the interim with Taoism gives *The Fountain* a much more Oriental tone than its predecessor.

"Forever Flowing, Ever Returning": *The Fountain*

Begun shortly after completion of *"Anna Christie"* in the summer of 1921, *The Fountain* offers its mysticism in a more concentrated form. The transcendent force glimpsed at the climax by Juan Ponce de Leon manifests the all-embracing love of the Christian God, and simultaneously reveals the *māyā*-like nature of our human distinctions. But while *"Anna Christie"* places a similarly eclectic mixture in a classical Greek context, *The Fountain*'s context is more Eastern. Both Juan's mystical vision and the play's central symbol assume that dualistic oppositions all engage in a larger cyclical rhythm that corresponds to the movement of the Tao. Dramatizing the spiritual journey of a divided European toward a mystical unity with nature, *The Fountain* represents O'Neill's quest for a religious experience that might sooth his own haunted soul. Juan looks to China to fulfill this need; the solution he discovers finds expression in a "forever flowing, ever returning" fountain that gives him an Oriental serenity in the play's closing scene.

While it is impossible to determine precisely when O'Neill began his study of the world's religions,[17] it is highly likely that it coincided with the years in which *The Fountain* was composed, 1921 and 1922. He could easily have obtained his copies of Müller's *Six Systems of Indian Philosophy* (1919), Coomaraswamy's *Buddha and the Gospel of Buddhism* (1916) and Legge's translation of *The Texts of Taoism* (1891) by 1921. Moreover, *The Fountain*'s action implies that O'Neill had acquainted himself with Oriental thought by the time he finished the play. Protagonist and playwright both pass over Western seas to arrive at mystical Eastern shores. For the first four acts, the plot focuses on the inner conflicts of a man of action (a soldier and governor) who is also a man of thought (a dreamer), the classic Platonic dichotomy. The play also shows its Western origin in its attack on the Catholic Church, a European in-

17. The only document in regard to this is vague. In the previously cited Sparrow letter of 1929, O'Neill asserted that he had studied the religions of the world "off and on for many years," but he does not explicitly state when he began (Sparrow, "Psychoanalytical Material"). Unfortunately, his library does not clarify the matter: no records exist as to when particular books were purchased in the early 1920s. Consequently, my conclusions are by necessity speculative, based on copyright dates and internal evidence.

stitution that O'Neill finds culpable in the harsh rule of the Spanish *conquistadores* over the native Indian population in Puerto Rico (where most of the play takes place). The concluding scenes, however, mystically resolve Juan's conflicts, and curiously overlook the Church's guilt. Indeed, the two final scenes emphasize the love Christianity preaches, not the hypocrisy Christians often practice. For ultimately, *The Fountain* does not affirm the superiority of Oriental religious approaches so much as it tries to reconcile them with Occidental ones.

The opening scene of this largely neglected play presents a Christian fanatic's murder of a Moorish poet who relates the "heretical" tale of a fountain of youth "in some far country of the East." [18] Juan Ponce de Leon discounts the legend, but soon sets sail with Columbus, seeking a Western route to the Orient. Twenty years later, as governor of Puerto Rico, he perpetually struggles with the Church, whose insistence on conversion of the natives, laments Juan, both "crushes their spirits and weakens their bodies," rendering them useless as laborers (p. 398). Dismayed by this and by the intrigues of Bishop Menendez, Juan also endures an inner tension between the soldier and dreamer within him. In his youth, he had imagined a glorious and benevolent Spanish empire; as a governor, he fights constantly with Spaniards whose actions frustrate that dream. The idealist in Juan is reinforced by the arrival of Beatriz, the beautiful young daughter of a woman whose love Juan had spurned in Spain. Falling in love with her, he now dreams of the fountain of youth described by the Moorish poet. An imprisoned Indian leader, Nano, relates a similar native legend, and promises to lead Juan to the mythical fountain in exchange for his release. Arriving there, Juan's party is ambushed by Indians, who leave Juan to die. But he has a miraculous dream vision which blends numerous allegorical figures (including poets and priests from East and West) into an eternally flowing cycle of becoming that unites man and nature. Several months later, Juan dies peacefully in a monastery after blessing the young lovers, Beatriz and his nephew Juan—a couple that succeeds where Juan and her mother had failed.

A textual matter is pertinent here, for it relates to the marriage of

18. *Plays*, 1: 387. Hereafter documented in the text.

different faiths depicted in Juan's vision. The play's final version (published in 1926) agrees in outline and most details with its 1921 scenario, but the intensity of the attack on the Catholic Church has diminished. In the original plot, for instance, Beatriz witnesses Indians in chains filing by. "Horrified, indignant," she asks "is this the way of Christ—of Spain?" The final version deletes this scene. Another change concerns the character of Luis, a young court poet and subsequent Dominican monk who is Juan's closest friend. In the scenario, Luis passionately rejects the fountain myth as heretical, suggesting the intolerance of even the best of Christians; in the final version, he is much less insistent. Luis's tolerance also figures in Juan's mystical vision. The scenario contains a "Spanish Cardinal-Warrior with a crucifix and sword"; the published play replaces him with Luis, carrying a cross. In the concluding scene another bigoted character—a young monk who is offended by the pagan fountain song sung by young Juan and Beatriz—is deleted altogether. This deletion is consistent with one other change in the conclusion, this one made on the publisher's galley sheets. The play's final moment mingles the recurrent fountain song[19]—"Love is a flower/ Forever blooming/ Beauty a fountain/ Forever flowing . . ."—with the monks' chanting after Juan's death. The original galley reads, "*the two strains blend with discord*," symbolizing the apparent irreconcilability of Christian and pagan approaches. But "*with discord*" is lined out and "*into harmony*" written above it, supporting O'Neill's final emphasis on the unity of different faiths: an approach more consistent with Juan's mystical vision, which merges East and West.[20]

The play's treatment of the Church's intolerance remains harsh despite these revisions. O'Neill pictures Columbus as a fanatical "chosen instrument of God" who wants to undertake a "Last Crusade" with the spoils gained from exploiting the New World (p. 394). Another bigot is Quesada, a hysterical young monk who shoots an Indian medicine man after confronting the latter's "blasphemous" inversion of the cross—which was intended as a pro-

19. The song appears once in the first scene and four times in the last two scenes, with minor variations in the wording depending on the specific dramatic context.

20. Manuscripts, scenario and galley proofs of *The Fountain*, O'Neill Collection, Firestone Library, Princeton Univ.

pitiation. Most menacing of all is Menendez. In the opening scene he kills the infidel Moorish poet for his fountain song; twenty years later, as Bishop of Puerto Rico, he has become "*an oily intriguer of Church politics*" who "*wants to be dictator to introduce torture and slavery*" (pp. 402–3). The villainy of these characters suggests that O'Neill at this time felt deep hostility toward the Church. Nonetheless, the play simultaneously pays homage to the Christian love ethic. Contrasted with the fanatics is Luis, who converts the natives through kindness rather than cruelty. Restless like Juan in the opening scenes, he displays a "*calm, peaceful expression as if he were at last in harmony with himself*" after joining the Church (p. 397). Luis's imitation of Christ results in charity toward others and personal serenity; so while O'Neill may have scorned the Church, he still embraced its primary value.

Respect for Christ's gospel also characterizes Juan's vision in scene ten. Before the miraculous vision, Juan confesses, "I prayed for a miracle which was not Thine. Let me be damned then, but (*Passionately*) let me believe in Thy kingdom! Show me Thy miracle—a sign—a word—a second's vision of what I am that I should have lived and died! A test, Lord God of Hosts!" (p. 438). The miracle that follows baptizes the penitent heretic into spiritual rebirth via the symbolic fountain. Moreover, Beatriz, the reigning spirit of the vision, recalls both Dante's Beatrice and the Virgin Mary whom she symbolized. At the vision's conclusion, Beatriz also brings to mind numerous Christian martyrs (and Christ himself) who are pictured ascending following their executions: "*Her arms are raised above her head. Her whole body soars upward. A radiant, dancing fire, proceeding from the source of the fountain, floods over and envelops her until her figure is like the heart of its flame*" (p. 442). Most significantly, Beatriz (again like Christ) stands for a personalized God of love who both initiates and satisfies Juan's spiritual quest. Given all these Christian elements, then, it seems appropriate that Juan's death in the following scene takes place in a Dominican monastery, peopled by Luis and other gentle Christians.

Enclosing the monastery, however—and enveloping Juan's preceding mystical encounter—is the wilderness. "*Beyond the wall nature can be seen and felt. . . . Palm trees lean over the wall casting their graceful shadows within. Vines in flower have climbed to the top and are starting to creep down inside*" (p. 443). Juan's final speech reveals him experiencing death not as a Christian's passage to personal immortality, but as a pantheist's absorption into nature. "Juan Ponce de Leon is past!," he cries, "He is resolved into the thousand moods of beauty that make up happiness—color of the sunset, of tomorrow's dawn, breath of the great Trade wind—sunlight on grass, an insect's song, the rustle of leaves, an ant's ambitions" (p. 448).[21] Juan finds peace in a loss of identity similar to that discovered by Anna in the fog. But here, union with God involves merger with a process, for "God is a flower / Forever blooming / God is a fountain / Forever flowing." This nature god has been anticipated by Juan's earlier declaration that "I believe in Nature. . . . She can perform miracles" (p. 421). And in scene ten, moments before the Indian attack he identifies Beatriz with nature, declaring that her "spirit inspires all things," and finding her in the four elements: "I hear you call in the song of the waves, the wind is your breath, the trees reach out with your arms, the dawn and sunset promise with your lips!" He concludes in despair, "You are everywhere and nowhere—part of all life but mine" (p. 436).

This pantheistic aspect of *The Fountain*'s god contradicts Christian dogma, but corresponds to Hindu teachings. Of course, numerous Western philosophers are also pantheistic, including Plotinus and Emerson (both familiar to O'Neill). Certain features of Juan's vision nonetheless point to a specifically Hindu influence. Beatriz—or rather, the divine force she represents—corresponds to Brahman, which projects itself into the false distinctions of the phenomenal world (*māyā*) while mystically binding all reality together in its dynamic unity. During Juan's vision, various distinctions vanish into a larger flow. After a masked figure representing death sits beside the dying Juan, Beatriz—"*the personified spirit of the fountain*" (p. 441)—materializes. She sings the fountain song and apparently vanishes. Actually, she disperses herself into a Chinese

21. *The Fountain*'s scenario also makes clear that Juan's rebirth does not involve his soul's continuance. "He realized he had known what Christ felt when he said, 'Why hast thou forsaken me,'" the scenario reads, referring to Juan's appeal to God in the wilderness; but now he has "thrown it off, renounced that last shred of personality, and now he is part of all things—and in harmony with them." (O'Neill collection, Firestone Library, Princeton Univ.)

poet, the Moorish minstrel of scene one, Luis in his earlier role of poet, and Nano. All join hands, indicating the transcultural nature of the fountain myth. The figures then disappear "*as if they were dissolved in the fountain*" which (like Brahman) obliterates all personal distinctions (p. 441). They shortly reappear, clothed now as priests (of Buddhism, Islam, Christianity, and Nano's primitive religion). This transformation blurs categorical lines between art and faith, and demonstrates the unity of all creeds: the priests dissolve into the fountain, leading Juan to exclaim, "All faiths—they vanish—are one and equal within—. . . God! Are all dreams of you but the one dream?" (p. 441). The next sight wipes out another distinction, one central to Juan's search. An old Indian woman appears, stretching out her hand; when Juan grasps it, "*her mask of age disappears*," revealing the young Beatriz. "Age—Youth—," Juan realizes, "they are the same rhythm of eternal life" (p. 442). Finally, the elemental distinction between death and life disappears: the masked death figure dissolves into the fountain and materializes as Beatriz, who undergoes the radiant transformation described earlier. Like the elusive Brahman, Beatriz transforms herself into a series of *māyā*-like manifestations, ultimately absorbing all disparate phenomena into herself.

By so doing, Beatriz demonstrates the meaninglessness of conventional distinctions between cultures, religions, age and youth, life and death. Moreover, her own dissolution into the flame and flowing waters suggests a deeper Oriental belief: that the separate personality is itself a fiction because of the constant flux of the universe. As Juan declares, "All is within! All things dissolve, flow on eternally! O aspiring fire of life, sweep the dark soul of man! Let us burn in thy unity!" (p. 442). The transfiguring flame and the love for which Beatriz stands may point to Christian sources, but the manner in which she obliterates distinctions, and then herself, points also to Hinduism.

The Fountain thereby offers a more concentrated, metaphysical application of Hindu thought than "*Anna Christie*." More pervasive than Hinduism, however, is an Eastern philosophy missing in the sea play. *The Fountain* hints at a Taoist influence in its repeated allusion to China as the home of the legendary fountain. During Juan's vision, the Chinese poet appears as the originator of the fountain myth. Moreover, Juan's quest for youth accords with Taoist values and practices. Taoism idealizes the youthful virtues of simplicity and spontaneity, and its central purpose of prolonging life through conservation of energy became translated (in popular Taoism) into various occult practices designed to restore one's youth. By far the most vital Taoist contribution to the play, however, lies in its rhythmic reconciliation of opposites. Juan's climactic vision and the play's imagery illustrate the Taoist treatment of apparent opposites as *yin* and *yang*, which by their cyclical alternation symbolize the dynamic unity of reality.

The famous *yin/yang* circle (or *mandala*) helps explain the numerous circles in *The Fountain*. Juan seeks with Columbus "the Western passage to the East" (p. 390), underscoring the world's roundness. Within this sphere, numerous other circles appear. Several settings are circular (including the clearing where Juan's vision occurs), with over half the scenes containing circular fountains. The play begins in one courtyard with a fountain (the Moor's house), circles back to end in another (the Dominican monastery). In addition, the apparently circular journey of the sun figures in various settings. Scene two ends with sunrise breaking over the New World; scene six takes place at twilight; scenes ten and eleven round off the play with (respectively) the dawn that follows Juan's epiphany, and "*a sunset sky of infinite depth*" that "*glows with mysterious splendor*" (p. 443). If these circles only suggested unity, one could argue that they simply manifested a universal archetype. But several circles express the unity of opposites in particular. First and foremost, Juan's travels West in search of the Orient culminate in a transcendent moment that philosophically reconciles East and West. Moreover, the sun's changing positions in the sky—rising East, setting West, reemerging East—symbolize the joining of the two contrary directions in a cosmic diurnal rhythm that governs both space and time. Yet another time cycle points up the alternation of opposites in human history. In the first scene, the Moor Ibnu Aswad, speaking of the decline of his people's empire, introduces the play's central symbol as a metaphor for the cycles of civilization. "The waters of the fountain fall—but ever they rise again, Sir Spaniard. Such is the decree of destiny" (p. 378); and such is the manner in which victory and defeat participate in a larger monistic rhythm.

The Moor's Islamic belief accords with the detached, passive approach of Taoism. If the alternation of *yin* and *yang* makes inevitable the succession of triumph by defeat, no faith should be placed in the apparent achievements of life—as Juan realizes after his mystical experience at the fountain. The fountain symbol also illustrates the Taoist connection between heaven (*yang*) and earth (*yin*). The song during Juan's vision makes this clear: "Beauty a fountain / Forever flowing / Upward beyond the source of sunshine / Upward beyond the azure heaven, / Born of God but / Ever returning / To merge with earth that the field may live" (p. 384). Combining heaven and earth in a divine rhythm of renewal, the central symbol conveys the dynamic Taoist view of reality. Finally, of course, the play offers a psychological variation on this theme in the personality of the protagonist, who combines equal parts soldier and dreamer. For most of the play, the inner conflict torments him, but his mystical awakening enlightens him to the hidden unity of opposites, thereby integrating his personality and bringing him peace.

From the Vedantic standpoint, Juan's vision reveals the unity behind all distinctions. From the Taoist perspective, that vision offers the rhythmic resolution of dualistic oppositions. The conflict between Eastern and Western cultures, for instance, vanishes as poets and priests join hands in a circle, symbolizing their unity. The duality of age and youth disappears when Juan comes to recognize them as "the same rhythm of eternal life" (p. 442). Life and death engage in an identical cycle. The fountain absorbs the allegorical death figure and replaces her with the vital Beatriz: life follows death, just as death stalks life. And surrounding all these individual circles are the waters of the fountain, whose cyclical movement dissolves these and all other oppositions into a rhythmic, cosmic flow.

Like his protagonist, the author of *The Fountain* was constantly plagued by conflicting impulses. In regard to Christianity, he deplored the historical intolerance of the Church, yet believed in Christian values. Hence, Luis and Beatriz personify the universal love that guides Juan to his epiphanic vision; but the institution that preaches that love is treated savagely, despite all the textual revisions. O'Neill's disillusion with institutionalized Christianity helped prompt the exploration of Oriental thought apparent in the play's climax and resolution. Picturing our categories as illusions,

Juan's dream reproduces the Vedantic notion that the phenomenal realm of *māyā* masks the pantheistic unity of the universe. Beatriz duplicates Brahman—assuming and shedding disguises, advancing and receding as she absorbs the entire spectacle into her being, finally transcending even her own personality. The Tao also informs Juan's vision. Its rhythmic conception of existence helps clarify the numerous circles in the texture and structure of the play, and the reconciliation of psychological as well as metaphysical oppositions.

Of all the oppositions in *The Fountain*, the most significant for O'Neill's subsequent drama was that between East and West. Like his protagonist, O'Neill was turning East. In the Orient existed religions that he hoped might satisfy his pantheistic urges and mystically heal his inner divisions. He nonetheless could not break the ingrained, subconscious attachment to a Catholic Church that preached love and rebirth. Consequently, he attempted to reconcile his conflicting impulses through a play whose God contained elements from East and West: pantheistic and cyclical, yet also loving and redemptive. The merger was a tenuous one, as the next O'Neill play about Occident and Orient would reveal.

East and West, *yin* and *yang*: "*Marco Millions*"

Like *The Fountain*, "*Marco Millions*" dramatizes the historical journey of a legendary European to an exotic land. Many of the play's scenes take place in medieval China, with Kublai Khan and his granddaughter Kukachin playing major supporting roles to the central character, Marco Polo. O'Neill in his drama thus realized Ponce de Leon's dream to find "Cathay," because the playwright himself shared that desire. Sheaffer's biography notes that O'Neill had from childhood "yearned to see India and the Far East," [22] and a letter written shortly after he completed *The Fountain* indicates his interest in visiting the Orient at this time. "Our plans for the winter remain chaotic," he wrote Kenneth Macgowan in September, 1922, so "we will probably, in a fit of desperation, wind up in

22. *Artist*, p. 310.

China. I'd like that, too, while Europe somehow means nothing to me."[23]

A similar attraction to the Orient and dissatisfaction with Western culture manifest themselves in "*Marco Millions*." In this blend of romance, tragedy and satire composed between 1923 and 1925, O'Neill for the first time explicitly contrasts the serene spiritualism of the East and the destructive materialism of the West. The conflict is epitomized in the love story involving Marco Polo and Princess Kukachin. Blinded to her love by his monetary monomania, "Marco Millions" unwittingly destroys the young princess, who clearly represents the Orient that he exploits. Pointing up the apparent incompatibility between Eastern wisdom and Western greed, the play thereby reverses *The Fountain*, which ended on a conciliatory note. O'Neill's manuscript revisions of *Marco* are correspondingly opposite in intent to those of the earlier play. Rather than toning down the attack on the West, the later play's changes, as John Stroupe concludes in his manuscript study, "have one overriding aim: to intensify the audience's apprehension of Marco Polo's corrupting influence upon the East."[24] Moreover, O'Neill now appears highly sceptical about the monism *The Fountain* embraced. The unresolved East-West conflict suggests one of two things. Either reality itself is founded on a struggle between irreconcilable opposites (the classical tragic position), or Western man—including O'Neill himself—is incapable of realizing and acting upon the mystical unity of the universe revealed by Oriental thought.

His study of Chinese culture in his research for *Marco*, however, simultaneously pushed O'Neill in a contradictory direction. Several of the volumes he acquired on Chinese art, thought and poetry covertly or overtly reflect Taoist beliefs.[25] His edition of the works

23. O'Neill to Kenneth Macgowan, 23 Sept. 1922; File Folder Za/O'Neill/to Macgowan, O'Neill Collection, Beinecke Library, Yale Univ.

24. John Stroupe, "O'Neill's '*Marco Millions*': A Road to Xanadu," *Modern Drama*, 12 (Feb. 1970): 382.

25. The following books relating to China are all inscribed in O'Neill's pre-1929 signature style, and almost undoubtedly were consulted by him in working on "*Marco Millions*" (published in 1927): Lawrence Binyon, *The Flight of the Dragon: An Essay on the Theory and Practice of Art in China* (London: John Murray, 1922); *Cantonese Love Songs*, trans. Cecil Clementi (Oxford: Clarendon Press, 1904); Li Po, *The Works of Li Po, the Chinese Poet*, trans. Shigeyoshi Obata (New York: Dut-

of Li Po, for example, reveals recurrently the poet's suspicion, shared by Chuang Tse, that life is a dream; and Lawrence Binyon's treatise on Chinese art focuses extensively on the "great cosmic rhythm of the spirit" that the Chinese call the Tao, the cyclical unifier of the universe. More important, "*Marco Millions*" clearly exhibits the influence of Legge's *The Texts of Taoism*. Several speeches of Chu Yin (Kublai Khan's spiritual advisor) allude to passages from Legge's translation, as does a poem uttered by the forlorn Kukachin; the final scene's treatment of death relies on concepts articulated in the *Chuang Tse*. Finally, the central characters subtly demonstrate in their personalities and relationships the reconciling rhythms of the Tao. Kublai Khan himself harmonizes opposing tendencies within his own nature, while the personality differences of Kukachin and Marco Polo correspond to those between *yin* and *yang*, faintly suggesting that they may in fact be united by larger cosmic cycles.

O'Neill's intuition of unity behind apparent contrasts also appears during the first act, though it does not operate here according to Taoist rhythms. In the scenes that follow the Polos on their journey through Persia, India and Mongolia to China, common structural elements hint at the universality of certain human patterns despite superficial cultural differences. The differences are exotic and striking: the Persian setting features a "*jeweled, high-colored, gorgeous background*";[26] the Indian scene contains a snakecharmer; the Mongolian episode offers a Tartar kettledrum accompanying a wordless chant. But in stage groupings, the three scenes are identical. Each contains a ruler seated before a place of worship, surrounded by attendants and a larger semicircle of squatting figures who represent six stages of life, from infancy to death. In each scene (and also in scenes two and six, set in a Papal Legate's Persian palace and in Kublai Khan's court), the ruler in the center is flanked by a warrior and a spiritual advisor. The sequence of events in scenes three, four and five is also identical. The Polos enter carrying sample cases and read their notes about the area; young Marco ob-

ton, 1922); and Arthur Waley, *More Translations from the Chinese* (New York: Knopf, 1919).

26. O'Neill *Nine Plays* (New York: Random, 1954), p. 228. Hereafter documented in the text.

serves the natives and encounters a prostitute (the same actress in three different costumes); a brief exchange unfavorably compares the local religion to Christianity; the Polos depart as the natives pray.

The similar stage groupings and character types symbolize the deep identity that makes understanding possible. The ecumenical thrust behind *The Fountain*'s final scenes here receives a more extensive application. In the earlier play, however, Juan's growth opened him to a mystical intuition of this unity; in "*Marco Millions*," the protagonist travels in opposite directions both geographically and spiritually, and thereby emphasizes the polar conflict between Orient and Occident. The farther he journeys East—through lands whose mystical creeds preach tolerance and renunciation—the more intolerant, ethnocentric and materialistic Marco becomes. Before the journey began, the teenaged Marco displayed enthusiasm and curiosity about the Orient. But by the time he reaches India, the maturing Marco glances at a sacred statue and mutters, "so that is Buddha!" in "*a smart-Aleck tone*" (p. 234). In Mongolia, he "*hardly glances*" at the local people in the background (p. 238). And as Marco departs for China from Mongolia, O'Neill highlights his pose to indicate the protagonist's emerging mythic status as the quintessential Western businessman. As he struggles through a gate, "*for a second he is framed in it, outlined against the brilliant sky, tugging a sample case in each hand*" (p. 241). Having gained his manhood, Marco is now prepared to assume the larger symbolic role ironically assigned him by the future pope in scene three: to "set an example of virtuous Western manhood amid all the levities of paganism, shun the frailty of poetry, have a million to [your] credit" (p. 227).

As a prime "example of virtuous Western manhood," Marco learns nothing from fifteen years in China, pointing up the apparently unbridgeable gap between East and West. His materialism intensifies: through taxing necessities instead of luxuries, he proudly delivers to the Emperor Kublai Khan "the unprecedented amount" he has "sweated out of" the city he rules (p. 255). His intolerance deepens: five hundred thousand inhabitants of the city sign a petition accusing him of "endeavoring to stamp out their ancient culture" (p. 256). Marco also dabbles in weaponry, inventing a cannon that (he claims) will save the Khan money, and incidentally bring Polo Brothers and Son one million yen. This behavior confirms the scepticism of Kublai Khan and Chu Yin about Marco's possession of "that thing called soul which the West dreams lives after death" (p. 243)—a Christian teaching Marco had promised to demonstrate to the Chinese ruler during their initial audience. Only Kukachin, who falls in love with him, believes in Marco's soul. When he sails with her to Persia, the Khan orders him to gaze daily into her eyes, believing that his "soul" cannot ignore Kukachin's despairing love. The Venetian remains blind. Only on the final night does he glimpse her desire, and respond with a "*voice thrilling for this second with oblivious passion*"; but the next instant, his uncle Maffeo is seen "*slapping a stack of coins into the chest with a resounding clunk*," which instantly returns Marco to his true beloved (p. 280).

The relationship between Kukachin and Marco dramatizes the polarity of the conflict between East and West. Marco exudes intolerance, while Kukachin radiates the supreme tolerance of one who loves a person totally unlike herself. Marco loves the treasures of this world, while Kukachin transcends them. Hence, in her final lines she bids farewell to Marco "*in a voice which is a final, complete renunciation.*" As with Marco earlier, O'Neill silhouettes her to illustrate her symbolic status: on the upper deck, she "*stands outlined against the sky, her arms outstretched*," looking away from the earth (p. 285). The fact that Marco cannot perceive her love, causing her initial anguish and eventual demise, would seem to offer the final proof that West and East are doomed to incomprehension, struggle and destruction. These qualities typify Western tragedy, of course, and the love story does possess tragic overtones (though the innocent Kukachin does not attain the stature of a classical heroine). Kukachin's death consequently allies her with numerous O'Neill tragic protagonists who strive against impossible odds and fail. Like Yank in *The Hairy Ape*, she confronts a dualistic cosmos where man is doomed to battle larger forces and lose. In this instance, however, the tragedy is international more than cosmic. Hence, Kukachin herself represents one larger "force," the Orient; her defeat is by a more powerful antagonist, progressive Western civilization.

Behind all this apparent dualism, though, the mystic in O'Neill strives to discover unity, and Taoism influences his efforts in this direction. The Oriental Kukachin, who is feminine, passive, and spiritual, corresponds to the *yin* principle in Chinese thought. The Occidental Marco corresponds to *yang*, the masculine, rational and active principle. The latter association is made explicit in the second act, when Marco is about to speak off-stage to a crowd. Chu Yin reports that one of his hands "rests upon—and pats—the head of a bronze dragon, our ancient symbol of Yang, the celestial, male principle of the cosmos" (p. 253). Moreover, Marco's behavior consistently underlines this identification. His countless clever schemes evidence a rational, technological mind that needs to keep busy. This obsessive activism is even announced, in his departing lines to Chu Yin before sailing to Persia: "If you look before you leap, you'll decide to sit down. Keep on going ahead and you can't help being right! You're bound to get somewhere!" (p. 271).

If the opposing personalities parallel *yin* and *yang*, so does their relationship. While Marco's insensitivity blinds him to Kukachin's passion, her love suggests an attraction corresponding to the bonds between *yin* and *yang*. The two figures also interpenetrate. Marco remains alive and successful after Kukachin perishes, but Kukachin finds life after death due to love. In the prologue, the dead Kukachin temporarily revives to proclaim, "I loved, and died; Now I am love, and live" (p. 218). That line subtly underscores the secret unity of the two characters: the soul's immortality was the very thing Marco had promised to prove. In addition, Marco and Kukachin sail away together on a sea voyage, like Chris and Matt in "*Anna Christie*." In the earlier play, the journey implied the secret union of all sailors in a transcendent force oblivious to individual differences. In "*Marco Millions*," the voyage instead suggests that Marco and Kukachin (like *yang* and *yin*) participate in the same larger, unifying process. If this is so, then the same may be said of the opposing cultures they represent—and, by analogy, of existence itself.

The monistic Taoist influence on the play also extends to O'Neill's portrait of Kublai Khan. The Emperor, called "son of Heaven, Lord of the Earth," harmonizes not only these realms but also the masculine rationality and aggressiveness of the West, and the feminine intuition and passivity of the East. An effective ruler of a vast empire, he periodically retreats to Xanadu to contemplate *"the vanity of his authority"* (p. 248), indicating a balance between active and passive, public and private, pragmatic and spiritual in his personality. O'Neill's opening description also emphasizes the harmony of opposites, picturing *"his expression tinged with an ironic humor and bitterness yet full of a sympathetic humanity. In his person are combined the conquering indomitable force of a descendant of Chinghiz with the humanizing culture of the conquered Chinese who have already begun to absorb their conquerors"* (p. 241). In this Oriental despot, O'Neill pictures both the integrated personality he himself lacked, and the harmonic universe assumed by Taoist thought. But the Khan's Taoist harmony is upset by Marco (the West) and his effect upon Kukachin (the East). Deeply attached to his granddaughter, the Khan cannot remain serene when he contemplates her love for Marco, whom he recognizes as "only a shrewd and crafty greed" (p. 251). In his attachment, the Khan violates Taoist precepts urging abstinence from relationship with anything but the Tao, and he suffers as a consequence.

In fact, only one Chinese character remains unperturbed, and consistently maintains the detachment of the Oriental sage: Chu Yin, the Khan's advisor. Not surprisingly, his advice accords with (and sometimes even paraphrases) the teachings of Lao Tse and Chuang Tse. Thus, Chu Yin advises the Emperor after their initial encounter with Marco to "let him develop according to his own inclination," reflecting the Taoist policy of non-interference with the spontaneous operations of nature (p. 246). Later, when Kublai Khan threatens to kill Marco rather than let Kukachin sail with him, Chu Yin recites *"in a calm, soothing tone"* that "the noble man ignores self. The wise man ignores action. His truth acts without deeds" (p. 265). Chuang Tse similarly observes that "the Perfect Man has no thought of Self," while Lao Tse expresses the doctrine of *wu wei* in his statement that "the sage manages affairs without doing anything." [27] In the same scene, Chu Yin tells the sorrowful Kukachin that "life is perhaps most wisely regarded as a bad dream between two awakenings" (p. 266), alluding to several Taoist

27. Legge, *Texts of Taoism*, 39: 169, 48.

textual passages. Chuang Tse maintains that "we are born as from a quiet sleep, and we die to a calm awaking"; he describes death as "the great awaking, after which we shall know that this life was a great dream."[28]

This Taoist connection of life to dream—also a belief of Hinduism and Buddhism[29]—appears again in Kukachin's poetic lament preceding her final departure from Marco:

I am not.
Life is.
A cloud hides the sun.
A life is lived.
The sun shines again.
Nothing has changed.
Centuries wither into tired dust.
A new dew freshens the grass.
Somewhere this dream is being dreamed. (p. 282)

The final line faintly echoes the concluding sentence in Chuang Tse's famous butterfly dream, where he admits that "I who say that you are dreaming am dreaming myself."[30] Viewing existence as illusion, Taoism is sceptical about the unique, separate personality: Chuang Tse realizes he may actually be a butterfly dreaming he is Chuang Tse. Similarly, Kukachin here proclaims "I am not," and wonders if she participates in another's dream. Other lines of the poem also reveal a Taoist influence. The cloud hiding the sun while "a life is lived" hints again at the obscure, dream-like nature of existence, and suggests the larger natural cycle formed by life and

---

28. Ibid., pp. 250, 195.

29. Doris Alexander's article on "*Lazarus Laughed* and Buddha" cites O'Neill's notes on "*Marco Millions*" to prove his familiarity with Buddhism when he composed *Lazarus Laughed* the next year. Buddhism was, after all, a prominent religion in medieval China, as O'Neill realized: witness the presence of a Buddhist priest in the concluding scene. Unquestionably, O'Neill conducted research on the Indian religion before or during the play's composition. However, the Buddhist teachings most evident in the play—concerning the impermanence and illusory nature of worldly existence—coincide with Taoist teachings on these matters. Hence, I have chosen to focus exclusively on Taoism as O'Neill's major Oriental source, which seems more fruitful in light of the allusions to Taoist texts.

30. Legge, *Texts of Taoism*, 39: 195.

death, which alternate like cloudy and sunny days. The expression "nothing has changed" likewise points to eternal cycles in which all apparent transformations (e.g., from life to death) mask the changeless nature of the Tao. And the image of decay ("tired dust") followed by one of renewal ("new dew") also calls attention to the merging of opposites into a larger divine rhythm.

The final scene of "*Marco Millions*" brings together the Taoist motifs of complementary polarities and life's illusory nature. The *yin/yang* symbolism is rendered visually. Before the entrance of Kukachin's corpse, nine aged masked singers appear, "*dressed in deep black with white edging to their robes. After them comes a troupe of young girls and boys, dressed in white with black edging,*" their costumes reversing the pattern of the elder's robes (p. 299). The complementary opposition resembles that found in the *mandala*, where a light dot (*yang*) surrounded by a dark semicircle (*yin*) complements an adjacent semicircle in which the pattern is reversed. The Khan's remark in the middle of his oration, "contain the harmony of womb and grave within you," relates to the symbolism of these costumes (p. 301). Just as the apparel of the old and young complement each other, so do birth and death harmonize in the rhythm of the Tao. The Emperor's final speech recalls another related Taoist teaching, since he (like Chuang Tse above) suggests that life and death may be opposite to what we believe: Kukachin's death may actually be life, while Khan's life may be death. Kublai Khan softly accuses Kukachin of feigning death. "Open your eyes and laugh," he pleads, "laugh now that the game is over. Take the blindfold from my dim eyes. Whisper your secret in my ear. I—I am dead and you are living!" (p. 303) His pathetic final lines, in which he bids Kukachin "welcome home," allude to a particular passage by Chuang Tse. The Taoist sage asks, "how do I know that the love of life is not a delusion? and that the dislike of death is not like a young person's losing his way, and not knowing that he is (really) going home?" [31] From this perspective, the Khan's apparent confusion about life and death contains wisdom as well as grief; and his final lines may betoken his knowledge of her awakening.

Brief mention should be made of the four priests in the final

31. Ibid., p. 194.

scene. A Moslem, a Confucian, a Buddhist and a Taoist are all asked by Khan to explain death, and each responds in accord with his religion before concluding "Death is." The Buddhist priest emphasizes the impermanence of life: "This is a thing which no god can bring about: that what is subject to death should not die." But the Taoist priest's reply is more pertinent to the anti-materialistic spirit of the play: "Which is the greater evil, to possess or to be without?" (pp. 299–300) The comparison suggests again that Taoism had more impact on "*Marco Millions*" than Buddhism, though O'Neill obviously had acquainted himself with both religions.

"*Marco Millions*," however, does not end on this Eastern note. In the epilogue, as the house lights come up, the audience sees a fellow theatregoer who is "*none other than Marco Polo himself, looking a bit sleepy, a trifle puzzled*" until he arrives in the lobby, where "*his face begins to clear of all disturbing memories of what had happened on stage.*" As he enters his luxurious limousine, he heaves "*a satisfied sigh at the sheer comfort of it all,*" and the car pulls away (p. 304). The protagonist's obtuse complacency and materialism is thereby projected onto the Western audience, and juxtaposed one final time with the Oriental beauty and wisdom displayed in the previous scene. The juxtaposition reveals the divided vision of O'Neill. He focuses on a relationship between two characters whose personalities resemble *yin* and *yang*; he portrays a wise Emperor who harmonizes opposites, and a spiritual advisor who expresses Taoist wisdom; and he suggests via costume and dialogue that apparent dualities—including that of life and death—may in fact be complementary, unified by a larger cosmic cycle. But O'Neill's Western side has the final word. The Eastern loveliness Marco (and the audience) has witnessed briefly baffles, then bores, him, and his incomprehension seems both inevitable and characteristic of Westerners. From this angle, East and West represent antagonistic approaches to life, and this antagonism does not simply govern the relations between Occident and Orient, but lies at the heart of the universe. However much O'Neill may satirize the Western greed and insensitivity of his protagonist, the playwright cannot divorce himself from the dualistic Western world view, since it constitutes the essence of his dramatic, tragic vision.

That dualism lies behind the two prevailing assumptions of each play discussed in this chapter: that every individual possesses a unique self (leading to inevitable conflict with others); and that every man engages in a perpetual battle with nature. The first assumption appears in the numerous personality conflicts in these works, and accounts for the attention paid to psychological questions in the development of Anna, Chris, Juan and Marco. The second assumption is reflected in Chris's distrust of "dat ole davil, sea"; in Juan's futile struggle against the aging process; in Marco's desire to technologically exploit nature, which he perceives only as a source of wealth. Other concepts and attitudes in these plays reveal O'Neill's Western religious heritage. Anna's and Juan's spiritual rebirths, produced by their love for another, obviously draw upon Christian teachings—and even the Oriental Princess Kukachin reflects this Western theme of renewal through love.

Despite their essential indebtedness to Occidental thought, O'Neill's early plays nevertheless evidence a growing attraction to Oriental mysticism. As a sea worshipper, the young O'Neill (like Eastern thinkers) imagined an ultimate reality that was calm, amoral and rhythmic. Thus, the Donkeyman in *The Moon of the Caribbees*, wise in the ways of this force, is himself serene and non-judgmental. Content to accept the ebb and flow rather than struggle against it like her father, Anna Christie displays a similar passivity when she makes contact with her sea god. Her play's god is intriguingly Brahmanic as well, weaving webs of *māyā*, absorbing individual identities in its all-encompassing embrace. By the time *The Fountain* neared completion two years later, Vedantic features had become even more prominent. In the wilderness, the hero encounters a pantheistic spirit that disregards our human distinctions, blending age and youth, life and death, heaven and earth in a flow symbolized by the play's title symbol. In addition, the play's attempt to rhythmically reconcile oppositions announces the advent of a Taoist influence on O'Neill that intensified with "*Marco Millions*." That play, however, stands *The Fountain* on its head. Despite its numerous allusions to Oriental wisdom, "*Marco Millions*" is sceptical about modern Western man's ability to embrace Eastern truths. A speech toward the end of the play indicates that the monistic philosophies of the East had not yet furnished O'Neill with the healing unity he sought. "My hideous suspicion," laments the grieving Kublai Khan, "is that God is only an infinite, insane energy which creates and destroys without other purpose than to pass eternity in avoiding thought" (p. 291). The American playwright remained trapped within a Western consciousness that led to despair, not liberation: the prophet behind these words is Schopenhauer, not Lao Tse. And the next four years, when O'Neill embarked on a series of overtly religious dramas, would pit the nihilism of Schopenhauer, Nietzsche and Strindberg against the serenity offered by Hinduism, Buddhism, and Taoism.

5

Oriental Thoughts for a Religious Theatre

During the period in which *The Fountain* and "*Marco Millions*" were composed, other O'Neill plays (like *The Emperor Jones* and *The Hairy Ape*) employed expressionistic effects which dramatized man's isolation in a hostile universe. In 1924, O'Neill paid tribute to the figure who inspired this departure from realistic conventions. "All that is enduring in what we loosely call 'Expressionism,'" he asserted, "can be clearly traced back through Wedekind to Strindberg's *The Dream Play, There Are Crimes and Crimes, The Spook Sonata*, etc." O'Neill's innovations had the same purpose he ascribed to his Swedish master: to "express in the theatre what we comprehend intuitively of that self-defeating, self-obsession which is the discount we moderns have to pay for the loan of life." That exploration of psychological questions was rooted in a religious impulse that also resembled that of Strindberg. Each writer hoped to discover (in O'Neill's words) "some as yet unrealized region where our souls, maddened by loneliness and the ignoble inarticulateness of the flesh, are slowly evolving their new language of kinship."[1] Yearning for communion and a release from alienation, both playwrights also turned East at the time they ventured into expressionism. Strindberg, in fact, had studied Buddhism and Hinduism fifteen years before he returned to them while composing *A Dream Play* in 1901. For O'Neill, however, his initial ex-

---

1. Playbill for *The Spook Sonata*, rpt. in Cargill, Fagin, and Fisher, *Criticism*, pp. 108–9.

amination of Eastern mysticism coincided with his technical experimentation, and the result was highly imaginative religious drama, particularly between 1925 and 1928.

In 1933 O'Neill expressed his desire for "a theatre returned to its highest and sole significant function as a Temple where the religion of a poetical interpretation and symbolical celebration of life is communicated to human beings."[2] O'Neill had already created plays for just such a theatre. Starting in 1925 with *The Great God Brown* and continuing with *Lazarus Laughed*, *Strange Interlude* and *Dynamo*, he made provocative use of expressionistic masks, split characters, thought asides and stop actions to communicate "the mystery I want to realize in the theatre."[3] Not coincidentally, this period of technical innovation also witnessed O'Neill's most concentrated research into world religions. In 1926, while working on *Lazarus Laughed*, he confirmed to Manuel Komroff that "I'm going in very heavily these days for the study of religion along certain definite lines I have mapped out as a sort of large background for certain work in the future."[4] Inevitably, O'Neill's drama continued to be indebted to his Christian background and to Western thinkers. Thus, behind *The Great God Brown* and *Lazarus Laughed* stand Catholicism, Nietzsche and Jung; behind *Strange Interlude* and *Dynamo* loom Schopenhauer and Freud. But another intellectual current, swollen by his desire to create a "supernaturalistic" theatre, was gaining momentum in O'Neill's mind. In the theories of his favorite European sources (Nietzsche, Schopenhauer and Jung) lurked some Oriental ideas about time, personality and ultimate reality. When reinforced and expanded by the Eastern texts he had read or was reading,[5] these mystical concepts waged

2. "A Dramatist's Notebook," *The American Spectator*, Jan. 1933; rpt. in Cargill, Fagin, and Fisher, *Criticism*, pp. 121–22.
3. O'Neill letter to New York newspapers, 13 Feb. 1926; rpt. in Barrett H. Clark, *O'Neill: The Man and His Plays* (New York: Dover, 1947), p. 106.
4. O'Neill to Manuel Komroff, 22 Mar. 1926; quoted in Sheaffer, *Artist*, p. 197.
5. Some of these texts are discussed in chap. 3. Other relevant texts acquired by O'Neill in 1926 include Frazier's *The Golden Bough* (New York: Macmillan, 1925); Max Müller's *Chips from a German Workshop* (London: Longmans, 1914); Albert Churchward's *The Origin and Evolution of Religion* (New York: Dutton, 1924); George Sale's translation of the *Koran* (London: Frederick Warne, n.d.); and Lewis Spence's *A Dictionary of Mythology* (London: Cassell, n.d.). All the volumes are signed by O'Neill and dated either March 1926 or April 1926.

ideological warfare with other, conventionally Western approaches. Because the tragedian in O'Neill continued to admire struggle, for instance, *Strange Interlude* pictures its characters struggling for nearly twenty-five years; yet his Oriental side yearned to transcend the strife, as the peaceful resignation of that play's final act reveals.

This conflict of East and West was also revealed in his techniques. In *The Great God Brown*, masks dramatize inner conflicts, following an essentially psychological (thus Western) purpose. Brown's assumption of Dion's mask, however, alludes to transmigration. Again, in *Lazarus Laughed*, the elaborate masking scheme seems very Western in its impulse toward psychological categorization. But from a Hindu perspective, those masks symbolize *māyā*, the multiplicitous and misleading distinctions created by our earth-bound minds.

When the conflicting philosophical tides are observed from a distance, they reveal the rapid advance and subsequent recession of Orientalism in O'Neill's work between 1925 and 1928. *Brown's* Eastern qualities are largely superficial: allusions to Nirvana and transmigration occur in a fundamentally Western context, though the play's rhythms recall Taoism. In *Lazarus*, the Orientalism is broader and deeper. Indeed, the focus on liberation from the ego and *māyā*—the major goal of Hinduism and Buddhism—makes this O'Neill's most Eastern play. *Strange Interlude*, however, finds this mystical influence ebbing. Freudian assumptions dominate a work whose characters constantly battle the guilt that accompanies sexual deviations from the prevailing social code. Yet an Oriental undercurrent nonetheless informs the play, for its other major Western source is Schopenhauer, whose Buddhist scepticism about wordly existence is apparent throughout. *Dynamo*, finally, repudiates Oriental thought by associating it with the modern electrical god worshipped by Reuben Light, whose devotion is psychotic and suicidal. Following *Dynamo*, O'Neill submerged his mystical impulses for over ten years, returning to traditional European models for his drama.

The above discussion largely excludes Taoism, because its permeation of O'Neill's art at this time requires a separate introduction. As was apparent in *The Fountain* and "*Marco Millions*," O'Neill's mystical intuitions had already begun to suggest to him

that a dynamic polarity structured and unified existence. This unifying rhythm becomes more pervasive in the four plays this chapter
analyzes. Though this phenomenon demonstrates an affinity that
goes beyond mere influence, two of O'Neill's sources should be
mentioned. The first is a book he owned by Lawrence Binyon, entitled *The Flight of the Dragon: An Essay on the Theory and Practice of Art in China and Japan* (London: John Murray, 1922). Since
the volume concerns China, O'Neill almost undoubtedly read it
while researching "*Marco Millions*," which he completed just before drafting *The Great God Brown* in 1925. Its treatment of
the rhythmic vitality of Chinese art, however, makes it particularly
pertinent to the plays under discussion. Listing six canons of Chinese aesthetics, Binyon asserts that "Rhythmic Vitality, or Spiritual
Rhythm expressed in the movement of life," is first and "all-
important." This primary law demands that the artist "pierce beneath the mere aspect of the world to seize and himself be possessed
by that great cosmic rhythm of the spirit which sets the currents of
life in motion." Indeed, "whatever rhythm is, it is something intimately connected with life, perhaps the secret of life and its most
perfect expression."[6] This "great cosmic rhythm" helps explain the
"conflicting tides" of *The Great God Brown*, illuminates the emotional vacillations of *Interlude*'s characters, leads *Dynamo*'s protagonist to his worship of electricity, and is ecstatically (and end-
lessly) proclaimed in *Lazarus Laughed*. One other observation by
Binyon relates particularly to the defiantly anti-representational
Brown and *Lazarus*. "It is not essential that the subject matter
should represent or be like anything in nature," he claims; "only it
must be alive with a rhythmic vitality of its own."[7]

The principle of rhythmic vitality, directly paralleling (because
based upon) the dynamic of the Tao, helped produce the thematic
cycles of all four plays. The second source encouraged their polaristic characterization. The theories of Jung suggested that fulfillment
lay in the reconciliation of opposites—particularly the contrary female and male aspects—within one's personality. This drive toward
psychological integration of opposing sexual forces, prominent in

6. Binyon, *Dragon*, pp. 11–12, 19.
7. Ibid., p. 21.

these dramas, also assumes metaphysical significance when the protagonists seek to reconcile competing mother and father gods.
Their wish is not always granted. The two most Western plays,
Brown and *Dynamo*, discover reconciliation only in death, but the
more Oriental *Lazarus* and *Interlude* manage to unite male and female deities by viewing them as polarities that participate in a
larger rhythm. The plays in which O'Neill's Eastern impulse is
strongest, then, have a mystical Taoist monism at their core, while
the two others conclude with Western dualism still triumphant.

"Conflicting Tides": *The Great God Brown*

After reading the famous letter O'Neill wrote to the New York
newspapers after *The Great God Brown* opened in 1926, one might
be inclined to regard the play as very Eastern in theme and tone.
Calling attention to "the mystical pattern which manifests itself
dimly . . . behind and beyond the words and actions of the characters," the letter identifies *Brown*'s central purpose as "Mystery—
the mystery any one man or woman can feel but not understand as
the meaning of any event—or accident—in any life on earth." [8] The
play also mentions Nirvana and transmigration, apparently dramatizing the latter in the transfer of Dion Anthony's personality to
Billy Brown. Finally, as O'Neill's letter states, *Brown*'s plot describes "conflicting tides in the soul of man," and the play's structural rhythms correspond to the cycles of the Tao.

Unquestionably, Oriental mystical religions influenced the play's
structure and ideas. Equally unquestionably, Christianity, Nietzsche and Jung had more impact on the play than Eastern thought.
And Dion's central conflict—his tortured movement between his
pagan and Christian impulses, "resulting in this modern day in mutual exhaustion" (according to O'Neill's letter)—dramatizes the
playwright's continuing Western obsession with tragic struggle.
Indeed, the psychological battles within and between Dion and

8. Rpt. in Clark, *O'Neill*, pp. 104–6. All subsequent quotations from the letter
refer to this source.

Brown consistently manifest a traditional dualism that is only transcended through death. Nonetheless, *The Great God Brown* serves as an important preparation for the more pervasive Orientalism of *Lazarus Laughed*, which proclaims similar mystical intentions. The earlier play, in fact, provides a kind of halfway house to *Lazarus*. While *Brown* remains largely within the confines of traditional Western thought and art, it gives more expression to O'Neill's Eastern intuitions than any previous O'Neill play. And some concepts from its major Western sources—Christianity, Nietzsche and Jung—are interpreted and applied in an "Eastern" manner. The "conflicting tides" of *Brown*'s characters, then, also appear in O'Neill's use of his sources, demonstrating an ambivalence between East and West in the soul of the playwright himself.

The Christian elements of the play prove least susceptible to Oriental interpretation. One can view *Brown* as a heavily moral parable about two sinners whose pride and envy make them stray from God, but who rediscover Him at their deaths. Dion Anthony sins by concealing his Christian soul under the mask of a scornful, proud, sensual young Pan. Pan turns into Mephistopheles as Dion gradually destroys himself through cynicism, self-doubt and self-indulgence. But his hidden spiritual dimension becomes increasingly saintlike and ascetic, and he shows love and seeks forgiveness when death approaches. Recognizing that his pride has isolated him and made him cruel, he dies with the opening words of the "Our Father" on his lips. The diabolical half of Dion lives on, however, in Billy Brown, whose cardinal sin of envy—of Dion's creativity and power to love—motivates his masquerade as Dion. As O'Neill's letter puts it, Dion's "devil of mocking doubt makes short work of him," as he quickly loses touch with his old complacent self. Once again, however, "out of this anguish a soul is born, a tortured Christian soul such as the dying Dion's, begging for belief, and at the last finding it on the lips of Cybel." Like Dion, Brown discovers the Christian paternal deity just before he dies.

This recapitulation highlights the basic Christian assumptions informing the play: the value of suffering, the isolating effects of pride, the destructiveness of envy, and the mercy of God. Another Christian motif inheres in the satire of Brown, the epitome of American materialism. Described in the letter as "the visionless demi-god of our new materialistic myth—a Success—building his life of exterior things, inwardly empty and resourceless," Brown represents the shallowness of those who lay up treasures on earth; Dion's hidden, world-renouncing soul is in deliberate contrast to this. This attack on materialism marks the only important correspondence between Christianity, Hinduism and Buddhism in the play. And obviously, O'Neill required no knowledge of Oriental mysticism to introduce this theme.

Moreover, the Nietzschean elements of the play contradict this renunciatory ethic. O'Neill's letter explicates the protagonist's name as "Dionysus and St. Anthony—the creative pagan acceptance of life, fighting eternal war with the masochistic, life-denying spirit of Christianity as represented by St. Anthony." The rejection of a "masochistic and life-denying" Christianity that inhibits the "creative pagan acceptance of life" echoes *Thus Spake Zarathustra*, with its numerous injunctions to joyfully embrace the material world. From this perspective, Dion's pagan mask represents "an integral part of his character as the artist," frustrated by the conventional Christian society that surrounds him, and consequently "distorted by morality from Pan into Satan." When Brown assumes the mask, the Nietzschean scorn it directs against his sacred bourgeois values of status and success causes him to doubt his accomplishments, and he disintegrates under the demands of a fragmented personality. However, Billy absorbs Dion's (and Zarathustra's) vital laughter from the mask. His final proclamation, delivered "*exultantly*," is that "the laughter of Heaven sows earth with a rain of tears, and out of earth's transfigured birth-pain the laughter of Man returns to bless and play again in innumerable dancing gales of flame upon the knees of God!"[9] This affirmative laughter is destined to become the theme of O'Neill's subsequent play, *Lazarus Laughed*.

The Zarathustran influence gives *Brown* a world-affirming, self-exulting tone that conflicts with both Christian and Oriental teachings. Oriental mystical faiths propose transcendence of this life, mainly through liberation from ego, rather than defiance of social morality through assertion of ego. Another Nietzschean element of

9. *Plays*, 3: 322. Hereafter documented in the text.

the play, however corresponds to Eastern thought. After Brown's death, the prostitute Cybel proclaims "always spring comes again bearing life," followed by "summer and fall and death and peace again," but "always, always, love and conception and birth and pain again—spring bearing the intolerable chalice of life again" (p. 322). This deliberately alludes to the seasonal cycles behind ancient Greek tragedy (discussed in Nietzsche's *The Birth of Tragedy*), and to Zarathustra's doctrine of the eternal recurrence, which envisions our lives as an eternal series of rebirths. But the eternal recurrence broadly parallels the Indian *samsara*, the cycle of reincarnations the soul must undergo until it achieves liberation from *karma*. While diverging on specifics, Nietzsche and the Indian faiths concur that life and death participate in an endless rhythm like that of the seasons; that rhythm acts as an Oriental counterpoint in *Brown* to the steady, linear decline of the two protagonists.

Brown's final Western source lends itself the most readily to Oriental redirection. The psychoanalytical theories proposed by Carl Jung were themselves, of course, influenced by Oriental thought. First, however, I will approach the play from a "Western" Jungian perspective, emphasizing those ideas of Jung shaped not by Eastern mysticism, but by Freud. From this perspective, the source of Dion's conflict is his Oedipal attachment to his mother, whose influence on him is reflected in his "shrinking, shy and gentle" soul (p. 264). This fixation is made explicit in Dion's feelings at her funeral, at which he "felt like a forsaken toy and cried to be buried with her" (p. 282). To replace her, he marries Margaret, who "became three mothers in one person" (p. 282). However, Dion's real mother and Margaret are both (in Jungian terms) "terrible mother" figures, who overprotect Dion while failing to nourish him, thus stifling his creativity. Cybel, on the other hand, represents the "good mother" who nurtures Dion while demanding nothing in return. Consequently, he can shed his mask and be vulnerable before her, as he cannot with Margaret.

The other prominent Jungian aspect of the play involves the polar oppositions within Dion and between Dion and Brown. Dion's health deteriorates because of the widening split between his feminized inner nature (his *anima*) and his sarcastic, masculine *persona*. This non-integrated *persona* becomes moody, irritable and childlike, gradually succumbing to the "shadow"—Jung's term for the inferior, evil side of one's nature that often assumes control of the neurotic personality. After Dion's death, Brown assumes the Satanic shadow, but also fails to integrate it. Possessing a personality opposite to Dion's—successful, materialistic, and unlovable— Brown had formerly formed with Dion one complete psychological unit. He depends on Dion for his emotional life; Dion proclaims, "he loves me because I have always possessed the power he needed for love" (p. 298). Dion depends on Brown for his economic survival. Their relationship thus illustrates Jung's theory of inevitable complementariness, as Cybel reveals in her observation that "you're brothers, I guess, somehow" (p. 289). Hence, when Dion dies, Brown cannot survive for long. But having assumed Dion's mask, he dies as Dion Brown, finally achieving integration in death.

The Taoist elements of Jung's thought come to the foreground in Dion's split personality. The polarities within Dion that should complement each other—his feminine *anima*, his masculine *persona*—resist integration and become dualistic oppositions. This places Dion in the familiar dilemma of the tragic hero, engaged in terrible conflict because of the dualistic nature of reality (here presented in psychological terms). A healthy personality, however, reconciles these oppositions by allowing their interpenetration, encouraging them to identify with each other. From this viewpoint, the alternating rhythm of Dion's personality between *anima* and *persona* resembles that of the Tao, which unifies *yin* and *yang* by engaging them in its transcendent process. But Dion, unable to perceive that unity, resists integration. Taoist/Jungian assumptions also help resolve an apparent contradiction in O'Neill's masking scheme for Dion. It appears at first that the Pan mask represents the public side of Dion that hides the genuine Christian soul underneath. Yet O'Neill's explanatory letter makes the pagan Pan mask stand for Dion's *true* nature, his creative imagination, that is distorted and inhibited by a superimposed Christian morality. The contradiction vanishes if mask and face are regarded as *yin* and *yang*, entities that reside on the same plane. Since both Christian and pagan are equally legitimate sides of Dion's personality—which the play itself demonstrates, whatever O'Neill's letter claims—the problem lies not in affirming one and denying the other, but in reconciling them. This conciliatory approach was absorbed by Jung from Oriental thought, which refuses to accept any dualism as ultimately real. This applies particularly to the moral dualism between Dion's "good" Christian and "evil" Mephistophelean aspects. Taoism would view any such moral distinctions as relative, conditional, and finally illusory. It therefore prescribes the maintenance of a balance between good and evil in order to achieve harmony in the soul. Jung, following Taoism, advises our acceptance of the "shadow" part of ourselves. Hence, Dion Anthony needs not an exorcism, but a liberated perspective that would enable him to integrate by accepting his "evil" pagan and "good" Christian sides.

The curious brotherhood of Dion and Brown represents another instance of unified opposites in *The Great God Brown*. As with Dion's inner conflict, it seems to persist as irreconcilable opposition throughout most of the play. In particular, the hidden "*dark, spiritual, poetic*" side of Dion contrasts with the masculine, active, materialistic body of Brown, who is "*tall and athletic*" (p. 257). But this polarity replicates *yin* and *yang*, and after Dion accepts employment from Brown, their hidden unity starts to become apparent. They assist each other in designing buildings; they love the same woman, Margaret; they have the same mistress, Cybel. At Dion's death, they become even closer, since one half of Dion now exists in Brown. Unfortunately, it is the wrong half—the masculine half—throwing Brown's personality completely out of balance. He shuttles violently between his masks of businessman Brown and Dion Anthony and the new (unmasked) soul that emerges from this conflict, until death brings integration of Dion and Brown in Cybel's arms. Together, Dion and Brown symbolize the complementary sides of human nature—soul and body, seer and doer, artist and pragmatist—that unite in the corpse on stage called (by Cybel) "Man!" (p. 323).

Separately and together, Dion and Brown thus embody the "conflicting tides within the soul of man" that O'Neill identified as the mystical meaning of the play. This rhythm constitutes *Brown*'s most pervasive Taoist feature. Interestingly, the two men alternate on stage with each other in the first half, joining only for important scenes (e.g., when Brown witnesses Dion's death). They thereby establish their own symbolic psychological counterpoint, with Dion representing man's spirit and imagination, Brown his pragmatism and acquisitiveness. Furthermore, Dion individually alternates between his pagan and Christian aspects in the first two acts, while Brown shifts between his two masks and his new-found soul in the concluding acts. Cybel and Margaret also vacillate between public masks and private faces, so the effect is that of numerous personal rhythms existing within the larger seasonal and cosmic rhythms mentioned earlier. Whether absorbed directly from Taoism or indirectly from Jung, these cycles and epicycles invest the play with the "rhythmic vitality" that Binyon's *Flight of the Dragon* identified as the key feature of Chinese art.

Hinduism and Buddhism also influence *The Great God Brown*, mainly in obvious ways. Dion alludes to Nirvana shortly before his death, when he hears no response following his fervent prayer to the Lord: "*suddenly, with a look of horror,*" he cries, "Nothing! To feel one's life blown out like the flame of a cheap match!" (p. 286). This simile reproduces the literal meaning of Nirvana (the extinction of a flame), so Dion's horror represents that of Western man facing the Buddhist void. His Dionysiac side—which exults in the ego's obliteration—strains to rejoice in this. Clapping on his mask, he laughs, "to fall asleep, and know you'll never, never be called to get on the job of existence again!" (286). The gold-hearted prostitute Cybel helps him accept this possibility, for she is herself overtly associated with Indian religion. On her first appearance, "*she chews gum like a sacred cow forgetting time with an eternal end*" (p. 278), alluding to a widely known feature of Hinduism. On numerous occasions, moreover, she is described as an "idol," referring to another familiar aspect of Hinduism, its idolatry. And while one cannot overlook the purely pagan touches to her personality—her animal nature, her connection to the seasonal cycles—Cybel's character also points East in more important respects. O'Neill's descriptions of her repeatedly insist on her serenity, acquired through her acceptance of the rhythms of existence. Unlike the others, for example, she does not suffer from the rhythmic alternation between her cynical, rouged public mask and her private face. "I gave my clients a Tart," she tells Dion. "They understood her and knew their parts and acted naturally. And on both sides we were able to keep our real virtue, if you get me" (p. 284). As this implies, Cybel maintains sufficient detachment from life to remain indifferent to its vicissitudes. Playing cards with Dion, she never loses. As she tells him, "you keep getting closer, but it knows you still want to win—a little bit—and it's wise all I care about is playing" (p. 285). This non-concern with goals corresponds to the path followed in *karma* yoga, in which indifference to the fruits of one's acts creates liberation into profound peace.

Dion lacks Cybel's indifference and serenity. He unhappily works for Billy Brown, for (he tells him bitterly) "one must do something to pass away the time, while one is waiting—for one's next incarnation" (p. 282). Margaret, in the epilogue, also alludes to transmigration when she declares that "after a thousand lives our eyes begin to open" (p. 325). These remarks, and Brown's assumption of Dion's mask, offer the play's most intriguing—and inconsistent—application of Oriental thought. The evil Dion does lives after him, as *karma* dictates it must. As a consequence of his cruelty to self and others, he returns as a lower form of life—Brown—leading to intense suffering for this remnant of Dion's soul. Oddly, though, Brown attains a measure of enlightenment as a consequence of Dion's mask; as Christianity (not Hinduism) teaches, suffering builds character and brings consciousness. He who hitherto had no soul develops one, and may even attain redemption at the conclusion.

Apparently, O'Neill either possessed an imperfect understanding of transmigration, or failed to apply it systematically to the play. A soul that returned in a lower state would hardly obtain liberation so quickly. Nor does reincarnation recognize split personalities. The play fails to indicate where the protagonist's St. Anthony side has wandered—perhaps to Nirvana?—but *karma* does not separately reward the good fragment of one's nature and punish the bad. Furthermore, if Dion has transmigrated, he would not take possession of a contemporary soul (with its own accrued *karma*), but would begin anew. O'Neill, then, toys with the notion of transmigration, but fails to apply it carefully. Indeed, the transference of personality from Dion to Billy, with its revenge motive and its grotesque consequences, is more consistent with the Gothic tradition that in-spired *Dr. Jekyll and Mr. Hyde* and *The Picture of Dorian Gray.* Ironically, the most obvious instance of Orientalism in *The Great God Brown* is the least Oriental in its application.

O'Neill's next two plays also consider reincarnation, but no more profoundly. Lazarus returns from death for a new life, but occupies the same body; *Strange Interlude*'s Ned Darrell bids final farewell to Nina by musing that "perhaps we'll become part of cosmic posi-tive and negative electric charges and meet again." [10] Other Eastern ideas in *The Great God Brown*, however, receive more attention in these works which aim (like *Brown*) to explore the mystical forces that shape our lives. Taoist polarities and rhythmic vitality (largely refined through Jung again) penetrate the structure and character-ization of *Lazarus*. Indian mystical doctrines become more promi-nent in both plays, and *Lazarus* in particular represents a more suc-cessful effort on O'Neill's part to integrate his diverse Eastern and Western sources into a unified, affirmative vision. *Brown*, after all, contains contradictions not just between Eastern and Western ap-proaches, but even *within* its Western sources. In *Lazarus*, the se-cret unity that binds together the fractured psyches of Brown and Dion advances downstage center in the integrated personality of the protagonist. But the Eastern serenity of Lazarus might never have been achieved had not the experimental, fragmented *Brown* paved the way.

"There is no death": The Mystical Monism of *Lazarus Laughed*

Despite its hints of the unity behind polarities, *The Great God Brown* concedes that only death can resolve the oppositions of exis-tence. Only at his demise do Dion Anthony's good and evil sides integrate; only at the conclusion may the dying "Dion Brown" reach the father god through the wisdom of the earth mother,

10. *Plays*, 1: 197.

Cybel. But *Lazarus Laughed*'s protagonist rises above good and evil, male and female, even life and death—all of which he views as simply different stages in the cosmic rhythm. Appropriately, the entire play is structured around the rhythmic activities (laughing, chanting, dancing) that accompany Lazarus's exuberant speeches about the eternal process of life.

As countless critics have testified, Nietzsche's influence stands behind the celebration of process, the personality of the protagonist, and the characters' ecstatic embrace of a primordial Dionysiac unity. In addition, Jung's philosophy contributes to the play's masking scheme, and (as in *Brown*) to the polarities of its character relationships. But O'Neill was reading widely in mythology, philosophy and comparative religion at this time. He acquired eight books on these subjects between March and May of 1926, while he was composing the play's first draft. One of them, W. T. Stace's *Critical History of Greek Philosophy*, reveals the affinities between pre-Socratic Greek and Indian philosophy; another, Samuel Angus's *The Mystery Religions and Christianity* (from which O'Neill copied passages) describes the Oriental invasion of Western religion during the early Christian era; a third, Max Müller's *Chips from a German Workshop*, includes several essays on Buddhism and Hinduism. Thus, Jung's and Nietzsche's theories contended with some Eastern concepts that both reinforced and contradicted them. If Lazarus is modelled on Zarathustra, he also resembles Buddha. If process rules the play, one of its forms of expression (the masking) yields as easily to a Vedantic approach as a Jungian one. And if the characterization is based on Jungian theories of complementary polarities, the play's pervasive cycles go beyond Jung to his ultimate sources, Lao Tse and Chuang Tse.

Of the three major Western sources for the previous play, one—Christianity—recedes in its influence on *Lazarus Laughed*. This is ironic, given the play's subject matter, but O'Neill's correspondence and revisions indicate his intention to wean the work from its Christian matrix. For instance, O'Neill drastically cut his typescript's first scene, which originally included both a lengthy recounting of Lazarus's rebirth and a speech by Lazarus that moralistically attacks the fear of death (calling it "guilty of all man's sin and guilt since time began").[11] O'Neill explained his motive in a letter to Kenneth Macgowan: "I have made what are very grave alterations and cuts—especially in the first scene which I have taken out of the Bible—all the Saint John Gospel stuff out, etc.—and most of Lazarus' talk, relying on a few sentences of his and his laughter. . . . There was too much in it of a regular Biblical play—a bad start for Laz."[12] O'Neill also abandoned his original intention to have his protagonist's final words allude to those of Jesus on the cross: "Father, I am thy son! Thou canst not forsake me!"[13] Despite the changes, the hero still resembles Christ: he exudes a radiance, is loving and forgiving, and (most important) suffers crucifixion after delivering a gospel that mankind cannot accept. O'Neill, however, discouraged identification of Lazarus with Jesus for two reasons. First, he desired a savior who would somehow represent *all* faiths—hence, his voluminous reading in comparative religion and mythology. "If *Lazarus* is anything," he declared in another letter to Macgowan, "it's absolutely non-sectarian." The same document exposes the second, more bitterly personal motive. Anticipating resentment of the play by Roman Catholics, he asserted that "if they are not stupid, it should hit them as a flat denial of all their fundamental dogmas."[14]

The reduced Christian influence prepares the way for an increased Nietzschean one. O'Neill's notes for *Lazarus* quote Zarathustra: "A God wilt thou create for thyself out of thy severe devils! Thou lonesome one, thou goest the way of the creating one."[15] Lazarus's death and rebirth have enabled him to overcome man's severest devil—the fear of death—and recognize an immanent, joyful God. Hence, Lazarus declares: "it is my pride as God to become

11. Typescript of *Lazarus Laughed*, File Folder Za/O'Neill/11, O'Neill Collection, Beinecke Library, Yale Univ.

12. O'Neill to Macgowan, 30 Dec. 1926; File Folder Za/O'Neill/to Macgowan, O'Neill Collection, Beinecke Library, Yale Univ.

13. *Lazarus Laughed* manuscript notes, File Folder Za/O'Neill/33x, O'Neill Collection, Beinecke Library, Yale Univ.

14. O'Neill to Macgowan, 7 Aug. 1926; File Folder Za/O'Neill/to Macgowan, O'Neill Collection, Beinecke Library, Yale Univ.

15. *Lazarus Laughed* manuscript notes, File Folder Za/O'Neill/33x, O'Neill Collection, Beinecke Library, Yale Univ.

Man. Then let it be my pride as Man to recreate the God in me!"[16] His proud belief in the potential god—or overman—within everyone makes clear another resemblance of Lazarus to Zarathustra. Also Zarathustran is his advancing youth, whereby his face and voice at the end possess the "*fresh, clear quality of boyhood*" (p. 365). In *Thus Spake Zarathustra*, the heavens tell the prophet, "the pride of youth is still upon you; you have become young late; but whoever would become as a child must overcome his youth too."[17] Lazarus also laughs triumphantly throughout, recreating the merriness of Nietzsche's prophet who "laughs at all tragic plays and tragic seriousness."[18] The laughter of Lazarus stems from his Zarathustran perception that the universe engages in eternal becoming. It is "of time and becoming that the best parables should speak," counsels Nietzsche's prophet: "let them be a praise and a justification of all impermanence."[19] Lazarus affirms our identity with this process, proclaiming man as "eternal change and everlasting growth, and a high note of laughter soaring through chaos from the deep heart of God!" (p. 309). And the "everlasting growth," finally, alludes to Zarathustra's definition of life as "that which must always overcome itself."[20]

Zarathustra, however, embraces the Western belief in man's "creating, willing, valuing ego, which is the measure and value of things."[21] O'Neill's prophet does not. Rather, he admonishes man to cast aside "our pitiable pretense, our immortal egohood, the holy lantern behind which cringed our Fear of the Dark!" (p. 324). This retreat from the self connects the protagonist to a second Nietzschean source, *The Birth of Tragedy*. Lazarus is worshipped by young Greeks who imitate the followers of Dionysus, and the choral dancing catalyzed by his laughter recalls the Dionysian choruses from which ancient Greek tragedy was born. The dancing always occurs to music, which (Nietzsche asserts) "alone

16. *Plays*, 1: 352. Hereafter documented in the text.
17. *The Portable Nietzsche*, ed. Kaufmann, p. 259.
18. Ibid., p. 272.
19. Ibid., pp. 198–99.
20. Ibid., p. 227.
21. Ibid., p. 144.

allows us to understand the delight felt at the annihilation of the individual."[22] Many individuals are annihilated during *Lazarus* to their own delight and that of their prophet, since they now have transcended the individuation that *The Birth of Tragedy* described as "the source of all suffering."[23] But in Nietzsche's treatise, the destruction of the ego is only temporary. The choral members (and the theatrical spectators) return to their individual lives following their ecstatic aesthetic immersion. During the performance, moreover, the Dionysian absorption is balanced by the Apollonian illusion, which aims at "a tranquil delight in individual forms."[24] Such is not the case in *Lazarus Laughed*. Here, the Dionysian takes over, returning man permanently to that primordial oneness described by Nietzsche, but celebrated by Lazarus.

The play's devaluation of the self, in fact, constitutes its sharpest break from the Nietzschean sources, which either affirm the ego or advise only a temporary retreat from it. Viewing egolessness as a desirable permanent state, Lazarus urges mankind to "let a laughing away of self be your new right to live forever" (p. 310). Following Zarathustra, he affirms life, growth, and joy; but identifying with the Dionysian principle, he does little to sustain his *own* life, since he has transcended identity (and hence the fear of loss of identity via death). This behavior is eminently Oriental—and emphatically Buddhist.

Previous scholars have noticed this Buddhistic aspect of *Lazarus Laughed*. Doris Alexander, pointing out the Indian origin of Lazarus's egolessness, also termed Buddhist his love for animals, asceticism, compassion, detachment from surroundings, and contemplative attitude.[25] Lazarus in fact resembles the legendary Buddha even more than Professor Alexander suspected. For instance, the sexual pleasure Pompeia offers Lazarus corresponds to Buddha's final temptation by Māra the Fiend, as recounted in Coomaraswamy's *Buddha and The Gospel of Buddhism*. Māra summons his three daughters, and they use "all the arts of seduction known to beautiful women. Again they offered him the lordship of the

22. *The Birth of Tragedy*, trans. Golffing, p. 101.
23. Ibid., p. 66.
24. Ibid., p. 141.
25. See chap. one, n. four.

earth, and the companionship of beautiful girls; they appealed to him with songs of the season of spring, and exhibited their supernatural beauty and grace. But the Bodhisatta's heart was not in the least moved,"[26] nor is the passionless Lazarus when tempted by Pompeia. Also like Buddha, Lazarus does not claim (like Christ) to be the son of God. Rather, he enlightens men to the impersonal divinity residing within all. The historical Buddha never claimed a unique status because that would have contradicted his Second Truth: God cannot become a particular self when the "self" is unreal. Buddha instead alerted others to the liberation inherent in the same egolessness preached by Lazarus. Furthermore, both Buddha and Lazarus practice passiveness for similar reasons. Following enlightenment, Buddha abandons active willing because he now understands that all desires are unreal. Better to contemplate Nirvana. Following rebirth, Lazarus permits the slaughter of family, wife, followers and finally himself, because he too recognizes the meaninglessness of our desires. Better to meditate, and laugh.

This contemplative quality points up Lazarus's most significant resemblance to Buddha. We first see Lazarus "*staring straight before him as if his vision were still fixed beyond life*" (p. 274), and throughout he is rapt in contemplation when not preaching or laughing. O'Neill's notes to *Lazarus* underscore the importance of these reveries. One note copies from Angus's *Mystery Religions* a quotation from Philo, a first century Platonist. "All things are provided (by God, life) that are necessary for man not merely to live but to live nobly: for the latter purpose the contemplation of the heavens induces in the mind a love of a desire for knowledge, which gives rise to philosophy, by which man, though mortal, is rendered immortal." Another note states that "Plotinus argues that the reverent contemplation of the universe brings the soul into contact with God of the Cosmos"; a third quotes Valerus, "I desired to obtain a divine and adoring contemplation of the heavens and to purify my ways from wickedness and all defilement."[27] This Gnostic approach to God constituted a major Oriental contribution to Western reli-

26. Coomaraswamy, *Buddha and the Gospel of Buddhism*, p. 34.
27. *Lazarus Laughed* manuscript notes, File Folder Za/O'Neill/33x, O'Neill Collection, Beinecke Library, Yale Univ.

gions during the early Christian era, though it was staunchly resisted by the Christian Fathers who espoused salvation through love. Hence, Lazarus is most Oriental, and least orthodox Christian, in his meditative nature. His temporary "death" has enlightened him to an Eastern truth: death is unreal, because the ego that perishes is illusory, inessential and non-eternal. Although he behaves compassionately, this is a *result* (not cause) of liberation, and he never preaches love as a path to salvation. Rather, his message reproduces that of Buddha (leavened heavily with Dionysian ecstasy): to discover bliss, release yourself from the illusory bonds of the ego.

With all the similarities between these two saviors, a fundamental difference remains. Lazarus believes peace follows recognition of our participation in a transcendent, eternal process; Buddha preaches liberation from that flux, since life's transience causes our suffering. Hinduism agrees with Buddhism that processes exist to be transcended, that beyond *samsara* lies a blissful stasis that approximates non-being. Liberation succeeds the realization that time's apparent processes are an illusion, as are all differences between sensory phenomena or individual personalities. These false distinctions result from *māyā*, which (Vedantists claim) obscures the unity of Brahman, the infinite, changeless, indefinable essence of all creation. At every man's deepest level, his impersonal *Atman* connects him to Brahman, but above that, *māyā* misleads us into accepting the spurious distinctions offered by our senses and our reason.

These Vedantic concepts inform the treatment of personality in *Lazarus Laughed*, whose ubiquitous masks correspond to *māyā*. The only unmasked figure is Lazarus, whom O'Neill described as "the one man who is real and true and alive in the midst of false, dead people."[28] The play's masking scheme thus spotlights the solitary vital character, fully alive because no longer obsessed with the fear of death. Undeceived by this ultimate false distinction between life and death, he manifests little regard for other discriminations. The barriers between nations, religions, and classes seem especially

---

28. O'Neill to Macgowan, 21 Jan. 1927; File Folder Za/O'Neill/to Macgowan, O'Neill Collection, Beinecke Library, Yale Univ.

inconsequential. When egohood is cast off, Lazarus exults, also "flung off is that impudent insult to life's nobility which gibbers: 'I, this Jew, this Roman, this noble or this slave, must survive in my pettiness forever'" (p. 324). Though these distinctions are reproduced quite precisely by the masking scheme, Lazarus perceives the unity beneath the disguises of *māyā*. "Now with laughter give we back that gift [life] to become again the essence of the Giver! Dying we laugh with the Infinite. We are the Giver and the Gift!," he proclaims in words recalling Emerson's "Brahma." [29] "Laughing, we give our lives for Life's sake!" (p. 324).

Unique in the recognition of *Atman*'s identity with Brahman, Lazarus wears no mask because he is closest to pure *Atman*. The other characters' masks correspondingly symbolize their entrapment in *māyā*, where age, cultural and personality differences seem all important. The masks' extreme multiplicity is one indication of this, for *māyā* is bewildering and manifold.[30] This excessive differentiation and categorization contrasts sharply with the solitary Lazarus, pointing up the play's Oriental variation on O'Neill's obsessive illusion/reality theme. Masks represent the multiplex, illusory realm of human personality; the unmasked protagonist stands for the eternal part of our nature that constitutes ultimate truth.

Probably the masking was influenced by Jung's *Psychological Types*, which also categorizes human personality. But as a psychoanalyst, Jung accepted the reality of personality differences, while *Lazarus Laughed* so exaggerates these distinctions that it implicitly ridicules the idea of categorization. The masks, then, do not simply symbolize different *types* of personality, but (taken together) stand for the very *concept* of personality. Hinduism views the individual

29. "They reckon ill who leave me out; / When me they fly, I am the wings; / I am the doubter and the doubt, / And I the hymn the Brahman sings" (*Selected Writings*, p. 809).

30. In each crowd, different masks represent each of seven periods of life, and within each period exist seven different masks for character types. Furthermore, there are several different kinds of crowds (Jewish, Greek, Roman), and distinctions occur *within* distinctions. Lazarus's followers, e.g., follow the scheme for Jewish features (in forty-nine combinations), but their masks resemble Lazarus also. The masks of the Roman soldiers, "*domineering*" and "*self-complacent*," differ from those of the Roman Senators, which convey "*strength degenerated, corrupted by tyranny and debauchery to an exhausted cynicism*" (pp. 291, 312).

personality as inessential and impermanent, as *māyā*, and *Lazarus* likewise associates the masks with impermanence. Certainly, the representation in the mobs of seven different life stages suggests the transitory nature of existence. Personalities also alter from moment to moment. The extreme fluctuations of every crowd member (and most major characters) in their response to Lazarus dramatize this instability, as characters shift between laughter and violence, love and hatred. O'Neill further implies the masks' impermanence in a symbolic lighting effect. As the flames consume Lazarus during his crucifixion, they *"flare upward and are reflected on* [the soldiers'] *masks in dancing waves of light"* (p. 367). The flame—a common symbol of impermanence in Indian scriptures—here plays upon the masks, suggesting again the *māyā*-like transience of human personality.

Underneath *māyā*'s veil, however, the divine *Atman* is possessed by all, which helps explain the universal response to Lazarus's gospel. Momentarily overcoming their individual preoccupations, Nazarenes unite with Jews, Romans embrace Greeks, and Caligula and Tiberius transcend their mutual hatred to laugh with Lazarus. Inevitably, however, all forget their ecstatic joy as soon as Lazarus departs, whereupon they fall prey to *māyā* once more. Their individual differences even push them to violent conflict with one another. "That is your tragedy," Lazarus tells them, "You forget! You forget the God in you" (p. 289). Recurring throughout the play, this sentiment is last expressed in Caligula's words at the final curtain, "Forgive me, Lazarus! Men forget!" (p. 371). Not coincidentally, this corresponds to the root definition of *māyā*: a cosmic nescience whereby Brahman forgets his true unity as he disperses himself into the particularized phenomenal world. More pertinent to *Lazarus*, it also alludes to the human equivalent of this—*avidyā*—which describes man's inability to consistently perceive, and be liberated by, his identity with the universe.[31]

Men's lapses in *Lazarus* are also open to a Christian interpretation, of course. The numerous unpleasant characters and the disgusting episodes—mob massacres, poisonings, assassinations and

31. These are the definitions offered by Müller in *Six Systems of Indian Philosophy*, O'Neill's chief source of knowledge about Hinduism.

finally crucifixion—can be viewed as the product of a Catholic sensibility that believes strongly in original sin. The play's solution to this, however, is Eastern liberation rather than Christian salvation. Catholicism demands that the individual soul earn eternal joy by good works in this fallen world, but Lazarus answers human evil by transcending it, reaching a realm where conventional conceptions of time and morality become irrelevant. Growing younger during the play and terming age and time "timidities of thought" (p. 354), he contradicts our standard notions of chronology. His other liberation, from morality, corresponds to both Nietzschean and Oriental thought. Zarathustra urges man to create his own moral code; Eastern mystical religions propose that conventional morality (even *karma* itself) no longer applies to the liberated soul. Following both sources, Lazarus disregards the usual distinctions between good and evil. "You are so proud of being evil," he counsels Caligula. "What if there is no evil? What if there is only health and sickness?" (p. 359) Consistent with this, the protagonist rarely renders moral judgments. While occasionally displaying disgust at man's viciousness and ignorance, he generally accepts whatever happens to himself, his followers and his loved ones with indifference. He does not mourn his parents' death, for example, nor blame Pompeia for her murder of Miriam. Moreover, Lazarus never judges his *own* actions, which are evil and destructive from a conventional moral perspective. The frenzy provoked by his gospel, after all, almost always precipitates the deaths of countless people. But we are not invited to judge Lazarus in traditional moral terms. First, if we accept his radical rejection of identity, the pain and deaths he causes are inconsequential. Indeed, morality itself becomes irrelevant, the product of a race of beings who take their actions too seriously because they assume their illusory "selves" to be real. Second and more important, moral definitions no longer apply to one who has passed beyond egohood. This is precisely where the play again breaks with Nietzsche. The superman has not transcended identity. Rather, his personal moral code affirms his unique self in opposition to society. Lazarus, though, preaches "that ultimate attainment in which all prepossession with self is lost" (p. 318), and morality disappears along with the ego.

In *The Fountain*, Juan did not transcend morality, and achieved liberation only at the price of his life. But his epiphany in the wilderness shares with *Lazarus* one fundamental feature, the Taoist reconciliation of opposites. More than any O'Neill play of this period, *Lazarus Laughed* perceives a dynamic unity binding together the opposing terms of apparent dualities. As in *The Great God Brown*, Jung's impact causes O'Neill to perceive character relationships as complementary opposition. Dynamic polarity, however, goes beyond the characterization to determine the play's structure and themes. The result is a work that alternates male and female, ecstasy and suffering, comedy and tragedy, and life and death, in a manner best understood from a Taoist point of view.

In the third act, Lazarus arrives at a Roman banquet and witnesses a grotesque reflection of the play's governing principle. Reclining on couches are forty-two masked young men and women, but *"there is a distinctive character to the masks of each sex, the stamp of an effeminate corruption on the male, while the female have a bold, masculine expression."* The lengthy stage direction then describes the feminine costumes, jewelry, wigs and voices of the young men, and the correspondingly masculine attire and manner of the young women. *"The whole effect,"* it concludes, *"is of sex corrupted and warped, of invented lusts and artificial vices"* (p. 336). Ostensibly, this group exemplifies the decadence of a Roman civilization that worships death. But O'Neill also offers here a distorted image of the interpenetration of sexual opposites. The immediate source for this, Jung, emphasizes the need to integrate male and female aspects within each psyche. In this particular instance, true integration is not achieved, only its warped semblance—as is appropriate in a play that discovers everywhere a grotesque imitation of existence, with true life residing only in the protagonist. The relationships of Lazarus with Miriam and Caligula, however, exhibit a deeper, more complex intermingling of opposites. In them we discover, beneath apparent contrasts, secret unities which testify to the dynamic oneness of reality which Lazarus preaches.

The opposition between the personalities of Lazarus and Miriam would seem to be polaristic and unresolvable. He experiences such joy that he actually grows younger; she dwells so on the death of her children and of Lazarus that she ages incredibly during the few months of Lazarus's second life. Just before her death, the thirty-five year old Miriam, "*in black, her hair almost white now, her figure bowed and feeble, seems more than ever a figure of a sad, resigned mother of the dead*" (p. 327). Her consistently black mourning garb contrasts throughout with the white robes of Lazarus. Finally, her loving attachment to others causes her grief over the death of Lazarus's family and followers, in marked contrast to his own serene detachment. Some subtle connections between the two, however, point to their rhythmic unity. Miriam's affliction by life's sorrows represents the former Lazarus, who wished for death's peace because "his life had been one long misfortune" (p. 276). Lazarus's past has thus become Miriam's present and future. More important, both drive directly toward death and accept it willingly, though Miriam does so by aging and Lazarus by growing so young that (as Miriam declares) "I felt new birth-pains as your laughter, grown too young for me, flew back to the unborn—a birth so like a death" (p. 345). Miriam's words suggest that the contrary processes the two experience, which ostensibly drive them apart, symbolically unite them. Lazarus prepares to re-enter eternity through Miriam's paradoxical "birth-pains," pains that immediately precede her own death. The peculiar rhythm of their relationship corresponds exactly to the *yin* and *yang* cycles of the Tao, which likewise seem contrary but are actually one. Moreover, the interpenetration of life and death in their relationship reinforces Lazarus's message: life and death cannot ultimately be distinguished because death (as we conceive it) does not exist.

The other major relationship, between Lazarus and Caligula, is also one of complementary polarity. Again, their opposition at first appears irreconcilable. If Lazarus fears no one and nothing, Caligula "must fear everyone," he admits, because of the precarious nature of power in ancient Rome (p. 301). If Lazarus radiates the serene beauty of one at peace, Caligula embodies the grotesque ugliness of one devastated by inner conflict. His malformed body, his prematurely wrinkled forehead and bulbous nose, his anemic complexion and ape-like legs together manifest the severe discord inside a man who both fears and loves death. He identifies with death, ordering his soldiers to "kill those who deny death! I will be Death!" (p. 319); but this perverse love stems from the terror of one who (as Lazarus perceives) "loves to kill because he fears to die"

(p. 308). Caligula's personality, in fact, radically expresses the inner tension besetting everyone but Lazarus. That conflict is founded upon the false dualism that views life and death as unalterably opposed: if they were regarded as a cyclical continuum, both the fear of death and the resultant neurotic worship of it would vanish. Hence, the opposition between Lazarus and Caligula ultimately symbolizes the central conflict between the all-embracing, vitalistic monism—with its Eastern roots—of Lazarus's message, and the death-centered dualism—with its traditional Western sources—of the fallen human race.

The victory apparently goes to Caligula (i.e., to dualism), who helps execute Lazarus. But Lazarus is the true victor, because he and Caligula are themselves secretly one, are doubles: the most blatant dualism is actually a unity. The colors associated with them hint at this. Lazarus appears throughout in a robe of white and gold; Caligula squats on a throne of ivory and gold. Caligula possesses boyish features, his curly blond hair "*of a child of six or seven*," his mouth "*childish*" (p. 299). Lazarus, of course, becomes ever more childlike during the play. Caligula's childishness expresses itself negatively in a "*boyish cruelty*" making him "*insensitive to any human suffering but his own*" (p. 299)—but this parallels Lazarus, who (for different reasons) is also indifferent to suffering. Additionally, Caligula's boyishness contains a desire for purity that attracts him to Lazarus. "I would be clean," he tells Lazarus. "If I could only laugh your laughter, Lazarus! That would purify my heart" (p. 358). Indeed, that craving for innocence motivates Caligula in his only honorable actions during the play, his several attempts to save Lazarus from death. He warns him of the dangers awaiting him in Rome, slays Flavius when he thinks Lazarus is in danger, and "*screams despairingly*" during the crucifixion, "Lazarus! I come to save you!" (p. 368).

He fails, however; in fact, he subsequently stabs Lazarus with his spear, proclaiming "I have killed God! I am Lord of Fear! . . . I am Caesar of Death" (pp. 369–70). For Caligula's personality moves here and throughout between his love/fear of death and his love of Lazarus, juxtaposing the intense conflict of the first with the liberation of the second. This personal rhythm in itself suggests a subtle connection to Lazarus, who preaches eternal cosmic rhythms and provokes rhythmic laughter and dancing. Caligula's cycle, moreover, alternates the death and life principles that he and Lazarus respectively represent. When beset by his obsession with killing, he symbolizes death. But when touched by Lazarus (as in the final act), he signifies the eternal life and joyous unity with the universe that awaits even the most depraved and divided of men. At the play's conclusion, Caligula is still vacillating. Moved by Lazarus's final burst of laughter, he shouts with "*a tender, childish laughter of love on his lips, 'I laugh, Lazarus! I laugh with you!'*"—and follows this immediately with remorse over Lazarus's death, pride in killing him, then remorse again (p. 371).

The interpenetration and alternation of life and death, as dramatized in these two major character relationships, constitutes the most significant Taoist contribution to the play. But *Lazarus's* most ubiquitous Taoist feature is its rhythmic vitality, which takes the form of a series of small rhythms wrapped within larger ones. The smallest rhythm is that of laughter, occurring in every scene in the choruses that respond to Lazarus's own infectious outbursts. The laughter is set within three broader rhythmic contexts. The first, dancing, follows the laughter's beat but does not occur as regularly. The second rhythm involves the alternation of laughter and dialogue throughout the play, where most scenes begin in conversation and conclude in ecstatic laughter.[32] The last context juxtaposes laughter with the numerous violent deaths that surround it. In the first act, Lazarus's laughter follows the deaths of his mother and sisters; in act two, Crassus reports the mass suicide of Lazarus's followers, who die laughing in each other's arms; act three witnesses the suicide of Marcellus, Caligula's murder of Flavius, and Miriam's poisoning—concluding with Lazarus's laughter; the final scene follows the suicide of Pompeia and Caligula's murder of Tiberius with the crucifixion of Lazarus, who expires laughing. Each act, in fact, contains enough corpses for a Jacobean tragedy. But

---

32. This rhythm also expresses the cycle between the rational and mystical approaches to life taking place within O'Neill's mind. The traditional Western dramatist in him appears in the dialogic exchanges of the characters, with language exercising its semantic function and providing the logical exposition, rising action and climax of the well-made play. The mystic in O'Neill, on the other hand, finds expression in the liberating laughter; it transcends language, and often leads to repetitious chants and dancing that unite men with each other and with the primordial oneness.

this violent, deadly current alternates with the repeated laughter of Lazarus and his followers, and sometimes the laughter and the deaths even commingle (as in the mass suicide in act two). The shifting tone of the play thus finds O'Neill applying the Taoist polarity principle to one final opposition, this time a generic one between the two traditional modes of Western drama, tragedy and comedy.

O'Neill hardly stands alone in modern drama in writing a tragicomedy—from Chekhov to Stoppard, this mixed mode dominates our stage—but *Lazarus Laughed* is unique in the nature of its blend. Most modern tragicomedy surrounds laughable characters with a bleak void (à la *Waiting for Godot*); *Lazarus Laughed* surrounds pathetic, tormented characters with a meaningful cosmos. And this uniqueness is connected to the play's Oriental sources. Hinduism concurs with Taoism in regarding the "tragedy" of life as a cosmic comedy. Where Western dualism tends to view existence as a contest of opposites concluded by death, Eastern monism pictures the world as a play of contraries.[33] (Thus, the Hindu term *lila*, meaning "play," describes the activities of Brahman in his eternal creation and destruction of the world.) Life only seems tragic to those who see *yin* and *yang* and all they represent—female and male, spiritual and material, non-being and being, life and death— as unalterably and eternally opposed. This describes the situation of the "normal" characters in *Lazarus*, beset by conflict over death because obsessed by their individual egos. As Lazarus admonishes Caligula, "tragic is the plight of the tragedian whose only audience is himself! Life is for each man a solitary cell whose walls are mirrors!" The tragic, dualistic impulse epitomized by Caligula is expressed in the countless deaths, and in the steady sorrow of Miriam. But a comic, monistic impulse resides in the death-defying (because ego-transcending) laughter of Lazarus. "I tell you to laugh in the mirror," he continues to Caligula, "that seeing your life gay, you may begin to live as a guest, and not a condemned one!" (p. 309) The secret lies in recognizing the hidden unity of life and death and of man and universe, in realizing "there is no death." From the cosmic perspective, the apparent opposition vanishes and

33. See Alan Watts, *The Two Hands of God* (New York: Macmillan, 1963), chap. two and passim.

becomes a play of interpenetrating contraries. And this divinely comic attitude is articulated by the protagonist and dramatized by the play, which mingles life and death in its characters and structure. *Lazarus Laughed* represents O'Neill's fullest expression of his mystical nature, so the work's accessibility to Oriental approaches is hardly surprising. Even its primary Western sources lean East. The world-affirming influence of Nietzsche's Zarathustra is heavily modified by Nietzsche's Dionysus, whose absorption of the individual ego demonstrates clear affinities with Brahmanic thought (as the philosopher himself admitted). And the dynamic psychology of Jung is applied in ways that go beyond character relationships, allowing us to glimpse the Taoist metaphysic that shaped Jung's own thought. Contraries—particularly life and death—engage in rhythmical alternation and interpenetration, supporting and refining Lazarus's message that existence is a ceaseless and unified process. The Indian religions contribute in somewhat more overt ways. Buddhism helps explain the contemplative passivity of the protagonist; the Vedantic concepts of *Atman* and *māyā* help explain the masking. Finally, the three mystical religions converge in the depiction of Lazarus's liberation from time, ego and morality, and in the unique tragicomic tone. That ultimately optimistic tone proved as transient and illusory as *māyā*, however, for O'Neill could not sustain his mystical monism for long. His next play, *Strange Interlude*, returns us to a universe where conflict prevails. Only after exhausting struggle do its characters attain peace; and that peace is not blissful, but resigned.

Strange Interlude:
Mother God, Father God, Neuter God

As *Lazarus Laughed* merged Buddha, Christ and Zarathustra into an eclectic Messiah, *Strange Interlude* again blends East and West. In *Lazarus*, however, the protagonist experienced a consistent mystical harmony in the midst of surrounding discord; in *Interlude*, that harmony is largely replaced by conflicts within and between the characters. Furthermore, the force of becoming that Lazarus affirmed so exuberantly becomes cause for despair in *Interlude*, whose characters feel themselves time's victims rather than its celebrants. For Nina Leeds, Charles Marsden and Ned Darrell, life's transience leads repeatedly to pain, confusion and neurosis. Not surprisingly, the, the play contains a stronger Buddhist coloring than did *Lazarus*. Viewing impermanence as the major cause of human sorrow, it proposes detachment from the transitory world as the only salvation.

The playwright doubtless encountered this idea in Coomaraswamy's *Buddha and the Gospel of Buddhism*, but his primary source was Schopenhauer's *The World as Will and Idea*, which he reread before composing the play in 1926. Schopenhauer also accounts for *Interlude*'s assumption that man is the plaything of an irrational, universal Will that finds expression in our sexual desires. Nina, Ned and Marsden struggle through a tragicomic drama in which the Will often fools and frustrates them. Only rarely does a character glimpse the secret unity of existence hidden behind the "veil of Maya"—Schopenhauer's phrase signalling his belief (borrowed from Indian religion) that our rational human values and distinctions are illusions. In *Strange Interlude*, those illusions center on the aggressive prime mover in the action, Nina Leeds. In her sexuality and willfulness, she symbolizes the Will; but her mysterious fascination and the delusions she engenders also associate her with *māyā*, which Buddhists and Vedantists emphasize as the source of our suffering.

This monumental drama, however, is not primarily Eastern. After all, Schopenhauer's emphasis on will and struggle typifies Western thought; and the play revolves around the sexual affair of Nina and Ned, which precipitates tension and inner division in all the major characters but Sam Evans. This psychoanalytical perspective places *Interlude* within the Freudian tradition of so much modern Western literature. Indeed, Freud's theories regarding id and superego dominate a work in which three central characters suffer guilt complexes due to socially prohibited sexual fixations. Only Sam suffers little, but he causes the anguished suffering of Ned and Nina, for he connects symbolically to the ultimate guilt producer, the father god of traditional Western religion.

Nina, however, juxtaposes this judgmental Judeo-Christian god with a mother god of Oriental features. Amoral and mystical, this maternal deity relates to the Taoistic rhythm that structures the life cycles of Ned, Nina and Marsden. Nina's vacillation between father and mother gods is crucial, for it duplicates O'Neill's own conflict between Occidental and Oriental world views. Nina returns to the father god at the conclusion, just as O'Neill gradually moves back toward his Western roots at this point in his career. The male god does not vanquish the female god, but incorporates her into himself, and this ultimately neuter deity symbolizes the uneasy marriage of East and West represented in the vision of *Strange Interlude*.

Three months after completing *Interlude*, O'Neill wrote to Kenneth Macgowan that "life is merely—and perhaps at its highest and holiest!—a game in which the best winning of the greatest winner is in regarding with a self-contempt the pain of his inevitable loss—a game of greater and lesser losers!" [34] The remark nicely captures the play's Oriental focus on life's impermanence, and the consequent wisdom of resignation and detachment. The opening acts, however, treat this theme of loss in a Freudian rather than Eastern manner. Nina suffers remorse over her failure to have sex with Gordon Shaw, her handsome and athletic fiancé, before he flew to his death in World War I. She blames herself and her father, who prevented her marriage to Gordon because of his own paternal possessiveness. Leeds' younger friend Charles Marsden also feels possessive of her, though he retreats guiltily from his underlying erotic motive because of a fear of sex that stems from an Oedipal fixation. Nina attempts to expiate her guilt by nursing crippled veterans at the sanitarium of Ned Darrell, Gordon's friend. There, she has intercourse with many of the wounded, but succeeds only in compounding her guilt and deepening her alienation. Freud would understand: a woman's unfulfilled sexual desires, blocked by the Victorian taboo against premarital sex and by jealous father figures, lead to guilt, promiscuity and self-punishment. Sadly, Nina's obsession with the dead Gordon continues for twenty-five years, as do the sexuality

34. O'Neill letter to Macgowan, 27 Oct. 1927; File Folder Za/O'Neill/to Macgowan, O'Neill Collection, Beinecke Library, Yale Univ.

and guilt his death engendered. Prompted by Ned, she marries Gordon's admirer Sam Evans to produce a child to love, but aborts the baby when informed of the Evans family history of lunacy. Nina then seduces Ned into a sexual affair that produces a healthy boy—named Gordon, of course. Their illicit affair, continuing intermittently for two decades, creates such guilt and anxiety for Ned that it destroys his career as a potentially brilliant neurologist. By the time Sam dies, however, Ned and Nina have purged themselves of sexual desire. Now Nina is ready to marry the waiting Marsden, who (as he says to himself), "passed beyond desire, has all the luck at last." [35]

Such a brief outline makes apparent the centrality of Freudian thought to the characters' struggles. The play's psychological complexity is deepened by its innovative thought asides, which expose a character's inner thoughts and conflicts to the audience as the action freezes. Marsden's sexual timidity, Ned's guilt and anger during his affair, and Nina's continuing obsession with the dead Gordon are all underscored by this device. One character, however, has far fewer asides than the others. While his early thoughts reveal Sam Evans to be plagued by self-doubt and guilt over personal and professional failure, his asides diminish drastically after young Gordon's birth. Sam becomes so secure, happy and prosperous that he virtually lacks inner conflict. His success also symbolizes the victory of the traditional Christian moral code—which dictates sacrifice, and the preservation of a marriage at all costs—over the needs of Ned and Nina. Refusing to reveal their affair to Sam and/or demand divorce, the lovers sacrifice their happiness and honor the code, which is associated with the dead Gordon. It was the "honorable code-bound Gordon" who refused premarital sex with Nina, causing her initial neurosis (p. 19); later, she remains with Sam (whom she does not love) because it would be dishonorable to leave him. She thinks, "Oh, Gordon, I'm afraid this is a deeper point of honor than any that was ever shot down in flames! . . . what would your honor say now? . . . 'stick to him! . . . play the game!'" (p. 71). After conceiving Ned's child, she again wants to leave Sam—but now Ned protects Sam by retreating to Europe, thinking

"that does it! . . . honorably! . . . I'm free!" (p. 106). That same
sense of honor inevitably extends into the next generation. Young
Gordon is also shielded from the truth, and adheres firmly to the
code himself. When he finally intuits that Nina loves Darrell, he
thinks admiringly that "she gave up her own happiness for his sake
. . . that was playing the game" (p. 189). The fact that Sam has
"madness" in his blood rationalizes Ned's and Nina's protection of
him, but it also offers O'Neill's ironic commentary on the insanity
of their obedience to an obsolete religious code that conflicts with
legitimate human needs.

Associated with traditional Christian morality, the character of
Sam also relates to two Christian philosophical assumptions. First,
unlike the others, Sam's movement through time is strictly linear.
"*Evans is simply Evans*," O'Neill notes about his final appearance,
"*his type logically developed by ten years of continued success and
accumulating wealth, jovial and simple and good-natured as ever,
but increasingly stubborn and self-opinionated*" (p. 159). He thus
ages in a fashion that duplicates the Western assumption that time
moves forward, a belief deriving from the Christian concept of a
God directing humanity toward the Last Judgment. The deity who
will judge us then is paternal, the second Christian belief that relates to Sam. Sam discovers his true identity in fatherhood. Until he
becomes a father (bogus though that paternity may be), he remains
unsure of himself and obedient to others. Indeed, his early mistaken
belief that he cannot impregnate Nina precipitates his emotional
distraction and professional failure. But following Gordon's birth,
"*there is a startling change in Evans. He is stouter, the haggard look
of worry and self-conscious inferiority has gone from his face, it is
full and healthy and satisfied. . . . He has matured, found his place
in the world*" (p. 111). Like the male deity of Christian theology,
Sam's significance reveals itself through the creation of a son, in
his own image. Possessed of "*a strength wholly material in quality*," educated to play the game, young Gordon develops into "*an
unimaginative code-bound gentleman*," who is "*too thoroughly
trained to progress along a certain groove to success ever to question it or be dissatisfied with its rewards*" (p. 184).

The guilt which their betrayal of Sam causes Nina and Ned further identifies Sam with the Christian God. The Ten Command-

ments lie behind the moral code that provokes their anguish, and retributive Old Testament morality characterizes the father god Nina broods about. When she encounters Ned in act eight, she thinks "our account with God the Father is settled . . . afternoons of happiness paid for with years of pain" (p. 165). Nina's sporadic search for judgment and forgiveness leads recurrently to her father-substitute, Marsden. In act two, full of guilt over her promiscuity, she crawls onto his lap and pleads for punishment because "now Father dead [sic], there's only you. You will, won't you—or tell me how to punish myself?" (p. 44) Twenty-five years later, addressing Marsden as "Father," she confesses her affair with Ned. She receives his forgiveness, and curiously forgives him in return, claiming "it was all your fault in the beginning, wasn't it? You mustn't ever meddle with human lives again!" (p. 180) The accusation refers specifically to Marsden's past support of Ned's plan to marry Nina to Sam; but it alludes broadly to Nina's conception of the father god as an interfering figure. Originating in her father's postponement of her marriage to Gordon, this notion receives its most dramatic expression when Nina is pregnant with Gordon and surrounded by her three adoring men. She suppresses "*an outbreak of hysterical triumphant laughter*" and literally knocks wood "before God the Father hears my happiness" (p. 135). Nina had earlier complained to Marsden about the male God "whose chest thunders with egotism and is too hard for tired heads and thoroughly comfortless" (p. 43); in the concluding act, she still imagines this distant god laughing contemptuously at their pathetic human antics (pp. 181, 194).

Connected to guilt and sexual repression, this Puritanical father god seems antagonistic to human needs. As she watches young Gordon fly off at the conclusion, Nina laments, "the Sons of the Father have all been failures! Failing they died for us, they flew away to other lives. They could not stay with us, they could not give us happiness!" (p. 199) Another line, deleted in the published version, appears in the *Strange Interlude* manuscript notes immediately following: "it is time a Daughter of God the Mother came on earth to try to save us."[36] This wish alludes to Nina's imaginary mother god,

36. *Strange Interlude* scenario and manuscript notes, File Folder Za/O'Neill/53x, O'Neill Collection, Beinecke Library, Yale Univ.

who compensates for the father's deficiencies. In contrast to the father's Western features, the mother displays Oriental characteristics. Under her mystical influence Nina feels beyond moral codes, and calmly proposes to Ned that he remain her lover while Sam remain her husband. While the father god is distant, the mother god (like Brahman) is immanent; Nina's strongest intuitions of her come while carrying a child in act five, when she explicitly compares her motherhood to that of God the Mother (pp. 91–2, 111). Like the Tao, this maternal deity is associated with a rhythm, symbolized here by the sea. As the pregnant Nina peacefully muses, "I am living a dream within the great dream of the tide . . . breathing in the tide I dream and breathe back my dream into the tide . . . no whys matter . . . there is no why . . . I am a mother . . . God is a mother" (92).[37] The speech's mystical sense of unreality and its passive acceptance of life correspond to Oriental thought, as does another line which intuits life's serene unity. "The world is whole and perfect," thinks Nina, "all things are each other's" (p. 91).

The maternal deity's most significant aspect is her association with rhythm, for cycles are ubiquitous in *Interlude*'s characters and relationships. The Ned and Nina affair, for instance, alternates for eleven years between passionate reunions and growing bitterness leading to separation. Similar cycles characterize individual lives. In act eight, Ned *"seems to have 'thrown back' to the young doctor"* of act two, with *"the air of the cool detached scientist"*; Marsden, mourning his deceased sister, is *"an older image of the Marsden of Act Five,"* who was mourning his mother (p. 159). Marsden's manner in act seven is compared to act one, while his paternal stance toward Nina at the conclusion recalls act two. Thus, Nina addresses Marsden as "Father" in her last speeches, declaring that she feels "as if I were a girl again" (p. 199)—thereby throwing *her* back to the time before Gordon Shaw's appearance initiated all the confusion.[38] And during the subsequent "strange interlude" represented by her obsession with Gordon Shaw, Nina's mind alternates

37. The water imagery recalls O'Neill's sea plays, especially *"Anna Christie,"* where the rhythmic sea is itself a god.
38. Note the resemblance to Mary Tyrone here, who at *Long Day's Journey*'s conclusion wants to return to her convent days, before she met Tyrone. Obviously, O'Neill's mother is a source for Nina as well as for Mary.

between father and mother gods. Worshipping her father as a girl, Nina presumably worshipped the father god as well. But as a disillusioned young woman, she invents a mother god that captures her imagination when she herself becomes a mother. The father god returns in acts eight and nine; Nina's final speech sees our lives as "merely strange interludes in the electrical displays of God the Father!" (p. 199) Ostensibly, the father god triumphs as Nina prepares to settle down with Marsden, a father figure.

Closer examination, however, reveals that this male deity has absorbed its female opposite. First, its "electrical displays" point to a rhythm of "cosmic positive and negative electric charges" (mentioned by Ned earlier) that inform existence—and rhythm characterizes the mother god, not the father. Second, Marsden himself represents mother as well as father. Nina will wed him because he offers the peace she earlier imagined in the mother god. His Oedipal fixation and *"indefinable feminine quality"* further counterbalance his fatherly role (p. 4). On first meeting Marsden, Ned sees him as "one of those poor devils who spend their lives trying not to discover which sex they belong to" (p. 34); O'Neill's manuscript notes concur, stipulating "in reality, [Marsden] is bisexual." [39] Thus, Marsden's personality merges male and female forces, like the neuter Tao that combines masculine *yang* and feminine *yin* principles.

If Marsden's bisexual personality allies him to Oriental metaphysics, so too does Nina's. Though apparently the essence of womanhood, even the eternal feminine (as critics have suggested), her *"broad square shoulders"* and *"handsome rather than pretty"* face are typically masculine (p. 12). Beyond this physical ambivalence, her life rhythms suggest affinities with the Tao. Vigorous activity (*yang*) and stillness (*yin*) are the two poles of the cyclical Tao, and Nina's life alternates between them. Acts one and two find her involved in the neurotic agonies of existence, at first nerve-wracked, later frantically promiscuous; act three describes *"an inner calm about her,"* quickly shattered after she discovers she must abort Sam's child (p. 48). Her act four movements *"are those of extreme nervous tension"* again before her seduction of Ned (p. 68). But her

39. "Notebook," 1925–26, File Folder Za/O'Neill/82a, O'Neill Collection, Beinecke Library, Yale Univ.

pregnancy makes her "*nerveless and deeply calm*" once more in the following act (p. 90). Her behaviour in act six mingles calm with exultation over Ned's return from Europe; in acts seven and eight, eleven and twenty years later, she is overwrought again; the final act finds her full of the peace of resignation.

Nina's cyclical movement also parallels that described in another Eastern system. Alternating between agitated participation in life's struggles and serene withdrawal from them, Nina duplicates Brahman's engagement and disengagement from the phenomenal world. A key thought aside of Nina's points up further similarities between her and Brahman. In a celebrated scene, Nina surrounds herself with Ned, Sam and Marsden, and thinks: "My three men! . . . I feel their desires converge in me! . . . to form one complete beautiful male desire which I absorb . . . and am whole . . . They dissolve in me, their life is my life . . . I am pregnant with the three! . . . husband! . . . lover! . . . father! . . . and the fourth man! . . . little man! . . . little Gordon! . . . he is mine too! . . . that makes it perfect!" (p. 135). Obviously, the speech relates Nina to various earth mother myths; less obviously, it connects her to the ultimate reality pictured by Vedantic Hinduism. Nina's overwhelming embrace obliterates normal role distinctions (husband, father, lover, son), as personal differences become meaningless during the merger into "one complete beautiful male desire." Dissolving individual identities—Marsden feels his life "queerly identified with Sam's and Darrell's" at this point (p. 135)—Nina declares her wholeness and (implicitly) that of these men who identify with her: "their life is my life." The absorption of personalities into a profound matrix recalls "*Anna Christie*," where the sea symbolically swallowed up the major characters without regard to their differences. Here, under Freud's influence, this act assumes explicit sexual coloring. But behind both plays lurks Brahman, to whom the unique self means nothing. Even Gordon Shaw, the ghost who controls Nina's destiny, means nothing to her at this visionary moment. As O'Neill's manuscript notes on this scene declare, "Gordon is forgotten as individual," because he too has been absorbed into the spiritual unity contained within Nina.[40]

40. *Strange Interlude* scenario and manuscript notes, File Folder Za/O'Neill/53x, O'Neill Collection, Beinecke Library, Yale Univ.

Hinduism makes clear, however, that Brahman manifests itself as *māyā*, a magic spell that obscures this universal oneness. For most of the play, Nina operates in this beguiling state. Her fascination is particularly apparent in the scene just discussed, where Marsden and Ned obey Nina and remain with her, despite their jealousy of each other and Sam. Nina's spellbinding nature is also dramatized in *"the strange fascination of her face,"* especially her *"unchangeably mysterious eyes"* (p. 48); the perceptive Marsden recognizes "her power to enslave men's senses," a key feature of *māyā* (p. 74). Also like *māyā*, the mysterious Nina is not what she appears to be, and assumes a series of delusive masks. Between acts one and two, under the pretense of loving the wounded soldiers, she tries to assuage her guilt for her chastity with Gordon. In act three, she pretends to love Sam, but really uses him to get her baby; in acts four and five, she first seduces Ned in order to provide that baby, then lures him into remaining with her. Sam suffers early and briefly from Nina's games, while Ned suffers later and longer as a consequence of their illicit affair. By act eight, twenty years later, he feels beyond her spell, but even then, she almost manages to enchant him into preventing her son's marriage by informing Sam of Gordon's true paternity. As *māyā*, then, Nina fools people and makes them suffer. Her chief victims, common-sensible Sam and rational Ned, are ill-equipped to penetrate her disguises. Only the intuitive Marsden—the most "Eastern" character in the play, as we shall see—possesses consistent insight into her behavior. And even he cannot resist the enticements of "the Nina I could never fathom," the Nina who herself has "strange devious intuitions that tap the hidden currents of life" (pp. 134–35).

Nina's personality does not represent *Strange Interlude*'s only correspondence with *māyā*. Another compelling illusion operates in the dialogue. The spoken word often conceals true feelings, as comparison between speeches and thought asides at any point in the play makes instantly clear. O'Neill, however, probes deeper than this. "How we poor monkeys hide from ourselves behind the sounds called words," laments Nina (p. 40), suggesting that language functions also as a tool of self-deception. Nina understands this when she cannot feel grief at her father's death: "I've suddenly seen the lies in the sounds called words. You know—grief, sorrow, love, father—those sounds our lips make and our hands write" (p. 40). By helping conventionalize our responses, language misrepresents our emotions to us. From this point of view, the thought asides are just as suspect as the speeches, for their words inevitably distort our inner reality and fail to grasp our lives' unifying, subconscious flow. In this they correspond to *māyā*, breaking down the unity of experience into the infinity of fragments that we take as reality. Indeed, the interconnections most basic to the play—between sex, birth, growth and death—cannot be adequately apprehended by language or by reason. The "extravagant and fantastic" things that happen to the characters, experiences they never anticipate or comprehend, testify to the *māyā*-like nature of existence itself—a "strange interlude in which we call on past and future to bear witness we are living," Nina muses (p. 165). By the conclusion, the three major characters agree on this. Nina refers twice to their "strange interlude"; Ned, reflecting on the events that gave him a mistress and son, reveals that "I can't think of these things as real anymore" (p. 165); Marsden tells Nina that "there was something unreal in all that has happened since you first met Gordon Shaw" (p. 199).

Buddhism also views life as *māyā*, and seeks happiness in the timeless void of Nirvana. Throughout *Strange Interlude*, one character unconsciously engages in a similar quest. Charlie Marsden suffers along with Ned and Nina from life's impermanence. But the lovers' anguish derives from the ebb and flow of their passions, while Marsden's pain stems from the loss of a beloved friend, mother and sister. Largely divorced from desire, and connected to death for much of the play—dressed in mourning in acts two, five, eight and nine—Marsden's lack of possessiveness and non-egoism identify him as the key to the play's Buddhist themes.

As mentioned earlier, much of *Interlude*'s Orientalism results from Schopenhauer's influence. Ned and Nina appear as the major carriers of the Will, the transcendent force that attaches us to life through our sexual instincts. Both are passionate beings: Nina regrets her chastity with Gordon Shaw and has a stormy affair with Ned, whom O'Neill's notes describe as one who "exudes sexuality and appeals strongly to all sensual women."[41] Ned's repeated seductions by Nina find him struggling against her stronger will and inevitably losing, because her desires accord with Schopenhauer's Will, being directed toward procreation—and as a rationalist, Ned is helpless against this force. Their sexual combat also reflects Schopenhauer's Western bias, since it embodies his vision of the world as a conflictive place where "the will to live everywhere preys upon itself."[42] Even Marsden, with his submerged sexual attraction to Nina, participates indirectly in this struggle. His personality, however, aligns more with the Buddhist aspects of Schopenhauer's philosophy. Unlike the lovers, Marsden maintains distance from the Will due to his fear of sex. Nina thinks of him as someone who "sits beside the fierce river, immaculately timid, cool and clothed, watching the burning, frozen naked swimmers drown at last" (p. 13). The river is life's flow, with the "burning" swimmers heated by the fires of desire that Buddha counsels man to extinguish. Marsden subsequently reveals that his fear of sex signifies this larger existential detachment when he admits to Nina that "I'm afraid of—of life" (p. 42). This alienation (despite its neurotic motivation) reproduces the response proposed by both Schopenhauer and Buddhism to the desires that cause human suffering. For men desire to grasp things that cannot be possessed, due to the law of becoming (*dukkha*) that rules existence. Our lives, relationships, and personalities are constantly in flux, dooming our desires to frustration. Nina holds on to Gordon's image, and later to Ned, with unhappy consequences. Ned cannot separate from Nina, despite the misery that inevitably follows interludes of happiness, and Marsden is overwhelmed by life's transience when he loses his mother and sister.

But Charlie Marsden is less possessive than the others. O'Neill's manuscript notes reveal Professor Leeds' wish for Nina to marry Marsden because he is "safe—sure—not possessive."[43] In the pub-

41. "Notebook," 1925–26, File Folder Za/O'Neill/82a, O'Neill Collection, Beinecke Library, Yale Univ.

42. Schopenhauer, *World as Will and Idea*, 1: 191. Also see Alexander, "*Strange Interlude* and Schopenhauer," *American Literature*, 25 (May 1953): 213–28; William Brashear, "O'Neill's Schopenhauer Interlude," *Criticism*, 6 (Summer 1964): 256–65; and Brashear, *The Gorgon's Head* (Athens: Univ. of Georgia Pr., 1977), pp. 88–103.

43. *Strange Interlude* scenario and manuscript notes, File Folder Za/O'Neill/53x, O'Neill Collection, Beinecke Library, Yale Univ.

lished version, Marsden responds to Leeds' confessed desire to hold
on to Nina by thinking, "forgive us our possessing as we forgive
those who possessed before us" (p. 21). Thus, Marsden does not
attempt to grasp life to the same degree as the passionate Ned and
Nina, or even the materialistic Sam. Consistently passive, he never
initiates action, but only responds to it: at the end, Nina proposes
marriage to him, not vice-versa. In his submissive non-possessive-
ness, Marsden represents the proper "lover" for Nina in the evening
of their years. Now "passed beyond desire" altogether, he can help
liberate Nina from her grasping of others. Her possessiveness of
Gordon Shaw, Ned, and young Gordon has always led to pain
as they died, changed, or grew—that is, as they demonstrated
the tragic impermanence of human life that is Buddhism's major
concern.

Marsden's goals and preoccupations also accord with Buddhism,
while those of the others do not. Sam attains happiness through
worldly success and his son; Ned and Nina frantically seek happiness through possession of each other. "I shall be happy for a
while," Ned thinks in their love scene, and Nina's thoughts concur,
"I shall be happy!" (p. 89). Only twelve years later does Nina briefly
muse, "I want to rot away in peace! . . . I'm sick of the fight for
happiness" (p. 138). When her mind turns this way permanently
after act eight, she becomes an appropriate match for Marsden,
who seeks peace rather than joy. His emotional life vacillates between his grief over the deaths of loved ones, and the contentment
of a detached man "living in comparative peace with himself and
his environment" (p. 146), his state in acts one, seven and nine. Admittedly, that peace does not duplicate Buddha's bliss: again, the
play's bias toward Schopenhauer's pessimism is revealed. But Marsden's contented withdrawal from life more closely resembles Oriental serenity than the American pursuit of happiness through possessiveness and passion. When Nina tells herself in act nine, "peace!
. . . yes . . . that is all I desire . . . I can no longer imagine happiness," she looks toward Marsden "with a strange yearning" because "Charlie has found peace" (p. 197). Her turn completes
the shift toward Eastern renunciation she unconsciously initiated
twelve years before.

As noted, the other pole of Marsden's life rhythm involves his grief over deaths. His association with death signifies his most intriguing correspondence to Buddhist thought. Nina thinks of Marsden in morbid terms in act five, when he appears dressed in mourning: "Black . . . in the midst of happiness . . . black comes . . . again . . . death . . . my father . . . comes between me and happiness" (p. 98). This connects Marsden to the meddlesome Western father god, but (as discussed earlier) his deeper affinities lie with the Eastern maternal deity. That mother god—like Buddha—identifies death with peace, because death means loss of self. Nina muses that death would mean "passing back into Her substance," and finding "peace of Her peace" (p. 43). Marsden himself cannot accept death until late in the play, but by enduring so many losses, he finally reconciles the two poles of his own peculiar life rhythm. Merging peace with death, he escapes the former cycles of his existence—another Buddhist aim. In the final act, Marsden is dressed in mourning once again (for Sam), but "*looks younger, calm and contented.*" He has reached "late afternoons in love with evening," in which there "comes no scorching zenith sun of passion and possession" (p. 187). Similarly scorning passion, the ascetic Buddha had no fear of death, which he viewed as an opportunity to experience Nirvana. Marsden looks forward to a similar annihilation, though he wants (paradoxically) to share the process with Nina. "Will you let me rot away in peace?," she asks, to which he replies, "all my life I've wanted to bring you peace" (p. 197). He views their lives as purgatorial preparation for purification and obliteration. an interlude "in which our souls have been scraped clean of impure flesh and made worthy to bleach in peace" (p. 199). This sounds more Christian than Buddhist, but earlier in the play, Marsden had thought (with typical self-contempt) that he and Sam Evans were moving "towards the same nowhere! . . . worse! . . . I'm not even going! . . . I'm there!" (p. 123). At the conclusion, he dimly intuits that the "nowhere" he describes resides within us, and that in that void lies hope for peace.

This thought is not uncommon in O'Neill's work. We recall Lazarus's egolessness, Larry Slade's yearning for death, and Edmund Tyrone's ecstatic immersions in the sea. No other O'Neill play, however, contains a figure quite like Marsden—effete, bisexual, detached and transcendent. His ultimate triumph points to the emergence of an Oriental world view at the conclusion. All three major characters agree on life's unreality, its *māyā*, and have transcended the desires that tormented them. Free from the cycles that have ruled their lives, they ease comfortably into an old age where the ego's demands count little. Ned's last lines ask God to "teach me to be resigned to be an atom," and death appeals to Marsden for the peaceful annihilation it will bring (p. 199). Moreover, the God they now serve is essentially neuter, and associated with the rhythms of their lives. Despite the strong Eastern finish, however, *Strange Interlude* is more in the Western tradition than its predecessor *Lazarus Laughed*. The internal and external struggles of its three major figures revolve around psychological conflict and sexual frustration. More important, the philosopher who prompted many of *Interlude*'s Oriental intuitions, Schopenhauer, pictures God as a Will that opposes man's happiness—a prevalent modern Western assumption. Schopenhauer's belief that the world is *māyā*, and his renunciation ethic, obviously ally him (and *Interlude*) with Oriental thought. But his solution involves divorcing oneself from the cosmic ruling principle, the Will, to find peace. This causes the fatalistic resignation of *Interlude*'s last act, where the pursuit of happiness is sacrificed in order to achieve contentment. In Oriental mysticism, however, happiness and peace both reside in the serenity that lies at the center of the cosmos. Obviously, the play's characters never achieve this bliss; and O'Neill's own inability to maintain contentment identifies him and this play as tragically typical of our modern Occidental world.

Dynamo: Repudiation and Retreat

Among O'Neill's plays, only *Lazarus Laughed* and *Days Without End* match *Dynamo* for overt religious purpose. The latter two plays were originally intended as part of a trilogy which (O'Neill proclaimed) would "dig at the roots of the sickness of today as I feel it—the death of an old God and the failure of science and materialism to give any satisfying new one for the surviving primitive religious instinct to find a meaning for life in, and to comfort its fears of death with."[44] Betrayed by his parents, *Dynamo*'s Reuben Light repudiates their Puritanical god and turns to the worship of electrical generators—the god of electricity introduced in *Interlude*'s final act. He seeks forgiveness from that deity after his desertion of his family contributes to his mother's early death. Identifying the dynamo with his jealous, possessive mother, Reuben feels intense guilt after sexual intercourse with the girl next door, shoots her, then commits suicide by grabbing onto the generator's brushes. He thus achieves union with the scientific deity that (as O'Neill's letter claims) has replaced the old Christian God. Unfortunately, Reuben's fanatical devotion to the dynamo strikes one as more ludicrous than profound. O'Neill's overzealous moralizing about the "sickness of today" prohibits identification with this psychotic protagonist, thereby defeating the playwright's declared purpose.

Despite its glaring flaws, *Dynamo* is an interesting companion piece to *Strange Interlude*, for its mother and father gods engage in a conflict similar to that found in the earlier play. In *Dynamo*, however, the mother god associated with Oriental religion catalyzes the catastrophe, and its worshippers are pictured as fools. Overtly, O'Neill claims to repudiate the modern Western god of science; covertly, he discredits the Eastern mysticism that had played a substantial, positive role in the preceding three plays. *Dynamo* also completes the larger swing in O'Neill's career back to Western sources and themes. Focusing on the guilt caused by parental conflict within the protagonist, the play presents a battle of wills culminating in psychic disintegration; this dissection of a personality constitutes the play's central (and very Western) concern. As the playwright insisted to Joseph Wood Krutch while revising the play for publication in 1929, "my intent . . . was psychological primarily, in spite of the published quotes from my letters on the trilogy."[45] The battle between father and mother gods consequently is more important for the light it sheds on Reuben's confusion than for its metaphysical implications, and the play's focus on character overshadows the Eastern elements it contains.

The play's Oriental features are nonetheless intriguing, for they

44. Quoted in Clark, *O'Neill*, p. 120.
45. O'Neill to Joseph Wood Krutch, 11 June 1929; File Folder Za/O'Neill/to Krutch, O'Neill Collection, Beinecke Library, Yale Univ.

point to other plays this chapter has discussed. As in *The Great God Brown*, an overt allusion alerts one to the Orientalism. The dynamo's oil switches, *"with their spindly steel legs, their square, criss-crossed steel bodies (the containers inside looking like bellies), their six cupped arms stretching upward, seem like queer Hindu idols tortured into scientific supplications."* [46] Like *Brown*'s Cybel, the dynamo has *"something of a massive female idol about it"* (p. 473). And as *Interlude*'s mother god was associated with O'Neill's beloved sea, so is this. "It's the sea rising up in clouds, falling on the earth in rain, made the river that drives the turbines that drive Dynamo!" Reuben exclaims (p. 477). Part of this god's appeal for Reuben lies in its *"hypnotic metallic purr"* that makes the heart *"strain with the desire to beat in its rhythm of unbroken, eternal continuity"* (p. 486). Similar to Lazarus, then, Reuben worships a god of process, and a bipolar process in particular—the ceaseless reaction between the positive and negative charges of the atom. Engaging opposite charges in an eternal rhythm that provides the energy behind the universe, the Great God Electricity corresponds to the Tao that unites *yin* and *yang*.

This dynamic force contains other oppositions as well. The creator of infinite energy, it can be awesomely destructive. It not only vanquishes old beliefs—"we have electrocuted your God," Reuben's blasphemous postcards to his parents announce (p. 456)—but claims two individual lives, and devours Reuben's identity as his dying cry *"merges and is lost in the dynamo's hum"* (p. 488). It also blurs the distinctions between good and evil. Fife refers to it as Lucifer, Reverend Light calls it "the devil," even Reuben compares it to "a devil fish" (pp. 481, 484); yet Reuben seeks security and forgiveness from it, and believes the waters that drive it are "washing all dirt and sin away! Like some one singing me to sleep—my mother—when I was a kid" (p. 476). While the maternal predominates in this deity, the dynamo also reproduces the father god worshipped by Reuben's father. Reverend Light's Puritan deity is wrathful, associated with the thunder and lightning that terrorize both father and son; the dynamo's anger frightens Reuben, and he seeks desperately to appease it after having sex with Ada. That sexual en-

---

46. *Plays*, 3: 483. Hereafter documented in the text.

counter illuminates another connection. Reuben's fundamentalist
father believes "the spirit decays in the sinful sloth of the flesh"
(p. 425), and Reuben incorporates this assumption into his jealous
dynamo god, which demands chastity. But this insistence on purity
derives also from the imagined jealousy of Reuben's dead mother.
Thus, the mother god becomes imbued with the judgmental, guilt-
inducing quality that O'Neill had largely limited to the father god
in previous plays.

Despite this Eastern mingling of opposites, *Dynamo* hardly regards this electrical god as a legitimate object of devotion. Driven
to it by psychosis, Reuben finds only death. Its other worshipper,
Mrs. Fife, resembles (as her husband observes) a jellyfish in her
obliviousness. She yearns for the condition of animals who "forget
to think they're living . . . they're just alive," and her "*moony
dreaminess is more pronounced*" when in the dynamo's presence
(pp. 454, 476). Through her, the play satirizes not only the worship
of science, but that obliteration of normal consciousness which
constitutes the mystical approach toward God. Her final lines and
actions (which conclude the play) expose the puerility of her mind-
less devotion. When she realizes Reuben is dead, she "*turns with
childish bewildered resentment and hurt to the dynamo*," and cries,
"I should think you'd be ashamed! And I thought you was nice and
loved us!" She then "*pounds the steel body of the generator in a fit
of childish anger*" and moans, "You hateful old thing, you," as she
begins to cry (p. 489).

Dynamo thus associates the mystical god of bipolar process with
psychosis, suicide and imbecility, discrediting it as an alternative for
Western (or any) man. O'Neill's ostensible object of attack may be
modern science and its failure to give meaning to life, but the science god's Eastern attributes place Oriental mysticism under the
same condemnation. Obviously, O'Neill no longer romanticized
Oriental faiths as alternatives to the guilt-evoking Puritan—and
Catholic—father god. Perhaps this explains the incorporation of
the father god's judgmental quality into Reuben's mother god. In
Strange Interlude, God the Mother offered Nina release from the
pain and guilt associated with God the Father; in *Dynamo*, Reuben's temporary relief is followed by a deepening of his madness
and an intensification of his guilt. If Reuben represents (in a dis-

torted fashion) O'Neill's own psyche, the play signals the play-wright's admission that his own father god was also inescapable. For all his efforts (especially in *Lazarus Laughed*) to embrace monistic Eastern thought, he could not escape the moralistic, dualistic tradition in which he was raised. The very presence of an Oriental mother god makes clear O'Neill's wish to believe (like Reuben) that tragic struggle might be transcended through discovery of a dynamic force that unites good and evil, male and female, life and death. When that god failed both protagonist and playwright, however, O'Neill's mystical side retreated from his drama for the next ten years.

If *Dynamo* did not purge O'Neill of his Eastern inclinations, the trip to China that followed its completion succeeded in doing so. He wrote Lawrence Langner in 1928 of his hopes to temporarily reside in the Orient with Carlotta: "where we'll settle there, whether we'll decide to remain there for any length of time—(we hope to)—all depends on conditions."[47] Conditions proved unfavorable. In Saigon in November, he lost money gambling, was scolded by Carlotta, and caught the flu. Before he had recovered, he began drinking again in Shanghai (further alienating Carlotta), and spent ten days in an English hospital there "teetering on the edge of a nervous breakdown" (as he later wrote Krutch).[48] His problems were compounded when he was discovered by reporters, causing him and Carlotta (with whom his affair was still clandestine) to leave Shanghai for Manila sooner than planned. There and in Singapore he resumed drinking, damaging relations with Carlotta even more. In Ceylon on the first day of 1929, she departed, leaving him alone on the cruise ship threatening to drink himself to death. She caught the next boat out and they reunited in Port Said, however, continuing together to their new home in France. Their relationship, then, survived; the mysterious East of his imagination did not. Describing O'Neill's unhappy December in the Orient, Louis Sheaffer speculates on one major cause of his troubles: "the Orient of reality was not living up to his romantic expectations."[49]

47. O'Neill to Lawrence Langner, undated (ca. 1928); File Folder Za/O'Neill/to Langner, O'Neill Collection, Beinecke Library, Yale Univ.
48. O'Neill to J. W. Krutch, 27 July 1929; quoted in Sheaffer, *Artist*, p. 316.
49. Sheaffer, *Artist*, p. 314.

Certainly, the plays that followed the journey showed little interest in the East. *Mourning Becomes Electra*, written from 1929 to 1931, drew on Greek tragedy for its themes, plot and characters. *Ah, Wilderness!* (1932), O'Neill's idyllic picture of small-town America, represented his first excursion into his personal past in Connecticut. The next play, *Days Without End*, presents a slightly more complicated case. Originally conceived as the second play (after *Dynamo*) in the projected religious trilogy, it employs masks, allying it with works like *The Great God Brown* and *Lazarus Laughed* which displayed varying degrees of Oriental influence. But the autobiographical protagonist, John Loving, explicitly rejects Oriental mysticism as a fancy he has long since outgrown—as the passage which opened chapter one of this study makes clear. The plot's Christian resolution underscores this repudiation. Much like Dion Anthony, "Loving" (a mask worn by one actor) represents the Mephistophelean side of the protagonist; "John" (played by another performer, unmasked) symbolizes his confused and frustrated soul that yearns for grace. When the Loving side attempts to destroy John's wife by revealing to her his current love affair, however, the spirit of Christ intervenes. The wife miraculously recovers from deathly illness as John slays his masked alter ego and heals his divided soul by rediscovering his Catholic faith.

O'Neill's purpose, he told Barrett Clark while composing *Days Without End*, was "to be clearly psychological and mystically clear, too," and he facetiously yearned for "the good old days when I was content to be either simple-minded or foggily mystical." [50] Unfortunately, the laudable desire for clarity resulted in a play that clearly reveals its Christian lesson, but does not seem informed by the complexities of life. *Days Without End*, in fact, misapplied the new aesthetic of simplicity that governed O'Neill's writing since the commercial (and artistic) failure of *Dynamo* in 1929. In that aesthetic lies one final cause, and effect, of the ebbing hold of Eastern mysticism on his imagination. Looking back over his work in 1929, he recognized his over-reliance on expressionistic settings and effects. He wrote Kenneth Macgowan in June of his consequent resolution:

50. O'Neill to J. B. Clark, 15 Nov. 1932; File Folder Za/O'Neill/to Clark, O'Neill Collection, Beinecke Library, Yale Univ.

"my trend will be to regard anything depending on director or scenic designer for collaboration to bring out its full values as suspect . . . Constructivism and such stuff is all right for directors but its [sic] only in an author's way. . . . Greater classical simplicity, austerity combined with the utmost freedom and flexibility, that's the stuff!"[51] A week later, he informed Barrett Clark that "you are a very accurate guesser when you think that my work will be simpler, more compact, and less theatrical. . . . By straining the collaborative possibilities of the theatre I feel I've at last won to what is my own technique, and it now remains for me to simplify and clarify that technique of its abortive growths and exhibitionism."[52] The play that followed these declarations, *Mourning Becomes Electra*, follows this new principle. While ambitious in scope, it contained no new innovative techniques. *Ah, Wilderness!* is equally non-experimental, while *Days Without End*'s only expressionistic device is Loving's mask—far simpler than the elaborate masking schemes of *The Great God Brown* and *Lazarus Laughed*. Finally, the various scenarios and scripts of the Cycle plays, which consumed O'Neill from 1934 to 1939, were all as realistic and traditional in technique as the late tragedies.

By so simplifying his technique, however, O'Neill straitjacketed his mystical tendencies. As we have seen, his Oriental side generally required expressionistic devices to reveal itself: of the eight plays we have considered, only the sea plays fail to experiment with distorted setting, characterization or dialogue. As his idol Strindberg had taught him, "supernaturalistic" techniques were necessary to reveal the ineffable mysteries that lay "behind life." But O'Neill's eventual disillusion with expressionism reinforced his disenchantment with Oriental thought. The playwright now returned to the naturalistic technique with which he began his career nearly twenty years before. By the time he composed *The Iceman Cometh* and *Long Day's Journey Into Night*, however, those naturalistic surfaces had acquired a spiritual depth that reflect the reemergence of Eastern mysticism in his vision.

51. O'Neill to Macgowan, 14 June 1929; File Folder Za/O'Neill/to Macgowan, O'Neill Collection, Beinecke Library, Yale Univ.
52. O'Neill to Clark, 21 June 1929; File Folder Za/O'Neill/to Clark, O'Neill Collection, Beinecke Library, Yale Univ.

6

Journeys Home

Withdrawals and Returns: *The Iceman Cometh* and *Long Day's Journey into Night*

O'Neill had concluded by 1932 that Oriental religion was (in the words of Father Baird in *Days Without End*) "not for the Western soul."[1] Neither *Days Without End* nor *Ah, Wilderness!*, which both explored O'Neill's personal past, considered the significance of Eastern philosophy in his life. For the next seven years, the playwright examined a national history that also paid little attention to Oriental mysticism. His projected multiplay cycle, "A Tale of Possessors Self-Dispossessed," intended to dramatize materialism's role in leading America from its revolutionary beginnings to its current disillusion and depression. O'Neill's emphasis, as the two surviving Cycle plays make apparent, was psychological and social rather than religious. *A Touch of the Poet* portrays the inner conflict of Cornelius Melody, an Irish-American tavern keeper torn between his peasant nature and his Byronic pretensions; a related conflict obtains between the Irish lower classes he represents, and the Yankee aristocracy symbolized by the mother of Simon Harford (whom Melody's daughter Sara wants to marry). *More Stately Mansions* examines the problems of the newly married Sara and Simon, focusing on his ambivalent feelings toward wife and mother, and on the tension between his Utopian idealism and his American materialism. Both works deliberately repress O'Neill's mystical tenden-

1. *Plays*, 1: 503.

cies, which are only faintly echoed in the Thoreauvian nature of Simon. Moreover, their realistic mode eschews the experimental devices common in O'Neill's theatre during the previous decade. Concentrating on secular themes, the two Cycle plays assume conventional, "common sense" attitudes toward personality and reality; as a consequence, O'Neill's Orientalism appears to vanish completely.

That disappearance was only temporary. For by the time O'Neill interrupted his work on the Cycle between 1939 and 1941 to compose two plays based on his personal past, his mystical side had reemerged. *The Iceman Cometh* and *Long Day's Journey Into Night* both feature characters who espouse or display the passive withdrawal from life preached so earnestly by earlier characters like Lazarus. Moreover, O'Neill's treatment of the illusion/reality theme in both works demonstrates his renewed suspicion that worldly existence is inseparable from *māyā*. The aging playwright who once again entertained these Eastern intuitions, however, was now too knowledgeable about himself to expect liberation from them. Absorbed by his own tormented history, he concluded that mystical escape from time and self was indeed "not for the Western soul," as these plays make clear. And the limited happiness available to man, they suggest, lies in following a Christian ethic of forgiveness and compassion which is contrary to the most fundamental teachings of Oriental mystical thought.

The renewed correspondences between O'Neill's vision and Eastern philosophy were partially prompted by the personalities of individuals who furnished models for characters in the two plays. Larry Slade, the leader of the derelicts in *Iceman*, was based on Terry Carlin—a mystic who preached Hindu and Buddhist precepts to O'Neill. Edmund Tyrone in *Long Day's Journey* was modelled after O'Neill himself in 1912—a young man who had recently experienced the mystical absorptions into the sea described by Edmund. But the immediate environment in which the two plays were composed also played a role in reviving O'Neill's Orientalism. After moving to California in 1937, Eugene and Carlotta had arranged to build a new residence in the Danville hills outside San Francisco. Decorating its interior with Chinese art and furnishings, they called it Tao House. Here O'Neill conceived and wrote these autobiographical plays, surrounded by Oriental artifacts collected by his wife. And that wife herself—O'Neill's sole companion for much of the time in their remote new residence—may have also reawakened her husband to Eastern thought. Around the time the couple moved into Tao House in October of 1937, she acquired two books that concerned Taoism: Dwight Goddard's *Lao-tzu's Tao and Wu Wei* (a gift received in September 1937), and Dorothy Graham's *Chinese Gardens* (purchased in March 1938). Containing numerous underlines and sidelines in Carlotta's hand, both were almost certainly read shortly after they were acquired, for she was curious to learn about their dwelling's name and wished to model their estate along Chinese lines.[2] In all likelihood, she discussed her reading with her husband; indeed, one of their habits was to read aloud to each other in the evenings, and this was a close time in their marriage.[3] Thus, in 1937 and 1938 O'Neill possibly found himself thinking about, even listening to, the Oriental teachings he had studied years before. And not coincidentally, certain passages marked by Carlotta involved Eastern concepts that emerge as motifs in *Iceman* and *Journey*.

The early chapters of Graham's *Chinese Gardens* repeatedly allude to the Taoist goals behind the Chinese gardening aesthetic. "Tranquillity bordering on oblivion was the ideal," Graham notes in a passage marked by Carlotta, "for serenity was conducive to introspection."[4] A subsequent marked passage mentions the related idea that "inaction is itself an art" (p. 7), the Taoist doctrine of *wu wei*. As we shall see, both *Iceman* and *Journey* raise inaction to the level of art, thereby manifesting the quietism of Oriental mystical thought. *Wu wei* also provides the title of Henry Borel's informal essay in Goddard's *Lao-tzu's Tao and Wu Wei*, in which Borel recounts conversations between a European visitor and a Taoist sage in the latter's mountaintop dwelling. The sage explains the title in a

2. See Gelbs, pp. 824–25; and Sheaffer, *Artist*, pp. 472–73.
3. Interview with Donald Gallup, curator of O'Neill Collection, Beinecke Library, Yale Univ., 13 Oct. 1978.
4. Dorothy Graham, *Chinese Gardens: Gardens of the Contemporary Scene, An Account of Their Design and Symbolism* (New York: Dodd, 1938), p. 4. On the inside front cover is Carlotta's signature and the date of signing, March 14, 1938. Hereafter documented in the text.

passage lined by Carlotta. "By strifelessness—Wu Wei—Lao-tzu meant: relaxation from earthly activity, from desire—from the craving for unreal things."[5] The human obsession with "unreal things"—the phenomenal realm termed *māyā* by Indian philosophy—also appears in another underscored passage in Borel's essay: "Things which are real to us are not real in themselves. What we call Being is in fact Not-Being, and just what we call Not-Being is Being in its true essence. So that we are living in a great obscurity. What we imagine to be real is not real, . . . All things appreciable to the senses and all cravings of the heart are unreal" (pp. 65–66). These lines enunciate the distrust of conventional attitudes common to Indian and Chinese mysticism. And a similar scepticism about "reality" informs both *Iceman* and *Journey*, which view man's hopes and desires as illusions that obscure the void at the heart of existence.

The Iceman Cometh's opening scene seems to dramatize the ideal of inaction articulated in Carlotta's books. "Dis dump is like a morgue wid all dese bums passed out," observes Rocky, the bartender in Harry Hope's saloon.[6] But even when awake, the derelicts instinctively follow the ideal of *wu wei* enunciated by Chuang Tse, in which "perfect enjoyment is to be obtained by doing nothing."[7] This indolence creates the "beautiful calm in the atmosphere" that Larry Slade, the introspective "foolosopher" among them, comments upon in the first act (p. 587). Able to harmonize because they eschew the competition and frustration attendant upon action, these dregs live in a state resembling the Taoist golden age. "I've never known more contented men," observes Larry (p. 594). Larry takes pride in being the most passive and serene of all, for he has (he believes) transcended the desires that propel men into activity. Formerly a member of the Anarchist-Socialist movement, he became disillusioned and "took a seat in the grandstand of philosophical detachment to fall asleep observing the cannibals do their death

5. Lao-tzu, *Lao-tzu's Tao and Wu Wei*, trans. Dwight Goddard and M. E. Reynolds (New York: Brentano's, 1919), p. 70. Inside the front cover is an inscription, "From Mai-Mai Sze. Sept. 1937." As indicated, Borel's essay on "Wu Wei" is appended to the Goddard-Reynolds translation of the *Tao Te Ching*. Hereafter documented in the text.

6. *Plays*, 3: 574. Hereafter documented in the text.

7. Legge, *Texts of Taoism*, 40: 149.

dance" (p. 579). Thus, he pursues the Oriental goal of "tranquillity bordering on oblivion" mentioned by Carlotta's volume on Chinese gardening, which also illuminates Larry's philosophical temper: "such serenity was conducive to introspection." Moreover, the other major character, the salesman Hickey, apparently corresponds to Larry in exhibiting the inner calm gained from transcendence of worldly strife. His gospel urges the derelicts to abandon all remaining desires, to "let yourself sink down to the bottom of the sea" where there is "not a single damned hope or dream left to nag you" (p. 625). For the derelicts' serenity, as both Larry and Hickey perceive, is ultimately inauthentic. It rests on "pipe dreams" about their happy pasts and productive futures: "they manage to get drunk, by hook or crook, and keep their pipe dreams, and that's all they ask of life," Larry comments (p. 594). And Hickey's mission to strip away all remaining desires intends to liberate the men into the more genuine serenity that follows transcendence of the world.

The theme of the pipe dream represents the other major connection of *Iceman* to Eastern thought. As Larry proclaims at the outset, "the lie of the pipe dream is what gives life to the whole mad lot of us, drunk or sober" (p. 578). The equation of existence with illusion (recalling Nina Leeds' identification of "life" and "lie") alludes to the doctrine of *māyā*, that our worldly existence involves a cosmic deception. "Things which are real to us are not real in themselves," as the sage in *Lao Tzu's Tao and Wu Wei* proclaims. *Iceman* applies this observation to all members of its microcosmic society, exposing their beliefs as self-flattering delusions about past and future. Thus, Harry Hope's conviction that he disengaged from life outside the bar due to grief over his beloved wife's death is contradicted by Larry's revelation that she "nagged the hell out of him" (p. 602); Jimmy Tomorrow's belief that he will regain his job the following morning overlooks the fact that he was fired for drunkenness. Similar contradictions characterize the pipe dreams of everyone, including Larry and Hickey. The former claims to desire death devoutly, but hangs on to life; the latter believes he murdered his wife out of love, while hatred was his true motive. Most profoundly, both claim to have discovered serenity through transcendence of illusion, while in fact illusion provides the foundation of their peace. Indeed, existence itself rests on illusion, on *māyā*, as the action demonstrates. After Hickey has pitilessly divested all of their pipe dreams, "*there is an atmosphere of oppressive stagnation in the room, and a quality of insensibility*" resembling death (p. 736). Only after Hickey's plea of temporary insanity permits the men to return to their illusions does life return; when Hickey himself departs, so does the reality that the play equates with nothingness and death. One person, however, has understood Hickey's gospel. As the derelicts sing and drink, Larry Slade stares into the void bequeathed him by the iceman of the title.

Long Day's Journey Into Night also offers a passive confrontation with the abyss which is so central in Oriental thought. The "Not-Being" which Borel's sage perceives as "Being in its true essence" permeates the play. It dwells in the long pauses that punctuate the action: the "*dead quiet*" when Mary is alone in the third act;[8] the stillness surrounding the "*sad, bewildered, broken*" Tyrone when Mary departs to inject herself with morphine at the act's conclusion (p. 123); the "*cracking silence*" that follows her final entrance (p. 170); the motionlessness of all at the final curtain. The play's prevailing tone of silence accords with its static plot. Following the second-act revelations of Edmund's tuberculosis and Mary's re-addiction, the situation does not change, but only intensifies. All gradually become resigned to the futility of any effort to escape a past containing Edmund's illness (the same disease which killed Mary's father) and Mary's drug habit. "All we can do is try to be resigned—again," laments Tyrone: "or be so drunk you can forget," responds Edmund (p. 132). The play's "action" is O'Neill's description of their paralysis, and their attempts to alleviate their misery through drink or drugs. Admittedly, their quietism does not produce the peaceful calm found at Harry Hope's saloon, but both plays manifest the same Oriental intuition that the wisest approach to existence lies in passivity, in "relaxation from earthly activity" and from the desire for change.

"The only way is to make yourself not care," Mary declares after her initial injection (p. 60). Liberated by morphine from her attachment to the world, she looks upon reality (according to O'Neill's

---

8. *Long Day's Journey Into Night* (New Haven, Yale Univ. Pr., 1956), p. 107. Hereafter documented in the text.

stage directions) as *"but an appearance to be accepted and dismissed unfeelingly—even with a hardy cynicism—or entirely ignored"* (p. 97). Despite its chemical source, her attitude corresponds to that of Oriental sages who view the world as *māyā*. In act four, her son Edmund recalls similar altered states of consciousness from his own past. The first occurred earlier that day, as he returned home in a thick fog along the shore. "Everything looked and sounded unreal," he relates, "nothing was what it is. That's what I wanted—to be alone with myself where truth is untrue and life can hide from itself" (p. 131). Edmund's other recollections describe his joy at momentary escapes from the source of *māyā*, the individual ego that perceives itself as separate from nature. Once, on the bowsprit of a square-rigger, he "dissolved in the sea, became white sails and flying spray, became beauty and rhythm, became moonlight and the ship and the dim-starred sky. I lost myself," he exults, "actually lost my life. I was set free" (p. 153). Other sea memories recall other absorptions, other intuitions that each self is part of the larger Self that Vedantists call Brahman. All these experiences, he remembers, were "like the veil of things as they seem drawn back by an unseen hand. . . . For a second there is meaning! Then the hand lets the veil fall and you are alone, lost in the fog again, and you stumble on toward nowhere, for no good reason" (p. 153). Significance lies only in the moments of mystical ecstasy; all else is illusion, a veil corresponding to the Vedantic *māyā* that conceals the oneness of man and universe.

While both *Iceman* and *Journey* point in some intriguing Oriental directions, it would nonetheless be misleading to call these plays "Eastern." For O'Neill's treatment of the characters mentioned above dramatizes his scepticism about the authenticity or efficacy of Eastern thought for Western man. As he confronts his personal past, the playwright simultaneously projects a desire for escape from that encounter onto Hickey, Larry, Mary and Edmund. None, however, attains the transcendence of time and self that they all seek. More important, all are judged according to a Christian ethic of compassion and mutual responsibility. In this Christian humanism, O'Neill reveals the primary shaper of his identity to be the Western religion he previously sought to repudiate; and in the courageous confessional mode of this drama, he signals his non-

Oriental determination to face himself and his past, in contrast to the desires of his characters.

The conflict between playwright and characters is clearest in *Iceman*. Hickey invites the derelicts to face the peaceful void of a life without illusion, and pleads with them in the final act: "You're free now to be yourselves, without having to feel remorse or guilt, or lie to yourselves about reforming tomorrow. Can't you see there is no tomorrow now? You don't have to care a damn about anything anymore!" (p. 705). Promising liberation from time ("tomorrow") and morality ("remorse" and "guilt") as well as desire, Hickey here echoes Buddha and other Oriental sages. But O'Neill is heavily ironic at Hickey's expense. Irony of event appears in the derelicts' despair after abandoning their pipe dreams: staring into the abyss hardly produces the serenity Hickey promised. This relates to the dramatic irony directed against the salesman, whose peace does not derive from facing reality but from embracing one last illusion. His inadvertent revelation of his final words to his wife—"you know what you can do with your pipe dream now, you damned bitch!" (p. 716)—clearly indicates that her murder was motivated by his bitter resentment of her pipe dream of reforming him. But Hickey cannot accept this, and quickly invents another illusion—that he "must have been insane" when he uttered those words (p. 716)—to maintain *his* pipe dream that he killed her out of love, to end her suffering. Were Hickey truly facing the void, free from guilt and desire, this self-deceiving charade would not be necessary. And one final irony is inherent in Hickey's gospel. Despite its apparent Eastern nihilism, he justifies preaching it by claiming he does so out of pity— a major Christian virtue.

Hickey, however, claims his is the "right kind of pity," designed to make the convert "contented with what he is" (p. 641); the "wrong kind," according to him, is practiced by Larry, who compassionately flatters the derelicts' pipe dreams. Despite his detached pose and "*mystic's meditative pale-blue eyes*" (p. 574), Larry involves himself with everyone in the bar. Consequently, after intuiting the dreadful implications of Hickey's gospel, he repeatedly implores him to spare the men's illusions and allow them to keep their faith. This accords with O'Neill's opening description of Larry as a "*weary, pitying old priest*" (p. 574), a role he also assumes for Don

Parritt. Parritt wishes to confess to Larry the betrayal of his mother Rosa (Larry's former lover, and a Movement leader) to the authorities. Guessing quickly what Parritt has done, Larry tries but fails to sustain his professed mystical detachment. By the end, "*convulsed with detestation*," he furiously urges Parritt to "get the hell out of life" (p. 720), and thereby reveals his moral disgust at the young man's act. "Look out how you try to taunt me back into life," he had warned Parritt earlier, "I might remember the thing they call justice there, and the punishment for—" betrayal, though Larry never says the word (p. 694). Ironically, Larry's fundamental belief in the Judeo-Christian morality of "justice" and "punishment" is precisely why Parritt sought him out, as a sinner desiring to atone for his actions. Unable to forgive Parritt's betrayal of his mother—a figure particularly sacred in Catholicism—Larry-the-priest hears his fragmentary confession and assigns him the ultimate penance of death.

The death sentence Larry pronounces is also prompted by his pity for the "mad tortured bastard" who came unto him in search of an executioner. And at the conclusion, he recognizes that he is fated to be "a weak fool looking with pity at the two sides of everything until the day I die" (p. 726). He thereby confesses the futile hypocrisy of his Eastern mask. Unable to believe in God's grace, he remains convinced of man's sinfulness, as epitomized by Hickey, Parritt, and perhaps himself (as Parritt's murderer). But he cannot avoid compassion for his fellow sinners, an admission which plunges him into the despair from which his detached pose had protected him. Praying sincerely now for a quick death, Larry at the curtain stares beyond *māyā* into the void of a life without sustaining illusions. That act offers no bliss, however; as a modern Western man, he perceives only emptiness, hopelessness and death.

The Irishman Larry Slade cannot escape his Catholic upbringing, nor can Eugene O'Neill, for his ironic debunking of Larry's mysticism represents an implicit admission of the futility of Oriental approaches for himself. Edmund Tyrone in *Long Day's Journey* shares Larry's desire to withdraw from the sufferings of earthly existence, as his fourth-act speeches about the sea reveal. Moreover, the lyrical intensity of these memories of ecstasy suggest that they do not simply represent young Eugene, the romantic dreamer of 1912.

They also stand for the mature O'Neill, who still experiences a profound sympathy with Oriental thought as a light on the path of existence. "For a second you see—and seeing the secret, are the secret," exults Edmund. "For a second there is meaning!" (p. 153). But as these lines admit—twice—these glimpses vanish quickly. As a non-Oriental, O'Neill can abandon the self and passively experience belonging only "for a second" before he is "alone, lost in the fog again." The play's central symbol, the fog, thickens during the play, pointing to the inescapable confusion and loneliness that were O'Neill's heritage as both a "haunted Tyrone" and a Western man. And the steady march of Mary and the other Tyrones into the past demonstrates—as does the very act of writing the play—O'Neill's inability to effect escape from history, despite his momentary mystical withdrawals from time.

While Edmund's evanescent escapes from time and self are exposed as futile, they are nonetheless harmless. The opposite is true in Mary's case. First, of course, her detachment is not spiritually achieved, but artificially induced. Mary has not passed *through* emotion to inner calm, but constructed a narcotic shield from anxiety and pain. Even were her detachment genuine, however, it would still cruelly intensify the sufferings of others. Her remote accusations of Tyrone, for example, reinforce his guilt over hiring the "quack" doctor who introduced her to morphine, and finally leave him *"overwhelmed with shame"* when she calmly tells Edmund how often her husband kept her waiting in "ugly hotel rooms" (p. 113). But Mary's effect on Edmund is the most devastating. In act two she pathetically confesses to him her desire to reach rock bottom, deepening his depression; she then acknowledges Edmund's shame of her, provoking his guilt; and in their next scene together, she reminds Edmund that his birth was the cause of her original addiction, prompting his *"shrinking into himself"* (p. 116). Sick and in need of comfort, Edmund feels emotionally deserted by his mother—just as he had been throughout his childhood.

From the perspective of her neglected son, Mary's self-absorption—the primary feature of the mystical state—is pathetic but reprehensible. Even if the Christian "God is dead" (as Edmund quotes Nietzsche), his teachings on sin and compassion still dominate O'Neill. In Christian dogma, man is by nature sinful; in *Jour-*

ney, everyone somehow provokes the misery of everyone else. But O'Neill's declared attitude (articulated in the play's Dedication) of "deep pity and understanding and forgiveness" is equally Christian (p. 7). These are qualities that Mary lacks. While she intellectually comprehends that "none of us can help the things life has done to us," she repeatedly deepens her family's misery with her accusations (p. 61). Mary thus offers a grotesque distortion of the Holy Mother whose name she shares. Aware of man's guilt, she lacks the courage for compassion and forgiveness. When she withdraws because she cannot cope with Edmund's sickness, she shirks a mother's duty. And her goal in so withdrawing is hardly admirable from a Christian perspective. She seeks to return to the pre-lapsarian state of her novitiate, and does so (in her imagination) at the end. Mary thus not only avoids taking responsibility for others, but for her present self as well. Reinforcing the guilt and pain of her husband and children, Mary fails to love: "she loves not you nor me as all we love her," as Jamie recites from Swinburne in the final scene (p. 173). In this *Lear*-like drama, where occasional expressions of tenderness mitigate the torment—where for most "*stung*" responses, there are corresponding "*moved*" ones—Mary is the chief sinner. Obviously, O'Neill found her the most difficult to forgive. Moreover, the fact that her sin both causes and results from a strange detachment, similar to that of mystics, demonstrates how far O'Neill had moved away from the ebullient Orientalism of *Lazarus Laughed*.

Despite both plays' overt repudiation of mysticism, they each possess one final Oriental feature. Like *Lazarus Laughed* and *The Great God Brown*, they attempt to reconcile oppositions by viewing them from a dynamic Taoist perspective, in which opposing terms alternate and interpenetrate like *yin* and *yang*. *Iceman* structures its larger oppositions in this manner. The play begins, for instance, in a scene of life, however minimal: Hickey brings death, as all eventually recognize; but in the final scene, life and death interpenetrate, as Larry yearns to die while the surrounding derelicts erupt into boisterous life. Similarly, illusion and reality alternate: the ubiquitous pipe dreams dominate the first two acts, truth (and consequent despair) takes center stage in acts three and four, but the conclusion finds the derelicts immersed again in happy illusion—except for Larry, who grimly faces the horrid truths about himself revealed by Hickey and Parritt. *Journey* also displays structural cycles: the diurnal cycle announced in the title points to the continuous alternation between present realities and past causes that is the play's major theme: "The past is the present, isn't it?" Mary declares. "It's the future, too. We all try to lie out of that, but life won't let us" (p. 87). Consequently, the further the Tyrones move into the future during the day the play takes place, the more deeply they immerse themselves in their past. Smaller epicycles alternate and interfuse the terms of other oppositions. Repeatedly, the Tyrones switch back and forth between love and hate, guilt and blame, demonstrating the closeness of apparently conflicting emotions. When Jamie vacillates characteristically between love and jealous hatred of Edmund in act four, he thrice alludes to the "dead part of me"—suggesting a mingling of life and death that also applies to the sick Edmund and the past-haunted "ghost," Mary. In both *Iceman* and *Journey*, however, the cycles do not convey (as in *The Fountain*, for instance) a mystical sense of the serene oneness of all existence. Rather, they suggest the entrapment of the major characters in situations of suffering and despair. For Larry Slade and the Tyrones, these circles are actually descending spirals, leading toward loss, deepening misery and death. Thus, the Taoist polarities which seemed so liberating in O'Neill's earlier drama are here another cause for despair; the playwright's only consolation is to turn to the fundamental teaching of Christianity, and discover in compassion some mitigation of man's destiny of sorrow.

Eastern Obit: *Hughie*

If the Tyrones and Larry Slade were not set free, their creator was—at least temporarily. After completing his "play of old sorrows," O'Neill experienced a burst of creative energy that produced outlines for six new projects.[9] One of them, a cycle of one-act monologue plays called "By Way of Obit," resulted in only one play, however: *Hughie*. Composed in the spring of 1942, *Hughie*

9. Sheaffer, *Artist*, p. 517.

(like *Journey* and *Iceman*) found O'Neill returning to his past, since its two characters were types O'Neill had encountered during his young manhood in New York City.[10] The plot, which alternates one man's spoken recollections of a deceased friend with another man's escapist fantasies, also focuses on the past. But Eastern touches qualify the Western obsession with history. Again, polar cycles of life and death, being and nothingness, structure the work; again, the void is briefly faced, with the characters retreating back to the *māyā* of existence. *Hughie* thus contains in capsule form three major elements of O'Neill's Orientalism, and represents his final judgment on it; we turn to it to conclude and briefly recapitulate this study.

The hotel setting of *Hughie* immediately recalls *The Iceman Cometh*. The "*seedy lobby*" of a "*third class dump*," is "about as homey as the Morgue," complains Erie Smith, echoing Rocky's description of Harry Hope's saloon.[11] In both plays, the setting fits the extreme situation: a morbid confessional monologue provokes an encounter with death, followed by a return to the human community. However, *Hughie*'s microcosmic society—here reduced to the garrulous Erie Smith and the taciturn Night Clerk—is pictured in terms of complementary polarity. *Hughie*'s two characters seem opposite in nearly every respect. The Night Clerk (thin, with a large nose and mouth on a long face) is married, quiet and passive; Erie (stout, with snub nose and small mouth on his round face) is single, verbose and active. Each, though, possesses a "*pasty, night-life complexion*" that symbolically unites them (p. 8). For both "night-life" men endure a dark night of the soul—the action transpires between three and four A.M.—which moves them to symbiotic union. By the end, the typical "Broadway sport" and "Wise Guy" Erie discovers a new "Sucker" in the Night Clerk to replace the recently deceased former night clerk, Hughie (pp. 9, 38).

A more uniquely Taoist aspect of *Hughie* is its cyclical rhythm of life and death. The silent Clerk is associated with the latter. De-

10. In a letter of 19 June 1942 to George Jean Nathan, O'Neill described the Night Clerk as "an essence of all the night clerks I've known in bum hotels," and called Erie "a type of Broadway sport I and my brother used to know by the dozen in far-off days." Quoted in Sheaffer, *Artist*, p. 521.

11. *Hughie*, pp. 7, 27. Hereafter documented in the text.

scribed as a "*drooping waxwork*" and "*corpse*," he listens not to
Erie but to urban night sounds that conjure up visions of murder,
catastrophic fires, and fatal accidents (pp. 14, 18). While his morbid
imagination rambles, the "*teller of tales*" Erie incessantly talks, for
(as the Clerk later realizes) this small-time gambler is "*awake and
alive*" (pp. 5, 20). The alternation of death (the Clerk's silent meditations) and life (Erie's long speeches) occurs in the play's larger
structure as well. *Hughie* begins in stillness, comes to conversa-
tional life with Erie's entrance, eventually falls to total silence as the
characters separately contemplate death, then resumes life again toward the end.

This cycle points to another one, between the void and being.
After the opening quiet, the first two-thirds of the play finds Erie's
conversation and the outside sounds (garbage cans, an el train, a
policeman's footfalls, an ambulance, a fire engine) filling the stage
with the noises of human existence. Then "*a rare and threatening
pause of silence*" falling outside coincides with pauses in Erie's
monologue, and "*enters the deserted, dirty lobby*" (pp. 29, 31).
However, "*the threat of Night and Silence*" recedes as Erie resumes
reminiscing while the Clerk commences fantasizing about gambling
(p. 32), until they converse about gamblers and shoot craps together as the play concludes. The alternation between the sounds of
being and the silence of the abyss, corresponding to the rhythm
of *yang* and *yin*, also characterizes the curious duet of Erie and
Hughie, of course. The compulsive talker and gambler represents
the activities and movements of existence; the nondescript Clerk,
whose physical features are uniformly "*without character*," stares
"*at nothing*" and wishes only to "*listen to the noises in the street
and think about nothing*" (pp. 8, 7, 13).

If *Hughie*'s cycles accord with the Tao, the Clerk's meditations
relate to those of Buddha. His fantasies about nothingness are explicitly connected to this source, in fact: as he listens to an el train,
he thinks that "*each one passing leaves one less to pass, so the night
recedes, too, until at last it must die and join all the other long
nights in Nirvana, the big Night of Nights*" (p. 19). Like that of
Hickey, however, his pursuit of the void is deceptive. His el-train
fantasies on Nirvana and his hope that a fire might obliterate the
city are pinned to the outside noises—signs of being. Once that

buffer vanishes and "*the spell of abnormal quiet presses suffocatingly upon the street*" and lobby, his "mind cowers away from it" (p. 31). As he tries desperately to recollect Erie's previous conversation, he recalls remarks on gambling, and now his mind "*pursues an ideal of fame and glory within itself called Arnold Rothstein*" (p. 32). That dream creates a bond between himself and Erie, who shortly recognizes that the Clerk—like his predecessor, the dead Hughie—is ripe for fiction. Contact is made, as the teller of tales spins forth his illusions for the newborn sucker and produces his dice.

As in *Iceman*, the void is not liberating, but unendurable. Hence, when Erie responds to the Clerk's confused query "What's the truth?" with "nothing, Pal. Not a thing," both verge on despair (p. 30). This Western retreat from nothingness back into being, however, reveals the final Oriental feature of Hughie, its view of existence as *māyā*. The Clerk's return to life coincides with the birth of an illusion, his "*Big Ideal*" of Arnold Rothstein (p. 34). Erie, who has minimal contact with the notorious gambler, gladly responds to the Clerk's need to picture him as Rothstein's friend. But the Clerk's life actually depends on illusion throughout. As his nocturnal fantasies sustained him earlier, he now fashions a pipe dream from Erie's boasts "to help me live through the night" (p. 30). The smarter Erie also needs illusion, though in a more complex way. He knows the tales he told Hughie were either outright lies or half-truths, "stories of big games and killings that really happened. . . . Only I wasn't in on 'em like I made out" (p. 29). Hughie's enthusiastic response, however, provided him with vicarious excitement and "done me [Erie] good, too, in a way. Sure. I'd get to seein' myself like he seen me," an important figure in the gambler's underworld (p. 29). Hughie's belief in Erie's tales gave the latter self-respect, confidence and good fortune. Hence, "when I lost Hughie I lost my luck" and confidence—the two qualities a gambler needs to survive (p. 35). All three characters, then, the dead as well as the living, demonstrate the inseparability of existence from illusion. Life is *māyā*, and the ultimate reality is the death, the "nothing, Pal," at the heart of the play.

Since Erie's past friendship with Hughie and his new camaraderie with the Clerk depend on lies and fantasies, the play suggests that human relationships rest on illusion, too; the final reality (as in so many O'Neill plays) is our isolation. However, this tragic view yields here to a larger—and traditionally Christian—affirmation of the human community. Because he loved Hughie, Erie never tricked his gullible friend out of money, and has even incurred risky debts to provide an expensive wreath at Hughie's funeral. Because he misses Hughie, he repeatedly exposes his vulnerability to the Clerk, and repeatedly the Clerk, his mind "*attending the obsequies of the night,*" ignores him or responds perfunctorily (p. 19). But these minimal responses make Erie "*grateful even for this sign of companionship*" (p. 19), and encourage him to remain. Just when Erie abandons hope of contact, the Clerk confronts the silence and begins to "*need company*" himself (p. 31). His nonsequitur replies to Erie's remarks on Hughie are first ignored, then rejected, by the gambler. Nonetheless, Erie "*is comforted*" at having made contact, and "*his face lights up with a saving revelation*" when he comprehends the Clerk's need (like Hughie's) for deception (pp. 33, 35). The diction of O'Neill's descriptions keys us to the tonal shift. The "Nirvana" and "nothing" of the first part give way to "companionship," "company" and "comforted." When Erie "*grins warmly*" and offers his hand "*generously,*" the Clerk responds "*gratefully*" (pp. 35–36). Human brotherhood may rest—like all existence— on *māyā*, the play admits; but brotherhood clearly has helped these former strangers endure the night. If *Long Day's Journey* demonstrates that hell is other people, *Hughie* unsentimentally asserts that other people are all we know of heaven, too. The primary Christian (and Western humanist) values of love and compassion are affirmed as Erie, "*purged of grief, his confidence restored,*" reaches out to the Clerk (p. 38). They play dice using Erie's money, gambling— but trusting now to love as well as luck.

A similar affirmation of compassion and communion characterizes O'Neill's final play, *A Moon for the Misbegotten*. Returning again to his family past, he dramatically recreates his alcoholic brother's determined pursuit of death following the loss of their mother. Like Hickey, Parritt and his fellow Tyrones, Jamie is driven to confession over a past deed: a sexual episode with a prostitute on the train bearing his mother's corpse. Like Erie and the Clerk, he finds some comfort in the companionship of another, here a maternal virgin named Josie. This half-ironic allusion to the Holy Mother, plus the central themes of guilt, confession and the human community, point up the Christian assumptions of the work. The play is also fundamentally Western in other respects. Time for Jamie moves, not in cycles, but in a tragic line toward slow suicide; the action revolves around his unresolvable inner conflict and alienation; and the plot subordinates the characters' illusions to the desperate realities of need and loneliness they recognize and express. O'Neill's Eastern impulse had apparently been exorcised by the preceding three plays, and he ended his career where he began—in the dualistic European tradition that emphasizes individual psychology, linear time, and unavoidable struggle.

If these emphases metaphorically constitute the *yang* side of O'Neill's divided vision, it clearly prevails over his Eastern *yin* in his final play. The same dominance inevitably characterizes the three Western traditions from which he emerged—Christianity, romanticism and American culture—and inevitably characterizes the playwright's work when viewed as a whole. But the shifting relationship between O'Neill's Eastern and Western sides gives an interesting shape to his career. From 1913 to 1925, the Western tragedian in O'Neill is in command, manifesting itself in the impossible dilemmas facing the protagonists of *Beyond the Horizon*, *The Hairy Ape*, *Desire Under the Elms*, and other plays. His mystical nature, however, apparent in early sea plays like *The Moon of the Caribbees*, aligns itself with Hindu and Taoist approaches to existence in "*Anna Christie*," *The Fountain* and "*Marco Millions*." The middle play's protagonist transcends life's struggles after a vision dramatizes the *māyā*-like artificiality of distinctions, and reconciles all dualities in a universal dynamic rhythm. While those monistic cycles fail to resolve the East-West polarity in "*Marco Millions*," the next phase of O'Neill's career finds him consistently viewing tragic conflicts within this larger unifying rhythm. From 1925 to 1928, four expressionistic, deliberately religious plays represent the high-water mark of his Orientalism. *The Great God Brown* ends (like "*Marco Millions*") in dualism; but its Western sources of Jung and Nietzsche combine with Hinduism, Buddhism and Taoism in *Lazarus Laughed* to reveal O'Neill's Eastern attraction to passivity, egolessness, and spiritual liberation. A similar yearning lies behind

Strange Interlude. That play's Oriental mother god, however, battles against the judgmental, Old Testament father god; and *Dynamo* repudiates both mother and father gods, submerging O'Neill's mystical urges until his final autobiographical phase from 1939 to 1943. Oriental and Occidental approaches again contend in *The Iceman Cometh, Long Day's Journey Into Night* and *Hughie*, but each play rejects Eastern paths and embraces Christian values of fellowship and compassion. And *A Moon for the Misbegotten* makes clear that the rejection—an inevitable consequence of O'Neill's Western identity—was indeed sincere and final.

However inconsistent his feelings toward Oriental thought, an understanding of O'Neill's relationship to it serves to explain both his work's uneven quality and its continuing relevance. Some of his least effective efforts are those which expressionistically indulge his Oriental intuitions, like *The Fountain* and *Lazarus Laughed.* O'Neill was on safer theatrical footing when he remained within the confines of Western naturalism, as *Beyond the Horizon* and *Desire Under the Elms* testify. Grounded in recognizable, concrete experience, these and other O'Neill plays in the realistic mode are more accomplished and emotionally powerful than the "Eastern" plays above. Yet his profoundest plays—*The Iceman Cometh* and *Long Day's Journey Into Night*—merge Oriental thought and Western naturalism. O'Neill's universal appeal has been attributed to various features of his work,[12] but one overlooked reason for his trans-cultural popularity may lie precisely in the peculiar combination of East and West evident in these late tragedies. His greatest drama probed the enduring concerns of Western man: the fear of death, the obsession with history, the quest for identity. Though it did so in a form familiar to Western audiences, it simultaneously raised the possibility of Oriental approaches to these problems, while remaining sceptical about Eastern philosophy's ultimate relevance to the Western mind. In this ambivalence, the American play-

12. The most recent book to address the question of O'Neill's universality limits itself to America and Europe, but represents many nations. *Eugene O'Neill: A World View*, ed. Virginia Floyd (New York: Ungar, 1979), devotes an entire section to the "European perspectives" on O'Neill, including several essays by Eastern European critics. Another section offers appraisals of O'Neill by prominent American critics, while a third focuses on the opinions of theatrical performers.

wright represents many modern Europeans and Americans alike—
and not just artists. As the communications revolution continues to
shrink the world, moreover, O'Neill's appeal will no doubt increase
for Orientals, especially those Westernized enough to experience a
similar conflict between their traditional values and the goals offered by another civilization. Universal as O'Neill's work may be, it
is of course unlikely to bridge the gap between East and West; but
his divided vision may further mutual understanding by offering
deep and subtle statements of the problem.

Bibliography

Index

Bibliography

(*Indicates volume in O'Neill's personal library)

Alexander, Doris. "*Lazarus Laughed* and Buddha." *Modern Language Quarterly* 17 (1956): 357–65.

―――. "*Light on the Path* and *The Fountain*." *Modern Drama* 3 (1960): 260–67.

―――. "*Strange Interlude* and Schopenhauer." *American Literature* 25 (1953): 213–28.

―――. *The Tempering of Eugene O'Neill*. New York: Harcourt, 1962.

*Angus, Samuel. *The Mystery Religions and Christianity: A Study in the Religious Background of Early Christianity*. London: Scribners, 1925.

Appleton, William. *A Cycle of Cathay: The Chinese Vogue in England during the Seventeenth and Eighteenth Centuries*. New York: Columbia Univ. Pr., 1951.

Babbit, Irving. "Romanticism and the Orient." *Bookman* 74 (1931): 349–57.

Baird, James. "Critical Problems in the Orientalism of Western Poetry." In *Asia and the Humanities*: Papers Presented at the Second Conference on Oriental-Western Literary and Cultural Relations. Danville, Ill.: Interstate Printers and Publishers, 1959, pp. 38–57.

Bermel, Albert. "Poetry and Mysticism in O'Neill." In *Eugene O'Neill: A World View*, ed. Virginia Floyd. New York: Ungar, 1979.

Bernard, Kathy Lynn. "The Research Library of Eugene O'Neill." Diss., Univ. of Massachusetts, 1977.

Berrigan, Daniel, and Thich Nhat Hanh. *The Raft is Not the Shore: Conversations toward a Buddhist/Christian Awareness*. Boston: Beacon, 1975.

*Binyon, Laurence. *The Flight of the Dragon: An Essay on the Theory and Practice of Art in China and Japan*. London: John Murray, 1922.

Bogard, Travis. *Contour in Time: The Plays of Eugene O'Neill*. New York: Oxford Univ. Pr., 1972.

Boulton, Agnes. *Part of a Long Story*. Garden City: Doubleday, 1958.

Bowen, Croswell. *The Curse of the Misbegotten: A Tale of the House of O'Neill*. New York: McGraw, 1959.

Bowie, Theodore R. *East-West in Art: Patterns of Cultural and Aesthetic Relationships*. Bloomington: Indiana Univ. Pr., 1966.

Braden, Charles S. "The Novelist Discovers the Orient." *Far Eastern Quarterly* 7 (1957): 165–75.

Bradley, Sculley et al., eds. *The American Tradition in Literature*. New York: Norton, 1974.

Brandell, Gunnar. *Strindberg in Inferno*. Trans. Barry Jacobs. Cambridge, Mass.: Harvard Univ. Pr., 1974.

Brashear, William. *The Gorgon's Head: A Study in Tragedy and Despair*. Athens: Univ. of Georgia Pr., 1977.

———. "O'Neill's Schopenhauer Interlude." *Criticism* 6 (1964): 256–65.

*Brooks, Van Wyck. *The Life of Emerson*. New York: Dutton, 1933.

*———. *The Flowering of New England, 1815–1865*. New York: Dutton, 1936.

Brustein, Robert. *The Theatre of Revolt*. Boston: Little, 1962.

Bussell, F. W. *Religious Thought and Heresy in the Middle Ages*. 2 vols. London: R. Scott, 1918.

Capra, Fritjof. *The Tao of Physics*. Berkeley: Shambhala Publications, 1976.

Cargill, Oscar, N. Bryllion Fagin, and William S. Fisher, eds. *O'Neill and His Plays: Four Decades of Criticism*. New York: New York Univ. Pr., 1961.

Carpenter, Frederic I. *Emerson and Asia*. 1930; rpt. New York: Haskell House, 1968.

———. *Eugene O'Neill*. Boston: Twayne, 1964. 2nd ed. Boston: Twayne, 1979.

———. "Eugene O'Neill, the Orient and American Transcendentalism." In *Transcendentalism and Its Legacy*, ed. Myron Simon and T. H. Parsons. Ann Arbor: Univ. of Michigan Pr., 1966, pp. 204–13.

*Cementi, Cecil, trans. *Cantonese Love Songs*. Oxford: Clarendon Press, 1904.

Chabrowe, Leonard. *Ritual and Pathos: The Theatre of O'Neill*. Lewisburg, Pa.: Bucknell Univ. Pr., 1976.

Chen, David. "Two Chinese Adaptations of Eugene O'Neill's *The Emperor Jones.*" *Modern Drama* 9 (1967): 431–39.

Christy, Arthur, ed. *The Asian Legacy and American Life.* New York: John Day, 1945.

———. *The Orient in American Transcendentalism: A Study of Emerson, Thoreau and Alcott.* 1932; rpt. New York: Octagon, 1969.

*Churchward, Albert. *The Origin and Evolution of Religion.* New York: Dutton, 1924.

Clark, Barrett H. *O'Neill: The Man and His Plays.* New York: Dover, 1947.

*Collins, Mabel. *Light on the Path.* London: Reeves and Turner, 1885.

*Coomaraswamy, Ananda K. *Buddha and the Gospel of Buddhism.* London: Harper, 1916.

———. "Buddhism." In *Religion in the Twentieth Century*, edited by Vergilius Ferm, pp. 59–79. New York: Philosophical Library, 1948.

———. *Hinduism and Buddhism.* New York: Philosophical Library, 1943.

———. *Selected Papers.* 2 vols. Princeton: Princeton Univ. Pr., 1980.

———, and Horner, I. B. *Living Thoughts of the Buddha.* Living Thoughts Library. London: Cassell, 1948.

Cox, Harvey. *Turning East.* Simon, 1977.

Danto, Arthur. *Mysticism and Morality: Oriental Thought and Moral Philosophy.* New York: Basic, 1972.

Day, Cyrus. "*Amor Fati*: O'Neill's Lazarus as Superman and Savior." *Modern Drama* 3 (1960): 297–305.

Deutsch, Eliot, trans. *The Bhagavad-Gita.* New York: Holt, 1968.

*Douglas, Sir Robert K. *China.* London: T. Fisher Unwin, 1920.

Durant, Will. *The Story of Philosophy.* 1926; rpt. New York: Washington Square Pr., 1962.

*Emerson, Ralph Waldo. *Complete Works.* 6 vols. Boston: Houghton, 1921.

*———. *The Heart of Emerson's Journals*, ed. Bliss Perry. Boston: Houghton, 1921.

———. *The Selected Writings of Emerson*, ed. Brooks Atkinson. New York: Random, 1950.

Engel, Edwin. *The Haunted Heroes of Eugene O'Neill.* Cambridge, Mass.: Harvard Univ. Pr., 1953.

Falk, Doris. *Eugene O'Neill and the Tragic Tension*. New Brunswick: Rutgers Univ. Pr., 1958.

Frank, Waldo. *The Re-discovery of America*. New York: Scribners, 1929.

*Frazer, Sir James George. *The Golden Bough*. New York: Macmillan, 1925.

*————. *The Magic Art and the Evolution of Kings*. 2 vols. Macmillan, 1917.

Frenz, Horst. "Notes on Eugene O'Neill in Japan." *Modern Drama* 3 (1960): 306–13.

————. "O'Neill and China." *Tamkang Review* 10, no. 1 (autumn 1979), pp. 5–17.

Gard, Richard A. *Buddhism*. New York: George Braziller, 1961.

Gassner, John, ed. *O'Neill: A Collection of Critical Essays*. Englewood Cliffs, N.J.: Prentice-Hall, 1964.

Gelb, Arthur and Barbara. *O'Neill*. 2nd ed. New York: Harper, 1973.

*Glover, T. R. *The Conflict of Religions in the Early Roman Empire*. 10th ed. London: Methuen, 1923.

*Graham, Dorothy. *Chinese Gardens: Gardens of the Contemporary Scene, An Account of Their Design and Symbolism*. New York: Dodd, 1938.

*Grantham, A. E. *Hills of Blue: A Picture Roll of Chinese History*. London: Methuen, 1927.

Guénon, René. *East and West*. Trans. William Massey. London: Luzac, 1941.

Guthke, Karl S. *Modern Tragicomedy: An Investigation into the Nature of the Genre*. New York: Random, 1966.

Haas, William S. *The Destiny of the Mind: East and West*. New York: Macmillan, 1956.

Hartman, Murray. "Strindberg and O'Neill." *Educational Theatre Journal* 18 (1966): 216–23.

*Hearn, Lafcadio. *Karma*. New York: Boni & Liveright, 1918.

Hinden, Michael. "*The Birth of Tragedy* and *The Great God Brown*." *Modern Drama* 16 (1973): 129–40.

*Hobson, R. L. *Chinese Art*. New York: Macmillan, 1927.

Hsia, An Min. "Eugene O'Neill and Tao." Diss., Indiana Univ., 1979.

Jung, Carl G. *Psychological Types*. Trans. H. Godwin Baynes, rev. R. F. C. Hull. Princeton: Princeton Univ. Pr., 1971.

————. *Psychology and Religion: East and West.* Trans. R. F. C. Hull. Princeton: Princeton Univ. Pr., 1958.

*————. *Psychology of the Unconscious.* Trans. Beatrice Hinkle. 1919; rpt. London: Kegan, Paul, Trench, Trubner, 1922.

Kaltenmark, Max. *Lao Tzu and Taoism.* Trans. Roger Greaves. Stanford: Stanford Univ. Pr., 1969.

Kaufmann, Walter. *Nietzsche: Philosopher, Psychologist, Antichrist.* Princeton: Princeton Univ. Pr., 1950.

Knowles, David. *The Evolution of Medieval Thought.* Baltimore: Helicon, 1962.

Langner, Lawrence. *The Magic Curtain.* New York: Dutton, 1951.

*Lao-tzu. *Lao-tzu's Tao and Wu Wei.* Trans. Dwight Goddard and M. E. Reynolds. New York: Brentano's, 1919.

————. *Tao Te Ching.* Trans. D. C. Lau. London: Penguin, 1975.

————. *The Way of Lao Tzu.* Trans. Wing-Tsit Chan. Indianapolis: Bobbs-Merrill, 1963.

Lewis, Leta Jane. "Alchemy and the Orient in Strindberg's *Dream Play.*" *Scandinavian Studies* 35 (1963): 208–222.

*Lewis, Wyndham. *Time and Western Man.* London: Chatto and Windus, 1927.

*Li Po. *The Works of Li Po, The Chinese Poet.* Trans. Shigeyoshi Obata. New York: Dutton, 1922.

*Lin Yutang. *The Importance of Living.* New York: Reynal and Hitchcock. 1937.

*————. *My Country and My People.* New York: Reynal and Hitchcock, 1935.

Lovejoy, A. O. "The Chinese Origin of Romanticism." *Journal of English and Germanic Philology* 32 (1933): 1–20.

Loving, Pierre. "Eugene O'Neill." *The Bookman* 53 (1921): 511–20.

*Mansel, Henry Longueville. *The Gnostic Heresies of the First and Second Centuries,* ed. J. B. Lightfoot. London: John Murray, 1875.

*Maugham, W. Somerset. *On a Chinese Screen.* New York: George H. Doran, 1922.

Merton, Thomas. *Mystics and Zen Masters.* New York: Dell, 1969.

Miller, Jordan Y. *Eugene O'Neill and the American Critic: A Summary and Bibliographical Checklist.* 2nd ed. Hamden, Conn.: Archon, 1973.

Miller, Perry. "From Edwards to Emerson." *New England Quarterly* 13 (1940): 589–617. Reprinted in *Interpretations of American Literature,* ed. Charles Fiedelson. New York: Oxford Univ. Pr., pp. 114–36.

——— et al., eds. *Major Writers of America.* Vol. 2. New York: Harcourt, 1962.

Miner, Earl. *The Japanese Tradition in British and American Literature.* Princeton: Princeton Univ. Pr., 1958.

More, Paul Elmer. *The Drift of Romanticism.* 1913; rpt. New York: Phaeton, 1967.

*Moulton, James Hope. *Early Zoroastrianism.* London: Williams and Newgate, 1913.

*Müller, Max. *Chips from a German Workshop.* London: Longmans, 1914.

*———, ed. *The Sacred Books of the East.* Vols. 39 and 40, *The Texts of Taoism.* Trans. James Legge. London: Oxford Univ. Pr., 1927.

*———. *Six Systems of Indian Philosophy.* London: Longmans, 1919.

New Haven, Conn. Beinecke Library. Yale Univ. Eugene O'Neill Collection.

Nietzsche, Friedrich. *The Birth of Tragedy and The Genealogy of Morals.* Trans. Francis Golffing. New York: Doubleday, 1956.

———. *The Complete Works of Friedrich Nietzsche.* Ed. Oscar Levy. Vol. 10, *The Joyful Wisdom.* Trans. Thomas Common, Paul V. Cohn, and Maud D. Petre. London: T. E. Foulis, 1910.

———. *The Portable Nietzsche.* Trans. and ed. Walter Kaufmann. New York: Viking, 1954.

Ollen, Gunnar. *August Strindberg.* Trans. Peter Turner. New York: Ungar, 1972.

O'Neill, Eugene. *Hughie.* New Haven: Yale Univ. Pr., 1959.

———. *Long Day's Journey Into Night.* New Haven: Yale Univ. Pr., 1956.

———. *A Moon for the Misbegotten.* New York: Random, 1952.

———. *More Stately Mansions.* Ed. Carl Gierow and Donald Gallup. New Haven: Yale Univ. Pr., 1964.

———. *Nine Plays.* New York: Random, 1954.

———. *The Plays of Eugene O'Neill.* 3 vols. New York: Random, 1954.

———. *A Touch of the Poet.* New Haven: Yale Univ. Pr., 1957.

*Pao-Ch'uan Wang. *Lady Precious Stream, An Old Chinese Play.* Trans. S. I. Hsiung. London: Methuen, 1934.

Parsons, Howard L. *Man East and West: Essays in East-West Philosophy.* Amsterdam: Grüner, 1975.

Princeton, N.J. Firestone Library, Princeton Univ. Eugene O'Neill Collection.

Quinn, Arthur Hobson. *A History of the American Drama: From the Civil War to the Present Day.* 2 vols. New York: Appleton, 1936.

Radhakrishnan, Sarvapelli. *East and West in Religion.* 1933; rpt. London: Allen and Unwin, 1949.

——. *Eastern Religions and Western Thought.* 2nd ed. Oxford: Oxford Univ. Pr., 1940.

Raghavacharyulu, I. M. *Eugene O'Neill: A Study.* Bombay: Popular Prakashan Pr., 1965.

Raleigh, John Henry. *The Plays of Eugene O'Neill.* Carbondale and Edwardsville: Southern Illinois Univ. Pr., 1965.

——. "O'Neill's *Long Day's Journey Into Night* and New England Irish Catholicism." *Partisan Review* 26 (1959): 573–92.

Richard, Rev. Ferdinand. *The 'Visualized' Baltimore Catechism No. 2.* Hudson, N.Y.: Trinity Guild, 1950.

Rieff, Philip. *The Triumph of the Therapeutic.* New York: Harper, 1965.

Riepe, Dale. *The Philosophy of India and its Impact on American Thought.* Springfield, Ill.: Thomas, 1970.

*Sadlier, J., trans. *The Great Day: A Souvenir of First Communion.* New York: Excelsior Catholic Publishing House, 1895.

*Sale, George, trans. *The Koran.* London: Frederick Warne, n.d.

Schopenhauer, Arthur. *The World as Will and Idea.* Trans. R. B. Haldane and J. Kemp. 7th ed., 2 vols. London: K. Paul, Trench, Trubner, 1887.

Sergeant, Elizabeth. "Eugene O'Neill: The Man with a Mask." *New Republic* 16 (Mar. 1927): 91–95.

Sheaffer, Louis. *O'Neill: Son and Artist.* Boston: Little, 1973.

——. *O'Neill: Son and Playwright.* Boston: Little, 1968.

*Sherab, Paul. *A Tibetan on Tibet: Being the Travels and Observations of Mr. Paul Sherap (Deye Zodba) of Tachienlu; with an Introductory Chapter on Buddhism and a Concluding Chapter on the Devil Dance by G. A. Combe.* London: T. F. Unwin, 1926.

Sievers, W. David. *Freud on Broadway: A History of Psychoanalysis and the American Drama.* New York: Cooper Square Publishers, 1955.

Sinor, Denis, ed. *Orientalism and History.* 1954; rpt. Bloomington: Indiana Univ. Pr., 1970.

Skinner, Richard Dana. *Eugene O'Neill: A Poet's Quest.* New York: Russell and Russell, 1964.

Smith, Huston. *The Religions of Man.* New York: Harper, 1958.

Smith, Winifred. "Mystics in the Modern Drama." *Sewanee Review* 50 (1942): 35–48.

Sparrow, Martha Carolyn. "The Influence of Psychoanalytical Material in the Plays of Eugene O'Neill." Diss., Northwestern Univ., 1931.

*Spence, Lewis. *A Dictionary of Mythology.* London: Cassell, n. d.

Strindberg, August. *A Dream Play.* Trans. Elizabeth Sprigge. In *Modern Drama: A Norton Critical Edition*, ed. Anthony Caputi. New York: Norton, 1966.

———. *The Ghost Sonata.* Trans. Elizabeth Sprigge. In *Classics of the Modern Theatre*, ed. Alvin Kernan. New York: Harcourt, 1965.

Stunkel, Kenneth R. "Indian Ideas and Western Thought During the Romantic Age: A Critical Study." Diss., Univ. of Maryland, 1966.

*Suzuki, Daisetz Teitare. *An Introduction to Zen Buddhism.* New York: The Philosophical Library, 1949.

Sypher, Wylie. *Loss of the Self in Modern Literature and Art.* New York: Vintage, 1962.

*Taylor, Thomas, trans. *Select Works of Plotinus.* Ed. G. R. S. Mead. London: G. Bell and Sons, 1912.

Thomas, Wendall. *Hinduism Invades America.* New York: Beacon, 1930.

Tiusanen, Timo. *O'Neill's Scenic Images.* Princeton: Princeton Univ. Pr., 1968.

Tornqvist, Egil. *A Drama of Souls: O'Neill's Supernaturalistic Technique.* New Haven: Yale Univ. Pr., 1969.

Urquhart, W. S. *The Vedanta and Modern Thought.* London: Oxford Univ. Pr., 1928.

*Waley, Arthur, trans. *More Translations from the Chinese.* New York: Knopf, 1919.

Watts, Alan. *Psychotherapy East and West.* New York: New American Library, 1961.

———. *The Two Hands of God.* New York: Macmillan, 1963.

Winther, Sophus Keith. *Eugene O'Neill: A Critical Study.* New York: Random, 1934.

Index

Adams, Henry, 79
Alexander, Doris, 13 n.5, 115 n.29, 136
America, United States of, 6, 34, 74–84, 168
Angus, Samuel: *The Mystery Religions and Christianity*, 43–44, 47, 137
"*Anna Christie*," 7, 16–17, 85, 87, 94–99, 100, 153 n
Aquinas, Saint Thomas, 39, 46
Atman, 15, 16, 97, 138–40
Augustine, Saint, 46

Baltimore Catechism (1885), 39
Bhagavad-Gita, 71, 82
Binyon, Lawrence: *The Flight of the Dragon*, 123
Birth of Tragedy from the Spirit of Music, The (Nietzsche), 57–59, 135–36
Borel, Henry: "Wu Wei," 170–71
Boulton, Agnes, 13 n.5, 17–18
Brahman, 5, 7, 13, 14, 15–16, 54, 57, 65, 70–72; in O'Neill's plays, 97–99, 104–5, 108, 118, 138–39, 155–56
Brahmanism (ancient Hinduism), 18
Buddha, Gautama, 17–22, 60, 66, 136–38. *See also* Buddhism
Buddha and the Gospel of Buddhism (Coomaraswamy), 18–22, 100, 136–37
Buddhism, 5–6, 8, 11–12, 13–14, 17–22, 25, 44, 54–55, 60, 63–64, 66–67; Hinayana (orthodox), 19–22, 35 n; Mahayana, 19; in O'Neill's plays, 115 n.29, 117, 122, 130, 136–38, 148, 157–60; Zen, 22. *See also* Philosophy, Oriental

Carlin, Terry, 12, 17, 19
Carpenter, Frederic, 2, 2 n.5
Catholicism, Roman, 37–50, 38 n.6;

and O'Neill (personal) 6, 33, 37–41, 43, 49–50 (in his plays) 45, 48, 50, 101–3, 134, 140–41, 166, 175–76, 178. *See also* Christ, Jesus; Christianity
Chinese Gardens (Graham), 170, 172
Chris Christopherson, 94. *See also* "*Anna Christie*"
Christ, Jesus, 1, 36, 38 n.6, 39–50 passim, 65, 103, 104 n, 134, 166. *See also* Christianity; God (Christian)
Christianity, 36, 37–50, 66–67, 70; and mysticism, 40–41, 43–49; and O'Neill (personal) 33, 38 n.6 (in his plays) 1, 93, 96–97, 101, 103, 107, 118, 124–27, 128–29, 133–34, 150–52, 161–62, 166, 174, 175–78, 182–84; and Oriental philosophy, 5, 19, 28, 50 n. *See also* Catholicism, Roman; Christ, Jesus; God (Christian)
Chuang Tse, 23–25; *Chuang Tse*, 27–30, 114–16
Collins, Mabel: *Light on the Path*, 12, 13 n.5, 81 n.79, 81–82
Conflict of Religions in the Early Roman Empire, The (Glover), 43
Confucianism, 25 n
Coomaraswamy, Ananda K., 33; *Buddha and the Gospel of Buddhism*, 18–22, 100, 136–37

Days Without End, 1, 166
Dionysian. *See* Nietzsche, Friedrich, Dionysian principle of
Dionysus, 57, 61, 126, 135
Dream Play, A (Strindberg), 62, 64–65, 67, 120
Dualism, 7, 19. *See also* Philosophy, Western, dualism of
Dynamo, 121–24, 161–65

197